FRESH SHOOTS IN STONY GROUND

The challenges of church planting

FRESH SHOOTS IN STONY GROUND

The challenges of church planting

Edited by
Stephen McQuoid and Neil Summerton

Copyright © Stephen McQuoid, Neil Summerton and the contributors 2012

First published 2012 by Church Planting Initiative and Partnership

Church Planting Initiative
3 Cedar Way, St Mary's Park, Portishead, Bristol BS20 6TT

Partnership
Abbey Court, Cove, Tiverton, Devon EX16 7RT

16 15 14 13 12 / 7 6 5 4 3 2 1

The right of Stephen McQuoid and Neil Summerton to be identified as the Editors of this Work has been asserted by them in accordance with the Copyright, Designs and Patents Act 1988.

All rights reserved. No part of this publication may be reproduced, stored in a retrieval system, or transmitted, in any form or by any means, electronic, mechanical, photocopying, recording or otherwise, without the prior permission of the publisher or a license permitting restricted copying. In the UK such licenses are issued by the Copyright Licensing Agency, 90 Tottenham Court Road, London W1P 9HE.

British Library Cataloguing in Publication Data
A catalogue record for this book is available from the British Library

ISBN 978-0-9570177-1-9

Cover design and typesetting by projectluz.com
Printed and bound by Gutenberg Press, Malta

Contents

Contributors   vii

Abbreviations   xii

Introduction   xiii

Part 1: Church Planting Explained

1. To plant or not to plant?   1
   Stephen McQuoid

2. Church plant or existing church—what's the difference?   11
   Stephen McQuoid

3. Am I a church planter?   17
   Stephen McQuoid

4. What is a church?   27
   Mark Davies

5. Lone ranger or team player?   39
   Stephen McQuoid

6. Stages of a church plant   51
   Stephen McQuoid

7. Different approaches to church planting   63
   Stephen McQuoid

8. Church planting models   77
   James Hyde

9. Thinking about starting points   89
   David Buchan

10. Cross-cultural church-planting in the UK   99
    Andy Gibson

11. Building an authentic community   111
    Martin Erwin

12. Discipling new converts   123
    Andy Gibson

13. The challenges of a building   135
    Giles Arnold

14. Developing and appointing leaders   153
    Roger Chilvers

15. Why size matters   169
    Stephen McQuoid

16. Handing over and moving on   177
    John McQuoid

17. Making decaying churches live *Graham Poland*	189
18. Encouraging the church plant to maturity *David Clarkson*	197
Appendix to Part 1: Church planting and emergent church *Stephen McQuoid*	207

Part 2: Ten Living Stories

19. Starting fresh—Liberty Community Church, Bellshill *David Buchan*	213
20. Mother and daughter—Kirkliston Community Church *Colin Haxton*	219
21. Mother and daughter—Bethany City Church, Sunderland *Dave Burke*	227
22. Mother and daughter—Abbey Church, Gloucester *Roger Chilvers*	233
23. Outreach to church—The Living Rooms, Inverbervie *Ken Dickson*	241
24. Purpose-driven style—Forest of Dean Community Church, Cinderford *Tim Cracknell*	247
25. A church-planting church plant—Lakeside, Brierley Hill *Andy Hodson*	253
26. Responding radically to decline—Strathaven Evangelical Church *Andrew Lacey*	259
27. The life and death of a church plant— The 145 Church, Hornsey, North London *Neil Summerton*	265
28. Growth delayed—Challenge Community Church, Hereford *Martin Erwin*	275
Further reading	279
Index	282

Contributors

Giles Arnold is married with two teenage children. He is a Chartered Surveyor. He is the General Manager for Church Growth Trust (a Trust Corporation set up to hold independent church buildings). He manages its church buildings, finding new churches to occupy when the existing congregations close, working closely with the occupying churches. He also specialises in advice on church and charity buildings, such as guidance on major projects, advice on leases, carrying out access audits, asbestos surveys and insurance valuations and help with unravelling Trust deeds. He has planted and led a local independent evangelical fellowship and is actively involved in his current church.

David Buchan was a social worker before joining the ministry of Gospel Literature Outreach (GLO) as a church planter in Viewpark, a large and socially-deprived housing estate on the east side of Glasgow. He then spent 12 years in France, living and working as a missionary and continuing to use the community involvement approach that he advocates in his contribution to this book, before returning to a social work career in Scotland. He is an elder in Lennox Evangelical Church in Dumbarton. He is married to Sheena and they have two daughters, who have given up trying to make him 'cool'.

Dave Burke was born in Sunderland in 1954. He read Zoology at the University of Wales before going on to Imperial College, London. Following a career in conservation and agricultural research, he moved into Christian ministry. He has worked with UCCF and a number of churches in the south of England. After almost 25 years living away from the region, Dave returned to the north east in 1997 to serve as Senior Minister of Bethany Christian Centre in Houghton le Spring. Dave helped to set up Wearside First Credit Union, a major initiative to serve the financially excluded in the city of Sunderland. Currently, he is leading a team of around 70 adults from Bethany who started a new church in

Sunderland, meeting initially at the Stadium of Light and now at the Quayside Exchange. He describes this new venture as, 'A church for people who have given up on the church'. Dave is married to Cathie, and they have two children and one dog. In his spare time, he enjoys binge running and kayaking.

Roger Chilvers works with Counties in Gloucestershire in evangelism and bible teaching and is a former Director of the Church Planting Initiative (CPI). He has worked extensively with the Billy Graham Evangelistic Association, with responsibility for training, counselling and follow up in missions and training programmes in the UK and other many parts of the world. He was also chairman of the Emerging Evangelists' Institute. Roger has served as a director–trustee of the George Müller Foundation. As a leader of Hillview Evangelical Church in Gloucester, he worked with others in planting Abbey Church in a large new housing area of the city where he is now a leader. Roger and his wife Hazel have three grown children.

David Clarkson was for 14 years headteacher of a large secondary school in the south of Scotland. Latterly, he was seconded to train newly-appointed head teachers. He has also been full-time worker and elder in a growing church in Glasgow. He is on the staff of Tilsley College (GLO) and is responsible for the development and leadership of Extension Ministries, focusing on the 'Learning to Lead' course which he has run in several countries. He is a BSc (Hons) in Chemistry from Glasgow University and has a DipRS from Cambridge University.

Tim Cracknell is married to Katrina. Linked to the Church Planting Initiative, they have re-launched an almost defunct Brethren church in Cinderford. They are particularly effective in connecting with their community where they have gained esteem and favour. By maintaining freshness and zeal in a growing congregation, they have helped new believers to maturity and incorporation into the body of Christ. They are also involved in visiting and encouraging other struggling churches.

Mark Davies and his wife Shirley served as missionaries in Zambia for 20 years, engaging in bible teaching, developing mission, and resourcing infrastructure and HIV/AIDS intervention, before coming to Tilsley College (GLO). Mark, a native of Swansea started a career in engineering, having qualified BSc from Bath University. He has recently completed a Master's degree in biblical interpretation at the International Christian College in Glasgow. He continues to be involved in bible translation work in Zambia and visits there regularly.

Ken Dickson has been married to Veronica for 35 years. They have four grown-up grandchildren and two grandchildren. They have lived in the coastal town of Inverbervie in north east Scotland for almost 30 years and are passionate about helping others to know Christ better. Ken worked in the pharmaceutical industry for many years, but now serves alongside a group of co-workers at 'The Living Rooms Christian Centre', where they endeavour to be 'God's Gloves' in the community.

Martin Erwin has worked as a Counties Evangelist since 1991. He leads Challenge Community Church, which he helped plant, and where he now devotes the majority of his ministry. He also developed and promotes 'Dying to Meet You', a church evangelism resource. He is also involved in leadership training, bible teaching and a variety of evangelistic opportunities.

Andy Gibson is married to Claire and they have two children. Andy served for 10 years as a Customs Officer, before training for Christian service with Claire at Tilsley College (GLO). Andy and Claire worked for 8 years in Hereford in a church plant linked with the Church Planting Initiative. Andy and Claire moved to Newcastle in 2007, where Andy is full-time elder at Regent Chapel. Andy is also a member of the Executive Group of Partnership.

Colin Haxton and his wife, Morag, along with their three children, have lived in Kirkliston on the edge of Edinburgh since 1997. Before that, they lived in Motherwell, where Colin was actively involved in a local evangelical church as a deacon, youth leader and worship leader. For over 20 years, he was a leader and latterly the Director of a Christian youth camp known as Maranatha Camp which has had a huge input into the lives of hundreds of young people. Colin has been a church elder for the last 10 years—first, at Bellevue Chapel in Edinburgh and then at the new church plant in Kirkliston. He enjoys travelling a lot, a necessity of his full-time job as Business Development & Marketing Director of GAP Group Ltd. He loves skiing, motor racing and playing the guitar

Andy Hodson leads the Lakeside estate Church Plant in Stourbridge (West Midlands), which meets at Nine Locks Community Centre. He was previously involved in another church plant in the area. Andy and Isobel joined Counties with Church Planting Initiative in January 2009 and have three daughters.

James Hyde is married to Debbie and they have two children, Chris and Ben. They live in the west of England. James has a passion for watching films, reading, and eating out. He was a solicitor in the water and waste industry until leaving to work at Grosvenor Church Barnstaple, where he was an elder. His desire is to live life as a gift to others in the global organic movement of biblical discipleship and missional church.

Andrew Lacey is married to Barbara, a social worker, and they are parents of three grown-up children. After a career in a number of retail outlets, Andrew joined the work of GLO as the Bookshop Manager in Motherwell in 2005. Over previous years, Andrew moved around a number of churches and denominations, before being involved in the setting up of an independent church in Strathaven, to the south-east of Glasgow. He is now an elder in the church, with a particular concern to develop the public gifts of the younger people of the church, and to seek ways to hand over the baton of ministry to a younger generation. Andrew is Assistant Editor of *Partnership Perspectives* magazine.

John McQuoid spent seventeen years as a missionary in Ethiopia, twelve years with a church in his native Northern Ireland, majoring in personal evangelism, seven years in pastoral ministry with a church in England, and has travelled widely, preaching and teaching during fifty years of Christian service.

Stephen McQuoid grew up in Ethiopia where his parents were missionaries. He then lived in Ireland, where he qualified as a nurse, before going on to study theology. He has a Dip.Th. from Belfast Bible College, and is a BA in Biblical Studies from Trinity College, an MA and a PhD in Theology from Trinity Theological Seminary, and a MTh from the University of Wales. He has written ten books. Stephen is the General Director of Gospel Literature Outreach (GLO), a missionary organisation based in Europe and on the board of the CPI. He is married to Debbie and they, along with their two children, fellowship at Liberty Community Church in Bellshill where Stephen is an elder.

Graham Poland is pastor of Grosvenor Church, Barnstaple, a church of about 400 with a strong emphasis on relationships and discipling. He formerly worked with GLO, leading teams in southern Europe and at the Training College in Motherwell. He has been an elder in churches in Weston-super-Mare, Southend and Bothwell, and is a Minister-at-large for Partnership. He is also involved in a teaching and internet ministry in Portuguese-speaking countries. In 2009, he completed a Masters degree in Applied Theology (Christian Leadership).

Neil Summerton is a first-generation Christian, converted as a teenager in Shropshire. He has been in Christian leadership all his adult life and was an elder of Cholmeley Evangelical Church in north London from 1972 to 1998. He is now chairman of the Leadership Team of King Street Chapel, Tiverton. He took part in planting a church in Crouch End in the 1990s. He has been a Council member of the Evangelical Alliance since late in the 1980s and has been involved in the leadership of a range of para-church bodies, including the George Müller Foundation, Partnership, and the Church Planting Initiative. He helps to organize the four-yearly International Brethren Conference on Mission which networks and encourages Brethren leaders worldwide. He was a career civil servant for over 30 years and led two research institutes in Oxford on environment and water between 1997 and 2003. He is an independent non-executive director of two water supply companies in England. He read history at King's College London, is a PhD in war studies, and is a chartered environmentalist. He has written extensively on church leadership, public policy, history, ethics and environmental matters. He is an Emeritus Fellow of Mansfield College Oxford and was appointed CB by HM the Queen in 1997. He has been married to Pauline (a business-woman and hospital chaplain) for 46 years and has two grown-up sons and three grandsons.

Abbreviations

CGT—Church Growth Trust

Counties—Counties Evangelistic Work

CPI—Church Planting Initiative

Echoes—Echoes of Service

ECM—European Christian Mission

GLO—Gospel Literature Outreach

Partnership—Partnership (UK) Ltd

Introduction

Stephen McQuoid and Neil Summerton

Any observer of church life in the UK will have noticed that churches are closing down in every corner of the country. This trend is likely to continue as so many existing churches are small and elderly. This fact does not threaten the future of Christianity in the UK, for, after all, there are also many vibrant and growing churches in the country as well. However, it is a serious situation and one that urgently needs to be addressed.

Some Christians believe that the way forward is to fortify those churches that are weak and struggling to ensure that they do not close. There is some mileage in this idea, but there also needs to be caution. When a church is in decline, there are always reasons for that decline. Unless the reasons are dealt with, growth will simply not happen. Even where relevant action is taken, it may fail because, humanly-speaking, the point of no return for the particular fellowship has been passed. Experience suggests that this is particularly so where a fellowship has fallen to a few elderly people. We could end up in the situation where we are pouring money and human resources into situations that will still fail. This is neither smart nor an appropriate use of the resources God has given us.

Another way forward is to plant new churches. While this may sound like a huge challenge, in practice, planting a new church is often easier that trying to turn around a church that does not want to change or adapt to contemporary life. As someone once said, 'Just as it is easier to have a baby than raise the dead, it is easier to plant a new church than rescue one that does not want to be rescued'. We urgently need to see new churches planted all over the country that will be a shining light in an increasingly dark culture.

This book has been born of a desire to see new churches come into being. It is one of the end results of strategic discussions that took place at the board of the Church Planting Initiative (CPI) in 2010. CPI is committed to supporting church planters and church planting all over the UK. It began in 1999 and is the combined effort of four member organisations—Counties, Gospel Literature Outreach (GLO), the Church Growth Trust and Partnership. The CPI strategy for church planting focuses on people, not buildings. The aim is to network church planters, and provide them with practical and pastoral support and, where necessary and possible, a measure of financial support.

The aim of this book is to open the reader's eyes to the challenge of church planting, but to do so in a down-to-earth and practical way. The authors have not been chosen because they are professional academics or polished writers. Rather, they are practitioners—people who have planted churches, or who are planting them, and consequently have much to share from their experience. They all share a passion for seeing God's kingdom extended by the planting of new churches. The book will function as an earthy and practical handbook on church planting, a 'how-to' tool kit designed to help anyone who wants to join the adventure of planting a new church.

The need for vibrant new churches is obvious. Our hope and prayer is that you will not simply take the time to read this book, but that you will think of what you can do to reverse the trend of declining churches by getting involved in church planting, whether by doing it, praying for it, supporting it, or funding it. We firmly believe that the UK, and indeed Europe as a whole, is a key mission-field, and that church planting must be at the very heart of any strategy. With bold vision and courageous leadership, we can make a difference and a new generation of churches can emerge to turn the tide.

PART ONE

Church Planting Explained

To plant or not to plant?

Stephen McQuoid

Evangelical Christians are by their very nature proactive people. It is part of their DNA that they are people who get things done, Christians who want to achieve by activity.

This proactivity expresses itself in a host of different ways. Many evangelical churches conduct a dizzying array of activities, such as Sunday school, mothers and toddlers, youth clubs, men's fellowships, children's clubs and coffee mornings. Equally, many are involved in cross-cultural mission, sending their brightest and best to distant lands across the globe. Some engage in social action, caring for the homeless, drug addicts and the broken. Indeed, such is the desire for evangelicals to do things that they have become the most vigorous and exciting grouping within Christendom.

There is one activity, however, that many evangelicals are hesitant to get involved in. Indeed, there is such a resistance to this particular activity in some quarters that they make a thousand excuses and even create problems for themselves, rather than get involved in this, to them, dubious practice. It is church planting.

In many ways, the resistance to church planting among some evangelicals is a contradiction in terms. After all, one of the defining features of evangelicalism is that it takes the bible seriously. Evangelicals believe that the bible is their authority for faith and practice. They are people who love the 'word' and eagerly desire to be truly New Testament Christians. It is here that the contradiction occurs. While they are often so reticent to get involved in church planting, the

New Testament is full of it. Indeed, it is threaded through with the theme of church planting. In the gospels, Jesus gives the assurance that he will build his church and the gates of hell will not prevail against it (*Mt.* 16: 18). The book of *Acts* records the planting of churches across the empire, some like Antioch being planted as a natural outcome of the witnessing of fleeing and persecuted Christians (*Acts* 11: 21). The epistles are the follow-up documents of Paul's church planting career. The fact is that the New Testament is so replete with references to church planting that it is impossible to be a genuinely New Testament Christian without being committed to the idea of church planting. That being the case, why are more evangelicals not actively involved in planting churches?

This is not an easy question to answer, simply because there are numerous reasons why many evangelical Christians and churches do not get involved in church planting. It is important to look at these reasons and ask if they have any real validity.

Church planting is too difficult

The first reason why more Christians do not get involved in church planting is that they think it is too difficult. There is a common perception that in order to be a church planter, you need to be an irrepressible character with significant spiritual gifting and a powerful sense of anointing. It is not a job for 'ordinary' Christians. Consequently, anyone who does not fit the bill in every respect should not even consider the possibility of being a church planter.

Of course, it is true that church planting is difficult; if that were not the case many more churches would be planted. Equally, those who do plant churches will need to be determined and appropriately gifted, with a sense of calling or at least a passion for church planting. However there is need to have a sense of perspective and to re-evaluate our assumptions. In doing this, two things must be mentioned.

First, we need to realise that, while church planting is challenging, it can also be difficult to make an already-established church grow. Indeed, sometimes it is harder to bring about growth in an existing church—which is why so many of them are in decline. One reason for this is that churches over time develop their own traditions and church culture. This is not necessarily a bad thing; indeed some church traditions can be positively helpful. Others, however, are not. Nevertheless, unhelpful traditions can become as much enshrined in the life of a church as helpful ones. It is not unusual to find churches that are so moribund with traditions that they are weighed down as by a ball and chain. Such churches often end up in a kind of self-imposed cultural exile within their own community, unable to relate the gospel relevantly to the very people they desire to reach. They may not lack sincerity or passion, but do lack the ability to really impact society. The reality is that it is at least as difficult to make these kinds of churches grow as it is to plant a church from scratch. Starting from scratch is indeed a challenge, but working on a blank canvas is certainly less complex that working with a very messy one.

Secondly, we need to recognise that not all church planting has to be done in the same way. There are times when a highly-gifted and motivated individual will go to an area to plant a church. In these situations, a fairly exceptional calibre of person will be needed in order to make the church-plant successful. However, more often than not, church planting is done by teams of planters. Consequently, the burden of the work does not fall on the shoulders of just one person. It also means that no one person needs to have all the gifts necessary to do the job, as the combined gifts and abilities of the team will suffice. It is also very common for a large church to send out not just one or two members, but an entire group of people, to plant a church. In effect, once this group begin meeting together, they have already formed a church, so the process of church planting can be greatly accelerated.

Given these two factors, we need to recognise that church planting, while challenging, is not an impossible task. Indeed, with the right people, the right attitude, the right strategy and of course the power of the Holy Spirit, church planting is something that can and does take place in Britain today.

There are already lots of churches

A second objection to church planting is that there are already many churches in existence. Consequently, the argument goes, we really don't need any more. Indeed, the UK Christian Handbook indicates that there are around 50,000 congregations already in existence within the UK; this would appear at first glance to be a healthy number. Surely, objectors might say, there can be no compelling reason to focus on church planting, given these numbers of churches. However, when the situation is given more detailed scrutiny, another picture emerges.

First, we need to note that, while 50,000 churches seems a lot, there are fewer churches in existence now than there were 20 years ago, and 20 years ago there were fewer churches than 20 years previous. Indeed, the actual number of churches in the UK has been in decline for several decades. What is more, many of today's churches are themselves suffering from declining numbers, an increasingly-aged membership, and a lack of real vision or penetration into the local community. It does not take a great statistician to work out that if present decline continues, a significant number of today's churches will be gone in another 20 years' time. Without significant church planting, the situation in the UK will become very serious indeed. Whole areas of the inner city and even leafy suburbs will be without a viable church. It is worth nothing that over the past 40 years church planting has been taking place. However, even with these new churches the overall picture is one of decline. That decline would be all the more marked if it were not for church planting that is being done.

Secondly, it is not only important that churches exist, but also that they exist in the right places. The last half-century has seen huge population shifts. Sparkling new housing developments have sprung up all over the country. Inner cities have either become derelict or have been rebuilt with retail and commercial developments, while the people who used to live there have now moved out to the suburbs. New towns have been created and planners and developers have managed to build significant numbers of houses next to some small villages. All of this means that many church buildings which at one point were in high-population areas are now in areas where few people live. These highly-unattractive locations make it difficult for the churches to reach out to others or have any sense of community.

Thirdly, we need to recognise the bare fact that 90% of the population of the UK simply do not attend church regularly. Consequently, however many churches we think we have in the UK, it is clearly not enough. The existing churches have made so little impact on our culture as a whole, and attracted so few members, that many more churches are needed as a matter of urgency.

A fourth and rather painful point that needs to be made is that many of the 50,000 existing churches are simply not suitable vehicles for evangelising our society. In some cases, it is because they are not evangelical, they do not proclaim a biblical message of salvation, and therefore have nothing to offer a fallen and sinful society. In other cases, churches might be evangelical but are so tradition bound, so wrapped up in the past, that they have lost their capacity to relevantly communicate the gospel within a rapidly-changing culture. There are also churches that have no real desire to reach out to their community. They are content just to remain an introspective 'holy huddle', unwilling to communicate the love of Christ to lost people. Such churches, while existing, do nothing else other than merely exist. But their existence does not help to counter the spiritual crisis that pervades society. Consequently, 50,000 churches is not nearly enough; more are needed to reach out into the darkness.

Church planting weakens existing churches

A third objection to church planting is that it weakens existing churches and will therefore be a counterproductive move. If too much expense and manpower is focussed on church planting, and therefore away from existing churches, they are bound to suffer. The overall gains will be limited because, while new churches emerge, existing ones will die out.

This may sound like a reasonable objection, but there is more to it than meets the eye. Existing churches do of course die out; that is a commonly known fact. However, in general the primary reason for this is not the drain caused by church planting. Rather, it is because those churches are not reaching out relevantly to their local community; in other words they are not truly missional. This is ultimately an internal problem. Had those churches been genuinely missional, they may well have continued to exist. On the contrary, churches that encourage and promote church planting do so because they are missional and, being that, they are more likely to survive and even thrive. This, of course is not guaranteed. Sending out a group to plant a church will inevitably have some negative impact on the sending church. However, this impact can be short lived if proper preparations have been made; and the missional desire of the mother church can lead to genuine growth despite the loss of some of its members. In that sense, church planting can actually help existing churches in the long term. Here the counter-intuitive applies. By developing a vision that enables a church to release members so that they can plant other churches, the sending church can experience increased growth.

It should also be stated that the planting of a new church should not necessarily involve just one existing or 'mother church'. Indeed, there is much to be said for several churches working together to plant a new church. If three or four churches in a locality each sent out half a dozen people from their membership to be part of a new church plant, this new church could emerge without the sending churches losing too many valuable members. A shared church plant could therefore be beneficial for all concerned.

Bigger is better

There is another issue that needs to be raised at this point. Often the people who object to church planting on the basis that it weakens existing churches are people who come from large churches. There has been a tendency in recent decades for Christians to find refuge in larger churches, believing that they are more likely to thrive and that they offer more to their members. This tendency is so compelling that it has even resulted in people leaving smaller churches where they are greatly needed, to shift their allegiance to larger churches where they are less needed. This situation while illogical is certainly understandable.

If you have a young family, there will be a natural desire to find a church where your children will have company and where their needs can be catered for. Equally, if you enjoy music or quality bible teaching and feel the need for pastoral care, there will be a great temptation to go to a church that is replete with musicians, a well-known bible teacher and a salaried pastoral team. These will usually be found in larger churches. Consequently, many people feel that bigger is better. A large church has more spending power, more talent and carries more visibility in the community. Leaders and pastors also like the idea of a large church, especially those with a gift of preaching or teaching. The bigger the church, the greater the audience to listen to the weekly sermon. This desire for big church means that any thought of church planting will be opposed because then the church will not be so big.

Before we get swept away with this argument, perhaps a word of warning should be sounded about the potential complications associated with large churches. While it is true that they have much to offer, they can also be plagued with problems. Large churches are particularly prone to having 'passengers', people who attend on a Sunday but don't actually use their gifts. This can happen in small churches too, but in a large church, where anonymity is easy to achieve, the problem is particularly great. Large churches can also lack a sense of community. This problem can be offset to some degree by organising house groups and social activities; nevertheless the dynamic of size remains an issue, so that a church of 200 members will simply not be able to have the cohesion and sense of community of a church of 50.

Large churches also find it more difficult to develop the gifts of their members. Generally speaking, a large church will be highly professional—a good thing of course. However, the standards set will make it very difficult for an individual to develop confidence and competence. The church can host lots of training events, but the best way of learning is to do the thing. The very professionalism of the programme will mitigate against allowing inexperienced practitioners to have the opportunities necessary to develop their gifts. Often this has led to the ironic situation where large churches, when looking for new staff members will bring in people from elsewhere because, despite their numbers, they have not properly developed their own people. Indeed, I have known of very large churches that have imported their pastoral team from churches half their size.

Furthermore, the suggestion that large churches are better at evangelism than smaller churches is a falsehood. Many large churches grow because of Christians transferring their allegiance from somewhere else. This is not real growth. A church can only say it is growing if people are becoming Christians either as a result of biological growth (children of believers becoming Christians) or because unchurched people are becoming Christians and then joining the church. Of course, many large churches do see converts and generally they have more converts than smaller churches. This is not necessarily because they are large; it has more to do the quality of the church. However, if a church of 200 people has three converts in a single year and a church of 50 people has only one, statistically the smaller church has shown itself to be proportionately more effective in evangelism. We consequently have to be cautions about making speedy assumptions about real church growth.

• •

Having dealt with some of the potential objections to church planting, we now need to ask why church planting should be a priority for us today. It is important to do so because we can only really engage in church planting if we are committed to the task. However, once the rationale for church planting has been firmly established, we can inspire each other, and our churches to take this ministry seriously. So why church plant?

It is an efficient form of evangelism

The first reason why we need to take church planting seriously is because it is an efficient way of reaching people who are not Christians. We have already noted that the vast majority of people in the UK do not attend church. Our society has become increasingly secular and the presence of today's churches has not done enough to alter the situation. The spiritual need is such that we need to take bold and adventurous steps to reach people for Christ. This will involve existing churches taking evangelism seriously, but it will also involves the planting of new churches. Any national evangelism strategy that does not incorporate the notion of church planting will be short-sighted and will not create sufficient impact to meet the spiritual needs of our nation.

There is a great deal of evidence to suggest that church planting is a highly effective way of doing evangelism. A new church plant if properly devised will be strategic and focused. People will be in place who are motivated and equipped to reach others for Christ. This mixture of commitment and preparation will enable a church planting project to bring a real spiritual impact to an area.

Some church plants do of course fail. Given the challenge, this is perhaps unsurprising, though, as we have noted, existing churches also fail. We therefore should not get discouraged when we hear stories of church planting projects that grind to a halt. The reality is that, while some fail, many others succeed and church planting has been greatly used by God, even in our generation, to bring many people to faith in Christ.

Church planting allows for a fresh start

A second reason why church planting is so important is that it allows the body of Christ in a particular location to have a fresh start. We have already mentioned the fact that many churches struggle with traditions built up over the years. While some of these are positive and constructive, others can become counterproductive over time. Indeed, some churches end up running services and programmes that might have seemed relevant 50 years ago, but now seem positively dated.

At times, it is possible to tackle these traditions and transform a church so that it becomes relevant once more. Sometimes, however, this transformation is not possible for a whole variety of reasons. The answer, therefore, is often to begin a completely new church. Church planting provides a completely fresh start. It enables the planter to design a structure that is relevant to the needs of the community he is reaching out to. With a blank canvas, it is possible to be creative and imaginative without having to deal with all the baggage of history. Just as the New Testament church was able to apply biblical principles to a Greco-Roman cultural setting as the church established itself, today's church planters will be able to apply biblical principles to the post-modern and secular society of the 21st century.

This fresh thinking is actually very exciting. So much of what we do in church life is because of tradition and culture rather than because the New Testament requires it. The New Testament does not demand that we conduct our meetings at 10 am, or 11 am, or even that we meet in the mornings. It does not ask us to wear a collar and tie or sing from a hymn book. We are not required to have 'mid week meetings' or take a Sunday collection every week. Nowhere does it tell us that we need a specially-constructed building in which to meet, or that we need a Sunday School, Youth Fellowship, Women's meeting or prayer breakfast. The truth is that the principles laid down for us allow for a great deal of flexibility and that means that the church planter will have the exciting task of applying the bible to his own cultural setting. This might mean that the new church will have an altogether different shape than the one from which the planter originated. It is here that church planting proves its worth as this 'fresh start' is something that an established church simply cannot do and is, in itself, a major rationale for continual church planting.

Church planting is targeted

A third reason why church planting is important is because it can be targeted. We have already noted that with shifting populations, existing church buildings can end up being isolated from population centres, which makes the job of evangelism for the churches that meet there even more difficult. Equally, new housing developments can bring large numbers of people into a location where no church presently exists.

Because church planting is a deliberate and planned activity, the planter can decide the best location to begin the work and use the initial mobility of a new work to his advantage. Indeed, this targeting can not only be location specific, but also specific in terms of the kind of people that the plant wishes to reach. For example, a church planting work could begin in an area of high immigration and focus particularly on one or two ethnic groupings in that area. This might result in a church that is primarily Asian or Iranian or Afro-Caribbean.

Church planting develops commitment

A fourth benefit of church planting is that it can demand and produce a high level of commitment among church members. One of the biggest challenges that churches face is that of apathy. Getting members to commit and sacrifice for the work of the church is difficult. If the church is large, it will be easy for some of its members to seek anonymity and be passengers, believing that there are lots of other people who can carry the burden of responsibility in the church.

In a church planting situation, no such luxury exists. The very nature of a church plant means that every gift is needed. Moreover, the structure and character of a church plant lends itself to allowing people to develop their gift and assume responsibility that they would never be able to in a more established church. It is not uncommon in a church planting situation to see both young people and young Christians engaged in significant ministries.

Church planting develops new leaders

The benefits of committed church members spill over into the area of leadership. In many established churches, the transition from committed church member to leader or elder is a slow and lengthy one. Very often, the leadership of an existing church will be people in their fifties and sixties. There is nothing wrong with this, of course. However, it does mean that leadership development often moves at a snail's pace.

This process tends to be quicker in church plants. The reason for this is that as a church comes into fruition, there are fewer people to choose from. Consequently, the planter is under pressure to find people willing and able to share the burden of leadership. Planters will therefore be constantly looking for and coaching potential leaders. An old adage states that 'necessity is the mother of invention'. This is certainly true of the process of finding leaders in a church plant. The planter either finds leaders or the project grinds to a halt. This incentive and pressure has a tendency to produce good leaders quickly.

By now, it should be obvious that church planting is not just a biblical thing; it is also something that is desperately needed. It is an exciting way of serving God and an important and strategic way of reaching people for Christ. It can be argued that, from a spiritual point of view, it is the biggest single need in the United Kingdom today. In any given society, people grow old and die. The same happens to churches. If that society does not produce new life, if children are not born, then there can be no future. Likewise as churches die, they need to be replaced with new churches, and the only way to do this is to church-plant. It goes without saying, therefore, that church planting should be a priority for the church in the United Kingdom today.

Chapter 2

Church plant or existing church—what's the difference?

Stephen McQuoid

Not all ministries are the same. This statement is so obvious that it hardly deserves a mention. Nevertheless in the context of a book on church planting, it is an important point to make, because comparisons can be assumed that are not necessarily there. For example, people who are involved in ministry within an existing church often assume that working in a church-planting situation will be fairly similar to working within an existing church. After all, the skills of evangelism, discipleship and bible teaching will be common requirements in both ministries. While this is true, it must be emphasized that work in existing churches and church planting are very different in many respects, and unless the church planter realises this, he or she will struggle a lot.

No recognition in the area

The first significant difference that needs to be noted is that existing churches have recognition in their locality; a new church-planting situation has none. The difference between these two situations is marked. Existing churches, by virtue of their history, have a profile in their local community, whether good or otherwise. Most people will be aware of the church's presence, even if they have never attended a single service. The majority of existing churches have their own building and, if it has been there for some time, it will be a familiar landmark.

If the church has a history of running a Sunday school or children's club, if there has been a youth club, then over the years many people from the local community will have experienced something of church life first hand, even if they never actually attended with any regularity. Equally, Sunday school teachers and youth leaders will be familiar figures for local people, especially if they live in the area. They will often be met with a smile and a greeting while walking down the street, and they will be considered by many to be trustworthy and upstanding members of the community. Their children will have gone to the local school, they buy their newspapers at the corner shop, and many people who have no association with the church will nevertheless know them at least vaguely.

Church planters and the church plant on the other hand usually enjoy no such visibility, especially in the early stages. If a team or group of Christians move into an area with the intention of planting a church, they will be comparative strangers. They will not meet grown-ups who have fond memories of attending kids clubs when they were young. Neither will they have the visibility of a building that has been a recognised place of worship for decades. If they have a name in mind to call their church once it gets established, that name will be meaningless to anyone who hears it. Indeed, even when they begin to conduct services, many onlookers will not think of these events as being 'church services' because the apparently casual gathering looks so different from the mental image that many unchurched people have of church. In truth, the job of gaining any kind of legitimacy and recognition from the local community for the fledgling church planting work is a big one. More often than not, the new church planters will be regarded with a degree of suspicion, and might even be perceived as a cult or some sort of 'weird' religious group.

No history

A second difference that exists between established church-life and a church planting situation is that the latter has no history to fall back on. If you were to go to an average church and ask average members why things are done in the way they are, they would probably shrug their shoulders and say, 'that's just the way we do things here'. In reality, so much of what we do in church life is just done as a result of habits built up over the years. There is no great theological or philosophical reason for doing many of these things; some will not even be very thought-out or even logical—we just do them because we do them!

At any given point, if people want to begin a new activity, or launch a new project, there is a whole history to call upon that goes back many years. This history can be utilised because of the lessons that have been learned. Planning meetings are often punctuated with expressions like, 'yes I remember trying that', or 'several years ago we did that…' Even if that history has not always been positive and mistakes were made, at least the lessons that were learned helped to shape the church and can now be fed into any strategic plan.

Church plants, on the other hand, have no such history. If questions are asked about how something should be done, imagination is called upon because there is nothing in the past that can be utilised as a point of reference. There is no good or bad in the past because there is no past. Of course, the church planter might have a great deal of experience of church life, but that experience, while useful, relates to other situations and not the present one. This is, of course, an exciting situation to be in. The planter can make a fresh start. Nevertheless the lack of history must be reckoned with because much more creative energy and imagination will be required to make the project work.

No building

A third and obvious difference between an existing church and a church plant in its early stages is the fact that usually existing churches have their own buildings while early church plants tend not to. There has been a great deal of discussion in recent years as to whether or not a building is a help to a church. Some have argued that while buildings keep you dry, they also keep people out. In this sense, a church building can be counter-productive because it puts a physical barrier between members of the church and the community outside. Those who hold to this position suggest that using a neutral venue for church services is much better. This neutral venue could include a leisure centre, a community centre, a school, or even a local hotel or pub. Some churches have also suggested that we should go back to the book of *Acts* and do exactly what the early church did by meeting together in homes.

Many others point to the advantages of churches' having their own building. To begin with a building can give a sense of belonging. Indeed, church members can build a genuine emotional connection with the building because they see it as the location of their spiritual home. A building provides facilities from which activities can be run at any time, whereas hired facilities may not be available when they are wanted. A building can contribute to the visibility and credibility of a church. Buildings can also be used by the community at large which elevates the church in the eyes of the community.

No doubt, this debate will continue and those who advocate not having a specific church building will be at loggerheads with those who believe that a specific church building is useful. It is true to say however that most churches in the UK to have their own building. Equally, most new church planting situations begin without having a building to call their own. This makes the two situations very different.

No weekly programme

Another issue which in the early stages of a church plant can be particularly frustrating is the complete absence of any weekly programme. This situation is unknown in existing churches because any church that has been around for a period of time will have developed a program which provides a framework by which the church operates. Indeed, there is a propensity in churches to have lots of activities which preoccupy the spare time of those members who are willing and committed. Anyone who is involved in an existing church will know instinctively what is happening on any given day. Monday could be prayer meeting night, Tuesday youth club, Wednesday toddler group and Friday youth fellowship.

Church plants operate differently. Any activity has to start from scratch and often this can take a great deal of time and energy. Until this happens one of the biggest challenges a church planter faces is how to fill his day. I remember visiting one church planting situation where the planter had become quite discouraged. He and his wife had moved into a large housing development to plant a church there. His very first day he set off around the area doing door to door work. He did this for three hours solidly and repeated the pattern every day that week. Soon he realised that it would be difficult to spend more than three hours a day doing such a difficult and often de-motivating activity, but also that the rest of his day needed to be accounted for. However, with the lack of any kind of structure or programme, he wasn't sure what else to do. By the time of my visit he was tired, disillusioned and struggling to pick up any enthusiasm for door-to-door work, or indeed anything else.

These early days in a church planting situation are key and, if the planter doesn't prepare properly for them, the challenge will be immense. Discouragement and frustration will become the norm. The planter will also need to be very disciplined and discover creative ways, not only of filling up his day, but creating a weekly programme that can achieve his aims. Even conducting a Sunday service is a challenge. After all, how meaningful can a service be if there is no one to attend?

No manpower

As well as a lack of a weekly programme, church planters also have to deal with limitations of manpower. Small existing churches face the same problem, particularly if they have an ageing congregation. However, many churches do benefit from a sufficient size of congregation to conduct a whole range of activities. What is more, larger churches also have the financial resources to employ staff and that greatly increases their work capacity.

When it comes to church planting, the lack of manpower can be a significant limitation. How great an issue this is will depend on how the church planting is being done. Some church plants happen when a sizable group leave a large existing church to form a new one. This mother/daughter model has the advantage of beginning the church plant with enough personnel to give the project momentum from the very start. Indeed, if the right people leave the larger church to begin a new one, then the new church can be even more dynamic than the mother church. But, even in this situation, manpower will still be at full stretch.

In other situations, an individual or small team will begin a church planting work and when this happens the lack of manpower becomes very evident. The reality is that so many evangelistic activities are heavily manpower dependant. Imagine trying to run a children's holiday Bible club or a youth club if you only have 3 or 4 people available to do it. Think of the problems that a couple, or even small team, would have trying on their own to put on an Alpha course complete with meal. With no church to support and staff these events, the challenge for the church planting team is evident. If anything is to be done, they have to do it because they have no one to call upon to help.

No immediate accountability

A final difference between working in an existing church and working in a church plant is the difference in structures of accountability. Typically, church workers, whether pastors, evangelists or youth workers, will function within a clearly-defined memorandum of understanding. Often they will have a contract that incorporates a regular review process. They will have a line manager or pastoral care group which will both support them and monitor their activity. They might even have to account for all they do in writing and have this read by those to whom they are accountable. Furthermore, all that they do is observed by the very church members who pay their salary and who expect service.

Church planters also frequently operate within a structure of accountability. Many are involved in church planting because they are associated with a mission organisation and it will provide accountability and direction. They may feel a sense of accountability back to the leaders of their previous church and work hard at informing them of their activity. Nevertheless, the atmosphere in which they function will be different because of the dynamic of a church planting situation. In a church plant, especially in the early days, the planter wields significant influence. The planter is surrounded by young Christians who have neither the experience nor confidence to analyze behaviour or critique ministry. Any accountability that comes from a line manager in a mission organisation, or indeed a group of elders from a sending church, will be accountability at a distance. It will involve the occasional visit as opposed to the constant presence of a leadership in an existing church. This situation gives a great deal of freedom which can be a mixed blessing.

On the plus side, there is no one looking over the church planter's shoulder, checking up to make sure everything is in order. The church planter will have the freedom to try new things, experiment and even fail without feeling that he has let down the line manager. However, it can have its downside too. There is a certain security that comes with accountability and the ability to know that you are doing the right thing. This accountability also feeds positively into the work that anyone is doing and produces good results. A good framework of accountability provides a sounding board to sift and critique new ideas. It can also eradicate complacency, and provide inspiration and give impetus to the project. If all of this is lacking, the church planter can feel both lonely and reticent. There can be the sense that he is working very much in isolation and in a ministry where no one else really cares about the work he does.

Getting the mind in gear

Clearly there are significant differences between working in a church planting context and working in an existing church. Almost every church planter I have met would have enjoyed the difference and found the experience of planting a church to be rewarding and exciting. However, the differences need to be clearly understood if the planter is to cope with the subtle pressure that comes from them. Church planting is no easy calling!

CHAPTER 3

Am I a church planter?

Stephen McQuoid

This chapter identifies the qualities that will be necessary if someone is to be suited to a church planting ministry. It also provides tools for discovering the kind of people we are.

It will be obvious by now that church planting is not only an important thing to do; it is also something that is achievable by the grace of God. That is not to underestimate the difficulties involved. However, the fact that churches are being planted all over the United Kingdom strongly suggests that this is not the impossible task that some think it is. Nevertheless the challenge is certainly an enormous one.

This begs the question, if I am to be involved in church planting, what qualities or gifts will be needed to accomplish the task? Clearly it is an important question to ask because, if someone is to commit themselves to church planting, they should have at least an idea as to whether or not they are suited to the task.

There is of course an inherent danger in trying to answer a question like this. Someone might feel that they don't tick all the boxes and therefore should not be involved in church planting. This would be a pity. God is great and we should live believing that He can enable us to do even remarkable things. The list of qualities should not therefore bind us overly, but such a list is useful and can even serve as a way of seeking God's guidance on the issue of whether or not we should be involved in church planting.

It should also be stated that the application of this list should be dependent on the way in which a particular church plant is being managed. For example, if an individual or a couple were to be doing a church plant on their own, they would need to be exceptionally able. On the other hand, if a team was to be doing the church plant, it would be sufficient for the abilities mentioned in this chapter to be spread throughout the team. In that way, any one member of the team could be someone with only relatively modest abilities. Equally, if a large group from an existing church left to begin a new church plant, this group would probably just representation an average cross-section of that church, though perhaps including a few highly-motivated individuals. An individual should not, therefore, be put off simply because he or she feels they have only a limited amount to offer. It is remarkable how God often uses the 'ordinary' to accomplish the extraordinary. I know of one retired couple who felt they would like to use their retirement to do something significant for God. There was a church-plant starting up not far from them and while they felt unable to take any kind of a lead, they offered their services to the team that was doing the church plant. They involved themselves in some of the routine work in the church plant, but it was all work that needed to be done. Their contribution was very significant, not least because when people began to become Christians, there was a mature couple there to bring stability to the fledgling church, as well as pastoral care and interest. These 'pensioners' were a key component in the church planting strategy.

In one sense there could be any number of qualities that we could point to that would enable a person to become a church planter. However, I would reduce the list to ten essential qualities that would need to be present either in the individual of the team. I will list them in no particular order.

Vision

The issue of vision is self evidently important when it comes to church planting. Indeed, it takes vision even to recognize that church planting needs to be done. This is why most Christians never even think about it. Once someone recognizes that a church-plant is needed, it takes another level of vision to conceptualize what the church-plant will look like. No two church-plants are the same and so vision is necessary to 'see' how this can be achieved and what needs to be done to make it happen. It might be quite a number of years before a church comes into being and so the vision must be clear, so that the project has proper direction.

Comfortable relationship with unchurched

A second quality necessary for church planting is that the planter needs to be able to relate well to unchurched people. Again, this is obvious because it is precisely these people that the church planter needs to reach out to, develop a relationship with and win for Christ. The truth is that many Christians are not comfortable in the presence of non-Christians, especially ones who never darken the door of a church. This discomfort can manifest itself in a number of ways. Some clam up and find conversation awkward and especially struggle to be natural about their faith. Others can be over-pushy in sharing their faith because they are not good at being relational. Still others are over-pious and distant, because they have forgotten what it was like to be an ordinary person who doesn't go to church.

Church planters need to know how to relate appropriately to people who don't go to church. They need to be able to build authentic relationships so that people warm to them rather than being repelled or afraid. However, they also need to be able to get the balance between friendship and proclamation. They should not be so relationally-focused that they are not prepared to tell people the truth about their spiritual condition. A true friend will be sure to share the good news of the gospel. This ability to be an evangelist and a friend is of great benefit in church planting.

A self-starter

The reality is that planting a church will require both stamina and determination. It involves hard work and persistence, often without receiving any encouragement. Anyone getting involved and in particular leading such a work would need to be highly motivated and willing to blaze a trail without expecting thanks or praise. This requires great self-motivation and the ability to overcome discouragement. When times are tough, church planters can feel very alone, as if they are the only people in the world doing church planting. This loneliness can be accompanied by feelings of frustration and disappointment when things don't turn out as intended. This is especially the case whenever converts who seem to be making good initial progress fall away. Such 'failures' cannot be allowed to derail the whole project, but often there is no one there to encourage and motivate the church planter. He or she will need to be the kind of self motivated people who pick themselves up and move on with renewed enthusiasm.

A healthy family life

Often overlooked is the importance of having a healthy and stable family life when church planting. People involved in church planting are often put under significant pressure. In many church planting situations, because there is no church building as a base, the home becomes the office. It is also a very important place to invite people. Hospitality is a key component in evangelism and that means having a home where visitors can feel welcomed and can relax. Having an open home inevitably puts pressure on the family and can strain a marriage. It is therefore imperative that there is a joint conscious commitment between husband and wife that they use their home in this way. There is also a need to remember that any disagreements or arguments are contained and they do not happen in the presence of others. Church planters should also talk to their children about their work and ensure that there is a good work/home life balance, so their children don't feel left out and get embittered. This can be achieved by planning each week so that, for example, not too many nights are used up in church activity and family recreational time is made a priority.

As well as making use of the home, another pressure that many church planters face is financial. Some church planting teams are comprised of people who have regular careers and they do church planting in their 'spare' time. Often, however, church planters will be people who have given up regular employment, or at least have taken up part time jobs, so as to give more time to the church plant. It is not uncommon for one marriage partner to work so that their husband or wife is able to devote all their time to a church plant. Where any of these situations is the case, finance can become a pressure. Existing churches are often able to give a reasonable stipend to their pastoral or full-time worker. But, if they branch out into church planting, it is rare that they can support a church planter to the same extent, unless they are a large or particularly wealthy church. Furthermore, there are very few mission organizations that are able to offer significant financial support to church planters. All of this can become a pressure. Planters need to exercise real faith, believing that God can meet their needs. They need to be willing to live modestly, to drive used cars, to take fewer holidays, and to have less money at Christmas to buy presents for their children. If they are spiritual people, this should not be an insurmountable problem, but it is a challenge. Having lived this way for more than 20 years, I am well aware of the significance of this issue and the real pressure it can exert on family life, especially in the highly materialistic cultures of the West. In such situations, an understanding and supportive spouse and willing children is a must.

Responsive to the community

Church planters need to know what is going on in their locality and to sense its pulse beat. They need to be aware of what people are thinking and something of their experience and worldview, so that they can learn to relate the gospel in a relevant way to the many people and situations within their community. This will necessitate the ability and willingness to integrate into the life of the community and get to know both people and structures.

There are many simple and obvious steps that can be taken to achieve this. One is to read local newspapers. They are less interesting than the national dailies and deal only with local issues, most of which are routine and of little wider significance. This, however, is exactly the point. Local newspapers are a window into the local community. Visiting community centres also pays dividends. It means that the church planter can see how people spend their leisure and social time, and is also a way of meeting people and community action groups. In addition, it is good to establish contact with the police, schools and the social work department. Each of these are integral components of the community, and knowing them and especially working with them will enable the church planter to be portrayed as someone at the very heart of the community, not at its fringes.

It should be stated that this interest in the community should not be forced and artificial. Church planters need to have a genuine care for the people of their community. They need to take an interest in people's lives and be concerned about the same things that concern people within the community. If there is an issue of teenage delinquency, poor housing, school closures or lack of play areas for children, church planters should be concerned and express that concern. They should want the best for the community and be motivated by a love for people. It is when this care for the community is public knowledge that local people will begin to accept the presence of the church-plant.

Flexibility

Another key quality is flexibility. By its very nature, a church planting situation will be unpredictable. There is no structure to force a routine and so the planter needs to be able to work in that kind of an environment. What is more, no two days will be the same. All kinds of opportunities will present themselves and these have to be seized. Equally, there will be disappointments and things which do not go according to plan, so a willingness to accept the situation and move on will be a must.

Of course, even a very flexible person can get annoyed and frustrated by things not going as planned. In a very real sense, this is unavoidable and a fact of life. It is also natural to feel this way as we are only human. However, the sign of a good church planter is that even though things annoy and frustrate, they do not discourage and the person has the ability to get on with it, without allowing the situation to get on top of them. Flexibility and a steely determination will prove to be a formidable combination.

A pastoral heart

Planting a church is all about working with people. It is said that wherever there are people there will be problems. There is certainly some truth in this. Human beings are not robots—they bring with them the hurts, idiosyncrasies, difficulties and ambiguities that make them what they are. It is therefore crucial that church planters care about people and have a pastoral heart.

It is important to differentiate between having a pastoral heart and having the gift of a pastor. Some Christians are very gifted at dealing with people and knowing exactly what to say in any given situation. Such a gift is very useful, though not essential in church planting. What is essential is that the church planter genuinely loves the people he or she is working with and is able to convey this in word and deed. This is important because, more than anything else, the thing that attracts people to church is the feeling that they are loved and cared for.

Pastoral care has always been important, but probably there has never been a time in British society where it has been more important than now. With the disappearance of a Judeo-Christian worldview and the fragmentation of family life, we now find ourselves as a culture in a situation where many people are emotionally scarred and confused, and lack any kind of moral compass. The clear implication is that we need to put a huge amount of pastoral care and attention into people's lives and play the role of shepherds. Unless church planters are prepared to invest in people's lives in this regard, they will find that either people don't stay, or if they do stay but they don't grow or experience transformation. A pastoral heart is consequently a huge need.

Encouraging gift in others

Of course, not all the work will be done by the church planter. Indeed if any church plant is to mature, develop and get to the point where it can stand on its own, the church planter will need to learn to encourage others into ministry. In all probability, the time will come when the church planter will move on and get involved in ministry elsewhere. In order for that to happen, there needs to be people identified who can continue the work and take responsibility for it. This does not happen automatically and so the church planter will need to be intentional in this regard.

There are a number of stages in this process, and the church planter will have to exhibit a number of different skills. First, there is the issue of identifying who can do what among the congregation. Sometimes this is easier said than done. Some gifts or talents manifest themselves easily. For example, someone might be an accomplished musician and therefore their abilities and the contribution they could make to the worship of the church would be easily recognized. Others are not so easy. How do you know if someone would make a good preacher? Some of the best preachers I know are quiet and fairly shy people, and their gift was only discovered by allowing them to have a go at preaching. The planter will need to be a careful observer of people and look for hints as to what a person might be able to do and therefore to contribute to the church.

Linked with the ability to identify gift is the ability to encourage. Often new Christians can be enthusiastic, but reticent about exercising their gifts. Their lack of confidence needs to be overcome if they are to be fully utilized. In a real sense, the church planter needs to be a spiritual parent who gently but firmly enables others to take their first steps in ministry.

An internal battle that the planter will have to face is their own reactions when their disciple either does things differently, or does things to a lower standard than the planter. I have often seen situations where a church planter will keep control of the church and all its activities, and will end up doing everything, because he feels it must be done his way or not at all. This will end up being counterproductive, as it means that the church will never reach the point where it can do without the planter because no one has been allowed to develop. Part of the sacrifice that a planter needs to make is that he or she will have to observe others doing things in their own way, and accept the situation. This requires both humility and patience.

Training

Having the ability to train is also important in church planting. If the planter is to do himself out of a job, he will need to ensure that there is someone who can credibly take his place. I have often seen the situation on the mission field where another missionary is called out to replace a missionary who has done a pioneer work. This is a luxury we cannot afford. In today's climate, we will have neither the finance nor the manpower. The planter must therefore find a replacement from among the membership of the fledgling church. One great advantage of selecting someone from the church-plant is that they will fully understand the heartbeat of the church and will be integrated into it already.

Training is not always an easy thing to do. It requires planning and purposefulness. There are also different levels at which training can be offered. At one level, there is on the job training. This is what Jesus did and it is possibly the most effective form of training. Such an apprentice can be asked to engage in ministry alongside the planter so that the apprentice can be instructed as they go along. At times, however, there will be the need of some formal training, especially if the apprentice will have a major role in bible teaching.

The issue of which college to send them to is very important. Being away for a prolonged period of time brings all kinds of complications. These apprentices can easily lose interest in their home church, once they experience life in another one. They can also let go of relationships with people in the home church. Generally, I would recommend a college that offers a dedicated one-year course. This is long enough for a good training, but short enough to avoid the problems already mentioned. My own church has made use of Tilsley College because we appreciate the very mission-orientated one-year course which it offers, and there is a second-year internship which students can do while working for their home church.

A key issue in the training that the church planter offers is to give a sense of ownership to the people being trained. When all is said and done, if the apprentice does not feel a great sense of responsibility towards the church plant, if he or she does not look at every challenge and problem and say, 'this is my challenge or problem', then the training has failed. Ultimately, churches are not built by teams, committees, ideas, strategies or creative methodology. They are built by individuals who are prepared to pour their hearts into the church. If the church planter can convey this sense of ownership, he will be able to walk away from the situation with a sense of confidence.

Piety

A final quality every church planter needs to manifest is a genuine piety. It is said that a church can never rise above the level of its leadership. While this is a generalization, it is also generally true. Church-planting is a spiritual work which must be done by spiritual people. No amount of cleverness or drive can compensate for a lack of genuine Christ-likeness. After all, the job of church planting is not merely to get a group of people meeting together regularly. It is about encouraging people to embrace the lordship of Christ and to meet in community so that the glory of Christ can radiate from the church community which is his home. This task is only possible for people who know Christ deeply, love him passionately and are surrendered to his will. A man or woman of God will produce a godly church, but if that piety is missing, the church will be divested of its essential power and meaning.

Am I a church planter?

These then are the qualities needed for church planting. Not everyone involved in church planting will manifest all these qualities to the same extent. More often, these qualities will be shared by the members of a team or group who will be a potent force as a result. However, the importance of these qualities must be stressed and any church planting project should take stock of what qualities are available and make sure that all the resources are in place to make a success of the church plant. The following checklist will be a useful guide.

Fill in the following chart on a scale of 1-5 indicating where you stand in relation to these qualities. 5 represents very great strength in the quality, 1 represents very little strength in the quality.

QUALITY	1	2	3	4	5
VISION					
COMFORTABLE RELATIONSHIP WITH UNCHURCHED					
A SELF-STARTER					
A HEALTHY FAMILY LIFE					
RESPONSIVE TO THE COMMUNITY					
FLEXIBILITY					
A PASTORAL HEART					
ENCOURAGING GIFT IN OTHERS					
TRAINING					
PIETY					

CHAPTER 4

What is a church?

Mark Davies

Grappling as we are with a seemingly innumerable and ever expanding range of definitions for the word "church," it may seem impossible to come to any kind of consensus on what it is we may be trying to "plant." Even as I write these words, the debate surrounding the "emerging" church rages on. However, like the Teacher of *Ecclesiastes*, students of church history will rightly note that 'there is nothing new under the sun.' So I will make no attempt here to deal with present-day debates about church: having dealt with various 'post-s' for a few years now, it may well be that 'post-emergent' churches will loom on the horizon before we get this book printed!

So, rather than tackling the present, we shall delve into the past, God's kind of past, and ask where the concept of 'church' came from anyway. Maybe finding the heart of God on this will help with defining and shaping the kind of 'church' that is worth planting where you are.

Ekklesia—a "calling out a people for himself"?

If we were to read the ancient scriptures (our Old Testament) in Greek, as the first Apostles evidently did, hearing a statement like 'the *ekklesia* (church) began at Pentecost' might well have given Peter or Paul sufficient excuse to write another letter to tackle a perceived errant thought. That something new happened at Pentecost there was little doubt, but God had been 'calling out a people for himself' a lot further back than that momentous day when the Father, at his

Son's requests, sent the Holy Spirit to inaugurate a new phase in a long established methodology.

It seems to me that 'creative continuity' best sums up the way God works in time and space. The concept of *ekklesia* undergoes a shift post-Pentecost, but it is not a fundamental change in definition. The Hebrew word 'qahal' was consistently translated by the Jewish translation team producing the Septuagint (*c.* 200 BC) with the Greek word, *ekklesia*. The two words are closely related in concept, as is apparent when Stephen describes the people of God passing through the wilderness (*Acts* 7: 38) as 'church' (that is, *ekklesia* in Luke's text).

The term *ekklesia* was in common usage by Greek speakers for several hundred years before the Christian era and was used to refer to an assembly of persons constituted by well-defined membership. In general Greek usage, it was normally a socio-political entity based upon citizenship in a city-state. Regarding its usage in the New Testament, however, it is important to understand the meaning of *ekklesia* as an assembly of God's people. The Greek word itself is not a specialist word, but a common word describing a group of people meeting together on some constituted basis. So careful study and reflection are needed on the context of the word when it is used, so as to understand the concept which the user may have been intending to convey. Given the central role of Christ and his command that his Apostles should focus on teaching all nations to obey all that he had taught (*Matthew* 28:19), then we shall start with Jesus own words. The only recorded uses that Jesus makes of the word *ekklesia* are both in *Matthew*.

A Universal Ekklesia…

In *Matthew* 16: 18, Jesus speaks on the assumption that as Christ, Son of the Living God, in fullest fulfilment of all Old Testament hopes, he will establish his people as a distinct entity. They are marked out not only as being his own, but also as enduring against all opposition, even death itself. Here we are faced with a body of people who span time and space, for while it would be a reasonable inference that Christ will do his building work on earth, the battle has metaphysical dimensions. These are sufficient grounds, with the Holy Spirit's inspiration, for Paul to teach the truth of a universal church with amazing characteristics, best described in his letter to the Ephesians:-

- A union of Jew and Gentile into one body forged at Calvary (*Eph.* 2:11-22)
- Built on the key revelators of old (prophets) and new (apostles) covenants (*Eph.* 2:20)

- A teaching tool directed at metaphysical realities—principalities and powers in heavenly places (*Eph.* 3:7-12)
- Presently growing as a living organism here on earth, with gifts equipping all the 'distinct ones' (saints), so that each acts as a body-part of a living body, growing up into the fullness of what Christ is (*Eph.* 4:2-16)

...With local expression

In *Matthew* 18: 17 Jesus speaks on the assumption that his *ekklesia* can be recognisable at a local level. Thus, if a couple of disciples have conflicts among themselves that can't be resolved one to one, then a distinct group of people in their local community may be consulted and may take action to seek either to resolve the conflict or to bring discipline to bear on an unrepentant disciple. In this context, Jesus makes the comment (which has been a defining watchword within the historical Brethren movement), 'For where two or three are gathered together in my name, there am I in the midst of them.' Again, the key verb, 'gathered', is not a technical term, but a common word for assembling together, whether people or things, whether for good or bad purposes. So, as with *ekklesia*, the meaning in the particular context is established by asking questions such as, who are the people meeting and for what purpose and in what way? Jesus answers succinctly, 'in my name'. Even a cursory reading of the Old Testament should cause us to realise that this is a significant expression—God talks a lot about the significance of His name. In a generic sense, doing something in the name of someone should clearly mean identifying yourself with that person and acting according to their wishes, and, where that person has some specific position or authority, it implies placing yourself and acting under that authority.

Deeper reading of Old and New Testaments teaches that the Name of God (YAHWEH) is both a summation of all that God is (a revelation of his character (*Exodus* 34: 5-7)) and a concentration of his power as he works out his purposes. That Jesus humbly but firmly considers his name to be that to which people gather and under which they function, draws together the incredible truth that the disciples of Jesus are the people of God. Where a grouping of such people, even as small as two or three, meet in humble but firm recognition of the reality of Jesus' lordship and deity, then a local expression of the greater reality of the whole church, the full body of Christ, comes into being.

While 'church planting', in the sense of establishing a larger group of people meeting with some organised leadership structure etc, is what this book has in view, the seriousness of drawing two or three (it is to be hoped, a lot more) to meet regularly under the authority of Christ should not be underestimated or belittled in any way. In God's reality, when two or three believers come together deliberately and regularly with a conscious submission to the authority of Christ, a local expression of the body of Christ (a local church) graciously and amazingly now exists on that piece of planet earth.

Not a new idea but creative continuity

Exodus 12: 6, 16: 1 and 35:1, for example, bring together two common Hebrew words used to describe God's gathered ancient people, Israel: *qahal* and *edah*, which are quite close in meaning. In English Bible versions of the more literal variety, *qahal* (used 170 times in the Old Testament) is most frequently translated as 'congregation' and *edah* (used 120 times) as an 'assembling together of people'. There are two often repeated expressions: one is 'the congregation of Israel' which has the sense of the *ekklesia* identified as 'Israel' i.e. the 'Israel-church'. The second is the 'whole congregation' which emphasises the union of the many into one entity. Although Israel was a nation of different tribes and many family houses and individuals, before God they were one people, one entity, one *ekklesia*-church. Occasionally, the expression 'assembly' or 'congregation of Yahweh' is used to describe this entity of God's own people.

This gives some historical background to what the disciples understood Jesus to mean when he said 'I will build my *ekklesia*, my assembly or congregation of people.' I doubt they would have thought of some entity divorced from Israel, but of the logical necessity that now Yahweh's Messiah had come, he would gather Yahweh's people to himself.

In addition to this *ekklesia* term and concept, the apostles were not slow in connecting the identities that Yahweh had intended Israel to fulfil, as being in essence what we now are to be in Christ. *Exodus* 19:3-6 (RSV) is worth quoting in full:

> Thus you shall say to the house of Jacob, and tell the people of Israel: You have seen what I did to the Egyptians, and how I bore you on eagles' wings and brought you to myself. Now therefore, if you will obey my voice and keep my covenant, you shall be my own possession among all peoples; for all the earth is mine, and you shall be to me a kingdom of priests and a holy nation. These are the words which you shall speak to the children of Israel.

Spoken as it is on the covenantal forging ground of Mount Sinai, this is a fundamental definition of what God desires here on earth—a people for himself. And in case there should be even the slightest shadow of doubt, these words are not spoken by some petulant, self-seeking deity who wants to grasp after more things than he ought. This is the Creator and Divine Redeemer lovingly embracing again that which had been lost. Peter grasped keenly the continuity for our times, when another mountain had been climbed and a new covenant made, and God again identifies his own in this world. Again a quotation with little comment will suffice, *1 Peter* 2:4-10 (RSV):

> Come to him, to that living stone, rejected by men but in God's sight chosen and precious; and like living stones be yourselves built into a spiritual house, to be a holy priesthood, to offer spiritual sacrifices acceptable to God through Jesus Christ....you are a chosen race, a royal priesthood, a holy nation, God's own people, that you may declare the wonderful deeds of him who called you out of darkness into his marvelous light. Once you were no people but now you are God's people; once you had not received mercy but now you have received mercy.

The uniqueness of the New Testament *ekklesia* lies in the sense of long-awaited fulfilment, that here at last is what God had always intended. This is what thrills Paul in *Ephesians* 3, the mystery now revealed. Through the awesome power of Christ's work in the cross, God is present in and communicates through his people on earth - not only to the rest of unregenerate humanity, but also to the spirit world that lies beyond our present comprehension.

A hint of a definition

By now we should have enough sense of the scriptures, the mind and heart of God, to see that *ekklesia* is God's use of a common human term to describe the core of his strategy on earth. He has always been and still is calling out a people to be his very own possession, who will live on earth, with his real presence among them, in such a way that there is an evident expression of God on earth. Whether this is in the fullest sense, transcending time and space, as the whole body of Christ—past, present future, on earth and in heaven (the 'Church catholic')—or else in the most intimate of local expressions as a few disciples of Jesus meet in fullest reverence for his name and glory, under and in his authority (*Matt* 28:19-20; 18:20).

A number of characteristics should be noted:

- **Divine Possession**: we are *his* people, this is *his* church not ours.
- **Appropriate humility**: We have not been chosen through any merit of our own, and so the fact of being God's special possession should give us a deep sense of security but not a hint of superiority or pride over others.
- **World Context**: we are not removed from or divorced from this world, but are his people in this world.
- **Missional Purpose**: We are not his people in this world for our own good (although there is eternal good in so being!) but for the communication of God's goodness to others. Implicit in the call of Abraham was the purpose that 'all nations shall be blessed through you'. This has been made explicit in Jesus command, 'go to all nations and make them my disciples.'

To be church then, whether in terms of identity or local functionality, must at least mean to bear out these characteristics in both our understanding and our actions.

From synagogues to local 'churches'

The New Testament concept of church in its fullest, most 'catholic' ('universal') sense lies in the Old Testament picture of God's calling of Israel to be his people on earth. Similarly, the functional principles of the New Testament local church owes much to a development that took place through the Exile in Babylon and the post-exilic period, when the Temple in Jerusalem was either non-existent or inaccessible, that is, the synagogue. It is amazing and intriguing that a phenomenon apparently not sanctioned in the Old Testament should, under the guidance, even encouragement, of the Spirit, have become a natural apostolic pattern for the local expressions of the universal church that Christ is building.

It is beyond the scope of this chapter, but it is worth studying the origins, purpose and functions of the synagogue, as it would have been familiar to Jews and Gentiles in the time of Jesus. The absence and then inaccessibility of the Temple was a real problem to the ten tribes of Israel scattered worldwide by the Assyrians, and to the remaining two tribes taken into captivity as Babylon destroyed both Jerusalem and the Temple. How could they maintain a relationship with God in foreign lands, and without access to the one place sanctioned as a point of meeting with and sacrifice to God? Pragmatically, the spiritual life of the people was kept alive through simply meeting together to encourage one another. The spontaneous gatherings of exilic Jews for Sabbaths and festivals, for communal worship and mutual support[1] were described later by the Greek word *synagoge*, which simply means 'to bring or come together, to congregate.' The linguistic overlap between the Hebrew *qahal* and the other Greek word *ekklesia* is obvious. In his letter, James (2: 2), writing to a largely Jewish group of Christians, does not hesitate to use the term synagogue to describe the local gathering of these early believers. If *ekklesia* became the common term to describe both universal and local expression of the entity of God's own people, it is not because the concept differed from synagogue, rather that the words meant the same thing to believing Jews.

So where does that leave us in terms of planting 'one of them' today?
I shall not start a debate about whether the term 'planting' is the correct term to use for the subject matter of this book. However, if we have grasped the core concept of 'church' then probably the more Biblically-accurate concept of 'congregating' a new church comes to mind. And we may note that the early Brethren spoke of 'gathering to his name' when they formed a local church! The art of 'Church planting' is found in the simple task of reconciling people to God and then in drawing them together into a recognisable entity, now that they are already a new entity—united into the one body of Christ by the Holy Spirit (*1 Cor.* 12: 13). In this sense, a church in a given locality of planet earth simply comes into existence the moment you have two or more believers together in one place. Human nature dictates that we should immediately start formulating our rules and regulations (which Protestantism has made an art-form for generations) as to how many people are needed (the Jewish exiles said ten males which may be a precedent!), how often they meet (Sabbath days and other high days?) and at what precise point the fourfold ministry of the local church does or can begin (teaching, prayer, fellowship and the Breaking of Bread) or whether we need to see the 7, 12, 21 or Heinz 57 varieties of 'marks' of a local church before we recognise a new group of believers as an ekklesia.

But lay aside our human summaries of sound New Testament principles for a moment and wonder at the awesome wisdom of God in the new covenant. Rather than using the model of Tabernacle/Temple (one exclusive place to which all must come,), the Holy Spirit takes up the concept of synagogue as model of a local church. However, the Temple concept as dwelling place of God must be fully understood too.

---

1 G W Bromiley, *The International Standard Bible Encyclopaedia,* Grand Rapids: Eerdmans 1988, vol. 4, pp. 676-684

A key theological aside—the 'dwelling place of God'

In *John* 14, Jesus uses the well-understood longstanding concept of 'temple' to explain to his disciples the seismic shift that was taking place during his days on earth. It is perhaps here more than anywhere else that the creative continuity of the church concept is most powerfully seen. Any local church planted should be founded on an understanding of the heart of God and his methodology in his mission here on earth. *John* 14.1-4 is very familiar territory for us, possibly so familiar we sometimes miss its central point. So also for those first disciples, the familiar term, 'house of God', was changed in a radical way. The word Jesus uses for house, *oikia*, was a common word to describe human dwellings, houses, and rarely used in a technical way for Temple or tabernacle. The expression 'Father's house' seems to convey a warm concept of a family home—not God's house, but the Father's house—and appears to be Jesus' distinctive way of referring to the Temple among other things! *John* 14.2 as an opening shot conveys a radical new idea to the disciples, because, after all, people did not normally live in the Temple. Jesus states that our future hope is as radical as living with God, our Father, in his house forever, along with himself. And in speaking of our future in 'many dwelling places', he uses the Greek word *mone*, which is a noun based on a frequently used verb 'to abide' or 'to remain' (see *John* 1: 33 and frequently in *John* 15). The noun form is only used twice in the New Testament; both of these occasions are in *John* 14 and therefore as you read the Greek you would link verses 2 and 23. The Lord's use of the noun seems to make a close connection between the eternal dwelling places we have with the Father in his home and the present dwelling the Father, Son and Holy Spirit have within each one of us. Long before we go to live in the mansions of glory, we are to be God's 'mansions of glory' here on earth—a very high precious calling that supersedes the specifics of any missionary or ministry calling we may have, as it touches all aspects of every believer's life.

Here is a reminder of what Jesus and the disciples to whom he is speaking were very familiar with:

(a) The presence of God is the sign that distinguished God's people from all others.

God living with His people was a well-known and deeply-appreciated truth among believing Jews. Although circumcision, the Law and the priesthood had their places, they were not as significant to the Jews as the presence of God among his people (*Ex.* 33: 7-23; 34: 29-35). Moses recognized the critical nature of this (*Ex.* 33: 15 & 16) as:

- the proof of God's pleasure in his people and their acceptance of him (relationship with God)
- distinguishing them from all other peoples as his special envoys to them (relationship with others).

(b) The place of the presence was in and on the tabernacle.

Essentially symbolized externally by the pillar of cloud (or column of fire at night) which rested on top of the tabernacle, God's presence was also specifically located within the holy of holies on top of the ark of the covenant, between the cherubim (*Ex.* 40: 34-38; *Lev.* 16:2; *Num.* 9:15-23 & 12:5). Significantly, a direct connection is made between the pillar of cloud and the Holy Spirit (*Is.* 63: 7-14 & *Neh.* 9: 19-20) whose function was:

- to give a real sense of the actual presence of God with his people
- for guidance
- to teach and instruct
- to give rest (defence and protection).

(c) The temple of Solomon became the place of the presence of God (1 Kings 8:1-13).

There was actual glory in that Temple, the cloud of the presence, the *shekinah*, the shining forth of God (*Ps.* 80: 1, 3, 7, & 19). We should note also that *shekinah* is a Hebrew word, the root of which is the word *sakan*, meaning 'to dwell'.

(d) The presence of God was lost by the persistent sin and idolatry of the people

This was described in graphic, painful reality by God in *Ezekiel* 9: 3; 10:3ff—the glory of God from off the cherubim to the Temple doorway, and 11: 22-25—from the doorway, through the city out to the eastern mountains. These are some of the most heart-rending passages of scripture, yet it is a sadly, an oft-repeated sequence of events in the history of the Church. Local churches or groups of churches (even whole denominations) who have lost the presence of God in their midst (see also *Rev.* 2: 5 & 3:20)!

(e) The post-exilic Temple never had the presence of God in or on it

Perhaps that was part of the reason why the old men wept (*Ez.* 3:12). Yet the promise remained that the presence would return to the Temple (*Mal.* 3: 1). The question is to which Temple and in what way? The answer was in the person of Jesus Christ, to the second Temple; not as a pillar of cloud but as Immanuel (*Matt.* 1: 23), the glory of God returned (*Lk.* 2: 9 & *Jn.* 1: 14). But this was temporary, as *John* 1:14 states, using the words *tabernacled among us*, a reminder of the dwelling place on the move in the wilderness.

(f) Christ himself is the house of God on earth

John 2: 19 contains a conceptual bridge between how the presence had dwelt in his people in the Old Covenant and how it would be in the New Covenant. Jesus Christ was the dwelling place of God, in whom was found the glory, the presence of God among his people. So we have a shift in the concept of the house (dwelling place) of God, from being a place or building to being a person. In *John* 1: 32-34, the Spirit descends and remains on Jesus and thus the body of Christ is the dwelling place of God on the earth. This was to be the distinguishing mark of the Messiah (*Is.* 11: 2; 42: 1; & 61: 1), the one upon whom the Spirit rested. Hence in *John* 2: 19, Christ sees his body as the Temple-dwelling place of God. In *John* 14, Jesus tries to convey to his disciples (vv. 9-11), that the Father has been dwelling in him all the time that they had been with him. But there was one more stage to go, which Jesus has already hinted at in private conversation with the Samaritan woman, that worship of God would not be limited to a place but could be done anywhere in Spirit and in truth (*Jn.* 4: 24). As he was soon to leave the world, where then would the 'Temple' on earth be?

(g) In the New Covenant the presence is in a new temple, in the way that was first demonstrated in Christ

In *John* 14, Jesus tries to convey to the disciples that not only did they have an eternal place in the Temple of God (the Father's house), but *they were to become the Temple of God* (*Jn* 14: 1)! The Father's house is Jesus' way of referring to the Temple (*Jn.* 2: 19 & *Lk.* 2: 49). The many dwelling places are the rooms described as part of the new Temple (*Ezek.* 42: 1-20; 44: 9-16; & 48: 11), reserved for the consecrated priests. Jesus is broadening the Jewish concept of a restricted priesthood among God's people, back to God's original intention that all of his people should function as priests and prophets (*Ex.* 19: 6 & *Num.* 11: 29) and that there is a special place for each one in the Temple of God. In *John* 14: 23, the Lord makes the final connection to what God intends to do now. Using the same word for 'dwelling places' (both 14.2 and 14.23), he states that the pillar of cloud was to descend again, not to a geographic place, but onto and into each of his disciples! As one of the phenomena of Pentecost, the tongues of fire resting on each head seem to give evidence of this, mini-symbols of the pillar of cloud as the Holy Spirit enters to dwell in each believer.

We are the Temple of God! This is how the apostles interpreted the teaching of Christ that the triune God is to dwell in us:

- The whole Church as one Body, the Universal Church (*Eph.* 2: 19-22)
- The local body of Christ in any geographic location, local churches (*1 Cor.* 3: 16-17)
- The individual believer, his own body, (*1 Cor.* 6: 19-20).

The profound simplicity of the concept of the dwelling place of God has awesome implication for what a local church is meant to be. A group of believers functioning together in Christ are assured of God's immediate presence and that they will be God's house in the community, his address, the meeting place for anyone there who desires to find God.

Recognising the limitless flexibility of 'synagogue' rather than Temple as the model for church

A remarkable concept emerges if we combine the theological concept of our meeting as believers, the mystical timeless/spaceless Church as being where God lives, and the pattern of multiple synagogues rather than a single Temple. The result is a flexibility that has enabled the emergence of local groups of believers world-wide, in any language or culture, unhindered by human hierarchies and national or international politics. This is truly amazing! Church history has demonstrated this time and time again, as the gospel goes to new regions and a distinctive 'Christ-like', yet different, expression of church appears. Intentionally lacking in earth-bound power and authority structures, no national or international government or army has ever succeeded in controlling, suppressing or wiping it out. With direct access to the Lord Christ through the imminent presence of God in Holy Spirit, each and every expression of this church can be led by the scriptures to grow and function as God intended. Local leadership (elders), along with gifted people who are called to minster trans-congregationally (*Eph* 4: 7-11—apostles, etc), blending together the local flexibility with a wider, cohesive strength.

If God can sanctify the human post-exilic creation of the synagogue and utilise it in the formation of first-century local churches, and has found it possible to use a huge range of evolving shapes of church through the past 2,000 years, then I don't think we need to worry too much about a precise 'shape' for any church plant that you may be involved in. I have always been a 'back-to-first-principles' sort of guy, and it strikes me that this is quite close to the mind of Christ in terms of mission in the world. Under Spirit-inspired reading of scripture, the focus should be less on shape and more on what enables the essential nature of church to take root. Whatever type or shape of church you may plant, seek by God's grace that it should become evidently a place where God can reliably be found and where His glory can clearly be seen.

A brief survey of key pictures of Church that relate to the growth of Church
We have focused on two Biblical concepts of what 'church' is meant to be—the people of God and the dwelling place of God. We have also focused on the starting point as being an understanding of what is the 'church' in the mystical universal sense, because local churches are expressions in time-space reality of what Christ is truly building for all eternity. It will be necessary to bear this constantly in mind, otherwise we will lapse into producing a grouping of people often reflecting more of our own preferences than Christ's heart, and when we do that, they often can become increasingly disconnected from the rest of the body of Christ.

But here are additional biblical pictures which powerfully describe the church and which space does not permit us to explore in this chapter. Here is a reminder of the key ones, as a challenge to study each of them and explore how these also should shape of local church that you are involved in developing.

- **People of God**: Bearing the character of God, for the sake of being his witness, salt and light, his ambassadors in this present world.
- **House of God** (Temple): the real presence of God on earth, God's address, found in three-fold forms of universal, local group, and in an individual believer.
- **Body of Christ**: The means by which Jesus continues his work on earth (*Acts* as a whole—the story continued …)
- **Bride of Christ**: the depth of intimacy to be developed between us and our God.
- **Children of God**: bearing the likeness and image of Christ, who is the eternal, unique Son of God (*Rom.* 8: 28-30 & *2 Cor.* 3: 17-18).
- **Family**: Intimacy of relationship one with another
- **Community**: Interrelatedness of members and their care for one another (*Acts* 2: 1-47 & 4: 32-35) and means of service outward through the fringes and into the world itself.
- **Royal Priesthood**: giving worship and praise to God and providing mediation and intercession for one another and for those not yet in the faith.

CHAPTER 5

Lone ranger or team player?

Stephen McQuoid

Church planting is not an impossible business but it is a tough one. It takes not only courage and determination, but also a range of different gifts and skills to plant a church and bring it to a point of maturity. When the work first begins there is a real need for people who naturally make friends and can share the gospel with them. Once a few contacts become Christians, then the work of discipleship begins. This runs alongside a developing teaching programme. Services begin and that requires people gifted in public presentation and worship leading. Finally leaders are chosen trained and empowered which takes insight and organisation. It is the application of all of these gifts, abilities and skills that enable a church to come to fruition.

There are times when churches are planted by individuals, but this is fairly rare. Very few people have all the gifts that are required to do the job, so several people need to learn to work together and that involves the important issue of teams and how they function.

Teams are formed in different ways. Sometimes a mission organisation will deliberately train and bring together a team of full-time missionaries to plant a church. On the other hand, a large church will send a group of its members out to form and plant a new church and informally teamwork will emerge so that the new church can become a reality. Sometimes several churches get together and assemble a team from their memberships and these church planters from several churches do the job. However, it is done, there can be no doubt that teamwork is a highly productive way of achieving a goal. If we can learn to work together, we combine our strengths and gifts; if we do not learn to work together, we will quickly discover the limits of our individual abilities. If teams work well they can be even more powerful that the sum total of their individual parts; if those same people work individually and in isolation, then their potential will be greatly diminished and dissipated.

It would be important to note that the idea of teamwork is a thoroughly biblical one. Indeed, a glance at Jesus' public ministry would reveal that at the very beginning, he chose a group of disciples to follow him and they became his team. Jesus formed his team by asking specific people to be part of it; in other words, he head-hunted the right candidates. There was nothing random about this process (*Lk.* 6: 12-16). He carefully selected them and then trained them for the task ahead. Interestingly, Jesus' method of training involved not only telling his disciples what to do, but showing them also. They learned by working together as a team.

As we look further at the ministry of Jesus and in particular his management of this team of disciples, we see a clearly-defined strategy in action (*Mt.* 10: 1-6). First, he organized them into manageable groups and then gave them the spiritual equipment necessary to complete their ministry (*Mk.* 6: 7). When it came to practical issues such as their support, Jesus dealt frankly with them (*Lk.* 10: 5-7). He ensured that they were culturally sensitive so as not to put any unnecessary stumbling block in the way of people hearing their message (*Lk.* 10: 8). He also made it clear that ultimately mission involves faith (*Lk.* 9: 3-5 & 10: 4-7). Jesus was careful to stress their accountability to himself as team leader and the need to report back all that they had done (*Lk.* 10: 17). This ensured good communication and co-ordination. As a consequence, their work had direction. What becomes readily apparent is that teamwork was at the very heart of all that Jesus did.

While Jesus is the key role model of good practice, there are others also. The apostle Paul is a good example. He too gathered teams to accompany him on his missionary journeys (*2 Cor.* 8: 23 & *Phil.* 4: 3). What is interesting is that, although Paul was unquestionably one of the most gifted and intellectually-able Christians of his generation, yet his inclination was not to be a loner, but to work with others in team ministry. His wisdom in this regard deserves reflection.

The biblical picture seems clear. It suggests that teamwork is at the very heart of mission. The ministries of Jesus and Paul are powerful evidences of this; moreover, there are few occasions in the New Testament where we read of mission being done by individuals working on their own. There are times when such a ministry is a necessity. Nevertheless, the principle still stands that teamwork is an important component of the work of mission. Certainly when it comes to a challenge as formidable as church planting, teamwork will be a valuable asset.

Having recognized the importance of teamwork, it is equally important to ask questions about what makes a team work well. After all, if teamwork is a feature of mission in general and church planting in particular, we would do well to reflect on how best to conduct team life. So what makes a good team? There are at least seven features of a good team that are worth pointing out.

1. A good team shares common goals

The first defining characteristic of a good team is that each member of the team shares a common set of goals. This is a self-evident quality because it stands to reason that if the different members of the team are not pulling in the same direction, then the team will become dysfunctional and may well fall apart. The implications of this are important to ponder. Anyone who has every worked on a team will know that 'ideas people' are worth their weight in gold. The creativity that such people bring makes the team dynamic. However, if the ideas that are produced and the strategy that results is not owned by everyone on the team then they will end up working at cross purposes. The ideas people should be encouraged to be creative, but time should be allowed for all the team members to own those ideas also.

On a good team, each member will be committed to the team's goals and be determined to ensure they are reached. They should not feel as if these goals are being imposed on them, but rather they are mutually agreed. Every team member will also be able to see how their particular gifts will assist in achieving these goals and will ensure they play their part.

2. A good team comprises members who have different roles to suit their strengths and weaknesses

A second feature of a good team is that it will be made up of members who fulfill roles that suit their strengths. We have already mentioned that when it comes to the job of church planting, no one person is likely to have all the gifts necessary. It is for this very reason that teams are so important. But a good team is one in which the different members will compensate for each other's weaknesses and therefore produce a strong unit.

Of course, this applies not only to the gifts that team members have, but also to their personality traits. Different people respond to situations in different ways and a team of people will usually be more able to meet the challenges that come from a range of different circumstances than an individual will. When new challenges arrive, the more creative members of the team will come into their own and will use their creativity to find a solution to the problem. When a situation becomes difficult and even unpleasant, the highly-motivated and rugged team members take the lead and confront the problem head on. If the situation in which the team finds itself becomes volatile and changeable, the more flexible team members begin to excel and enable the others to accommodate themselves to the situation. If the challenge becomes momentous, then the experienced and mature team members will find that their contribution becomes indispensable. When there is tension within the team, or indeed the whole church-planting project, those who are more disposed to being peacemakers will play the vital role of keeping everyone together. These qualities will never be found altogether in the same person, but if the church plant is being done by a team, then it is possible that each of these helpful qualities will be present.

3. A good team is mutually supportive

A third feature of a good team is that its members are mutually supportive. It is said that no man is an island and this is certainly true. Human beings are by their very nature social creatures and, while many of us do like our own space and company, no one can properly exist devoid of meaningful relationships. Equally, while some people like working on their own for periods of time, no one can successfully work in complete isolation from everyone else. After all, even the Lone Ranger was never really alone; he always had the company of Tonto.

This will certainly be true when it comes to church planting. It can be a very lonely calling. There are times when the planter will experience great discouragement and disappointment. Some situations which church planters will encounter will be almost unbearably hard. There will be heartbreak and setbacks, times when things seem to be going well and times when nothing seems to be working properly. What is more, our own human fallibility has to be reckoned with. It is all but impossible to separate what we do from our personal situations. If a church planter is going through a personal crisis or hardship; perhaps it is a family problem, or a health issue, it might even be a spiritual issue, it is impossible just to focus on the job and shut out all the pain that is being experienced. Sooner or later those personal issues will crowd in and begin to affect the work being done.

If a good team exists, however, this discouragement and these issues can be dealt with. Good team members support one another and look out for each other. They will take a genuine interest not only in the work their colleagues do but also their personal lives. They will work hard at developing harmony and closeness within the team and growing their friendships. They will also pray for each other, show loyalty and be committed to helping one another in practical everyday things. Sometimes it is this kind of support that will keep team members from becoming discouraged and giving up altogether.

4. A good team gives priority to development and training, both on an individual and team basis

Another feature of a good team is that its members recognize that they are not the finished article and that they can always do better individually so that the team as a whole can improve on what it does. This quest for excellence will permeate the team and motivate each member to be the best they can. This is an important feature to have in team life, because complacency is one of the greatest dangers we can face in Christian ministry. It is easy to feel that we are doing well enough and don't need to improve. There is also the temptation to rely on other team members to carry the burden and not to feel a sense of personal responsibility. Equally, it is easy to assume that we are able enough to do what we are doing rather than looking actively for ways of improving our levels of skill or developing further through training.

If members of a team fall into this trap of complacency, they will eventually lose their edge and that will ultimately lead to the team itself becoming a little stale. A good team will be comprised of individuals who demand the very best from themselves and their colleagues. They will challenge each other to improve and to achieve excellence in every situation.

5. A good team believes in a relationship of equality, although leadership is essential

A fifth quality of a good team is that the members of the team respect each other and treat each other equally. That is not to say that no distinctions are made in the team. Every team needs leadership and so in that sense there needs to be a first among equals. But this leadership position is one of function, not status. Unless the leader is willing to be treated in the same way as everyone else, then the team will not function. A leader who acts in an elitist way, who doesn't think about the needs of others, who is not willing to listen to their opinions; such a leader will eventually demoralize his team. Servant leadership is the key, because people are motivated when they are treated well. Only when everyone feels respected and their voice is heard will the team function properly.

6. A good team maintains a high level of mutual communication

A good team requires good communication. This again is self evident. If there is not good communication then the team will be reduced to a collection of individuals who are engaged in their own pursuits, but with no reference to each other and no coherent strategy. Worse still, where there is no communication, misunderstandings are bound to occur. This in turn will lead to hurts and friction building up in their interpersonal relationships.

With good communication, however, each team member will know what the other is doing. They can interact with each other and also iron out any possible misunderstandings. It will enable each member to feel they are engaged in the whole work of the team and will certainly give great stimulus to prayer in team life. What is more, it will mean that team members will take an interest in each other's life and ministry.

This communication needs to take place at several levels concurrently. First, there needs to be good communication from the leader to each of the team members. This is because without communication in this direction, the team members will be unaware of the leader is thinking, where he wants the team to focus its attention or what specific goals he would like to set. Team members need to know what is expected of them and should not be put in a position where they are surprised by events because they have not been told about them.

Equally, communication needs to go from team members back to the leader. They need to give honest feedback about what they have been told. It is highly damaging to team life for a team member to have concerns about something, but not to articulate those concerns. This will lead to disappointment and even bitterness. Equally, team members need to be able to positively express their support of good initiatives that the leader takes, both to encourage the leader and to lend weight to good judgment calls. If team members maintain a silence, they do not hold their leader accountable, neither do they encourage him.

There also needs to be good communication between team members. They have the dynamic of their own relationships to maintain. If the leader is communicating with each of them but they are not in touch with each other, there is a danger that everything is centralized around the leader with no cross-fertilization of ideas across the membership of the team. This will result in a fairly sterile team life. What is more, with the team leader being at the centre of everything and being the only link with each team member, the possibility of favoritism or at least the perception of favoritism is very real. All that would be required would be for one team member to feel that the team leader considers his or her opinion to be of less value that that of another team member. The result would be that the team member would become demoralized and de-motivated.

Finally there needs to be communication between the team and those they are working with in the church plant. This becomes particularly important as the church plant grows and begins to involve a number of people who are not part of the team. It is essential that team members learn not to work in isolation, but to openly communicate with everyone in the church so that the agenda and goals of the team are shared by everyone who is involved in the church plant. This will be especially important when the church begins to appoint elders. Often elders will be appointed who have not been in the church planting team. They will feel very isolated and somewhat left out if there is good communication within the team but they are not included in this. It will make the transition from church plant to established church more difficult and volatile than it ought.

7. A good team is constantly adapting to change

Lastly a good team is constantly adapting to change in a dynamic way, not just carrying out policy from above. In any work, conditions can change over time and with change comes the challenge of how to respond to a different situation. Individuals working on their own often find it difficult to deal with change; this problem is multiplied when a whole team has to deal with the experience of change—but deal with change it must.

A good team is able to re-invent itself and deal with new situations in a united and positive way. Change will be seen as an opportunity not a disadvantage. The individual members of the team will encourage and stimulate each other's thinking so that they can all adapt to whatever new situation they face. There will be sufficient coherence in what they do that no one member will be left behind, trying to solve yesterday's problem. Rather they will all be up to speed and ready for today's issues.

The question that needs to be asked is, how does such a team come together? What is it that will enable the team to function well and work as a genuine unit? Ultimately the success of a team will depend on two vital factors, without which no team can function well. These are accountable team members and a good team leader.

Accountable Workers

There is a real sense in which a team simply does not exist until its members recognize that they need to submit their will to that of the team as a whole. This is self-evident but often overlooked. A team cannot be a mere collection of individuals—there must be a willingness to work for the benefit of the whole, not just be focused on self. Each team member must recognize that while they have a voice and have something to bring to the table in the church planting project, there is also a leader who needs to give the team direction and ensure that the work gets done. Without the humility and determination to recognize this, a team will never come together.

Leadership

But as well as team members who are prepared to follow, there also needs to be a leader who will provide impetus for the church planting project. Indeed the single most important issue in teamwork is that of leadership. Good leaders can do an enormous amount of good and make things happen, but equally they can hamper a work. No two people will lead in the same way, as different leaders will each have their own style. However there are at least four things that a good leader will do:

- a good leader will transfer the ownership of the work to his team members. This is important because, until they really own the project, they will not give it their all. Only when they are as passionate about the project as he is, will he be free to concentrate of the vital issue of directing the team.
- a good leader will create an environment in which team members will thrive. People will work at their best when they are valued, happy and secure. These conditions must be created by the leader. If he does not provide encouragement for the team and encourage an environment which is mutually supportive, no one else will. Some leaders are less concerned about the conditions in which their team members work and only think of what they achieve. This, however, is shortsighted because if team members enjoy what they do, then they will do much more in the long run.
- a good team leader will develop the potential of each member of his team. This is easier said than done, because everyone is an individual and each person will bring a different set of skills to the team. Moreover, different

people are excited and motivated by different things. The leader will need to learn what makes each person 'tick' and then use that knowledge to get the best out of them. If he does this, he will reap the benefits.
- a good team leader will be a role model for his team. No true leader will expect something from a team member that he is not prepared to do himself. What is more, he should set the standard for conduct and commitment. No team will rise above the level of its leader, so the job of leadership is firstly to ensure personal standards are maintained and then ensure the team follows.
- A good team leader makes himself accountable to his team. If accountability is to be effective, it works in both directions. Every leader has the right to have high expectations of his team; they also have the right to have high expectations of him and to hold him accountable for his actions. When leaders give the impression they are above criticism, or that they do not welcome input from others, they automatically alienate their teams. Good leadership involves being open to constructive criticism from those you work with.

The dynamic of team life

When all of this comes together the dynamic of team life begins. A team will be a finely-balanced unit in which each person plays their part so that the team is greater than the sum of the individual parts. Any default in any direction will cause the balance to be shifted and the team will function less effectively. The diagram below demonstrates how this works in practice.

In a situation where team members are effective in what they do, but the team leader is not, the end-result is a team that keeps itself busy because of the calibre of the membership, but one that lacks direction. Where both team members and leader are ineffective, the team will achieve very little. Where the leadership is good, but the team members do not play their role, the result will be a leader exerting himself but struggling because of the burdens he bears. Where both leader and team members are effective, the team will be a powerful and dynamic unit.

```
                      EFFECTIVE MEMBERSHIP
                         ↙          ↘
            Effective team          Busy but ineffective team
                  ↗                         ↖
EFFECTIVE                                        INEFFECTIVE
LEADERSHIP                                       LEADERSHIP
                  ↘                         ↗
            Follower team           Sleepy team
                         ↖          ↗
                      INEFFECTIVE MEMBERSHIP
```

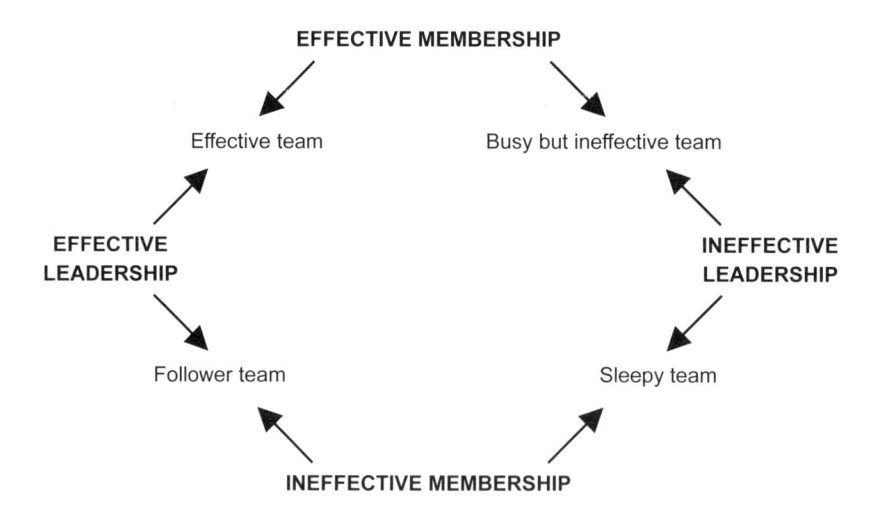

Dangers of Team life

The lesson is clear: both the team leader and the team members have their part to play in order to ensure that the team works well. Even when this does happen, there is no room for complacency because there are several factors that can frustrate and derail even the most balanced of teams.

First, a team can be destroyed by members who are too independent. Where the impulse for autonomy becomes more pronounced than the desire for cooperation, the team will begin to fragment. There is nothing wrong with team members who are independent thinkers—indeed this can be a real help for the team as they bring a different perspective. However, this needs to be tempered by the requirements of team life. If it is not and the independence goes unchecked, the team will end up being no more than a collection of individuals who share the same basic beliefs and commitments.

Secondly, team life will be destroyed by cliques. These can form easily but are difficult to disband. It is inevitable that team members will relate better to some of their colleagues than to others. Indeed it would be unsurprising in a team of any size if some team members did not naturally warm to each together. However these differing personalities need to be reckoned with, as they impact on the dynamic of team life. Cliques form when teams allow their personal feelings to interfere with team life. Team members who get on well together can form exclusive relationships in which other team members are treated as outsiders. While they might justify this exclusivity on the basis that it is a 'social' relationship, it can nevertheless dissolve the working unity which the team tries to build.

Thirdly, a team can be destroyed by people who are too combative. Of course there should always be a place for healthy debate. Indeed, it is essential that all team members are willing to express their opinions and argue their corner. However, the spirit in which debate takes place is all important. Not only should everyone pick their battles wisely, they should also express disagreement in a gracious way. If team members are overly-aggressive and even intimidating in the way they deal with colleagues, then team relationships will inevitably be badly damaged.

The fourth thing that destroys team life is when team members are so malleable and co-operative that they neither have strong opinions on anything nor express themselves vigorously. Differing opinions well expressed make for highly-creative teams and ones where important issues can be thrashed out in the search for solutions. If team members refuse to engage in what is being discussed, for whatever reason, the team will lose its sparkle and there will be nobody to hold the team leader accountable.

A fifth thing that can destroy a team is when team members are business-orientated and not relationship-orientated. While a church planting team is there to do a job—namely plant a church, nevertheless the team lives as a result of relationship. Consequently, interpersonal relationships are of great importance. If relationships on a team are allowed to weaken, then the team as a whole will be weakened.

CHAPTER 6

Stages of a church plant

Stephen McQuoid

Church planting is in some senses no different than many other activities in that it occurs in stages as part of an overall process. In this respect, it is a bit like building a house. Anyone in the construction industry will tell you that when you are building a house, you do not begin with the roof; rather the starting point is the foundations. Once they are completed, the builder then goes on to build the walls, then the roof, and finally put in all the windows, doors and fixtures. So too with church planting; it is a process that takes place over several stages. In this chapter we will outline the typical stages that go into a church plant.

Pioneer

The first stage in any church plant can well be described as the pioneer stage, because it involves the initial impact that the church planters will make in the area where they are planting. Obviously there are different ways of doing a church plant as next chapter indicates. Likewise, there can be different starting points, as some church plants might involve a sizable group of people starting the church, while others might begin with a small team of just two or three couples. Nevertheless, the pioneer stage will necessarily involve the task of trying to ensure that people get to hear the gospel. Unless people hear and believe, then a church will never be established. It is this need that will drive the agenda during the pioneer stage.

Of course, ensuring that people hear the gospel is easier said than done. The challenge for the church planters is how to get an audience? Before you can proclaim the gospel to people, you first need to establish a relationship with them. This, however, takes time and is not an easy thing to do when you are new to an area. What is more, doing evangelism in a pioneer situation is very different from doing evangelism in the context of an existing church. To begin with, a typical church plant in its pioneer stage will not have a building to operate from. If the planters wish to hold evangelistic services, bible studies, children's clubs or a youth club, they will need to find facilities in the local community to host these events. These might include a school, a community centre, a pub or even the church planters' own home. The challenge here is that these 'public' buildings will not always be available at the most appropriate times, so a degree of flexibility and compromise will be necessary.

As well as having no building, church planting in its pioneer stage will not have a service structure to utilise. Most existing churches have a whole menu of things that they can invite non-Christians to. These might include a Sunday service, and Alpha course, a women's coffee morning or a prayer chain ministry. If anyone expresses any interest in the Christian faith, the church member just needs to point the person in the right direction and an opportunity to share the gospel is available. Church plants do not, in their early stages, have this facility. There is nothing to invite people to, so a different methodology needs to be incorporated. In any case, even if the church planters had a building and plans for constructing a church menu of activities, they generally don't have the manpower to maintain this activity. A church of 100 people will be able to find the manpower to do a lot; a church planting team of three couples will inevitably be much more limited. How do you run a youth chub with 40 noisy teenagers when you can only get 3 leaders? How do you launch a full-blown Alpha course, replete with three-course dinners, when you only have a handful of people? This challenge is a very real one.

The biggest challenge in pioneer church planting, however, has nothing to do with programmes or events. Rather it is the enormous challenge of just getting to know people so you can share the gospel with them. Unless the planter gets to know people and establishes a relationship with them, he will never be in a position to really communicate the gospel.

A very good example of someone who moved into a new area and began sharing the gospel with the people there, was the apostle Paul when he went to Athens, as recorded in *Acts* 17: 16-30. Paul arrived in Athens during his second missionary journey and, while he was waiting for the rest of his team to catch up with him, he noticed that Athens was a city that was 'full of idols' (v. 16). This fact spurred him on to engage with and evangelise the city. He began to witness in the synagogue, as was his custom, but then went out into the 'market place day by day' (v. 17) to witness to those who were there. The reason for this is obvious. Only a few Athenians were likely to enter the synagogue, so, if Paul confined his evangelism to the synagogue, he would only reach the few. To reach the many, he had to get out to the market place, the centre of public and business life where he was most likely to meet people.

It is this same factor that church planters today face. In a generation where people don't come to church, the church must go to them. Church planters need to learn to be where people are, to make contacts and to engage with people who have no intention of going to church. Unless this initiative is taken, it is unlikely that a church will ever be planted.

Paul's message

It is worthwhile noting the way in which he communicated, once he had made his contacts. Paul had aroused some interest as he mingled with people in the marketplace and was then invited to present his case at the Areopagus which was the chief court and main administrative body in Athens. His address there is a model of how to communicate to unchurched people. Paul began by noting that the Athenians were 'very religious'. This was not a complement; rather he was beginning to build a thought-bridge between the biblical position and theirs, by establishing some common ground. In short, he was being sensitive and courteous, so that he would be in a position to bring the gospel to them with clarity.

The same kind of presentation is required today. With all the confusion and doubt which our culture is causing, it is simply not tenable to proclaim the gospel from a distance. If we are perceived to be arrogant and self-righteous, we will drive people away, not attract them. Church planters need to learn to establish some common ground which will then lead to the presentation of the gospel.

Having established this bridge, Paul then mentions the altar to 'an unknown god' (v. 23). This kind of altar was common in Athens, so Paul's audience would easily have identified with what he was saying. He uses this inscription as a means of introducing to them the true God who is unknown to them. This was a powerful object lesson and demonstrates one of the reasons why Paul was so successful as an evangelist. It was because he spoke their language. He ensured that he presented God to them in a way that they could understand.

This is something else that church planters need to learn. It does not take long for someone who goes to church to pick up a great deal of jargon. So much of the vocabulary, and so many of the expressions that Christians use, are incomprehensible to people who are unchurched. We get so used to using this religious jargon that we do not even realise we are doing it. It is vital, therefore, that we find object lessons and modes of expression that will enable us to communicate the gospel to our peers so that they fully understand what we are saying to them.

Next, Paul went on to explain who the true unknown God is. He deals with the issue of creation (v. 24), establishes the fact that we as human beings are accountable to God, and asserts that God wishes a relationship with us (v. 27). But then the crunch comes in verse 30! Having built bridges and ensured that he is speaking in their language, Paul ultimately had to challenge the false notions held by the Athenians. They were idolaters and this needed to be dealt with. Though Paul was preaching in a culture that was highly pluralistic, he did not succumb to it.

This courage is needed while church planting in our pluralist and relativistic society. Though we need to demonstrate love, understanding and grace as we interact with our non-Christian friends, this should never be at the expense of presenting the uniqueness of Christianity. Ultimately, the only way of getting to heaven is through the person of Jesus Christ, and those to whom we witness need to know this. We need to hold our nerve and insist, gently but unwaveringly, that salvation comes only as a result of Christ's work on the cross. Paul knew when to play the diplomatic card and when to dig his heels in and contend for the truth, and this is a skill that we need to develop in our witnessing.

It is also significant to note when Paul brings Jesus into his message. What Luke records for us is obviously an abbreviated version of Paul's sermon. Paul talks about God as creator and builds an entire biblical world view before he mentions the person of Jesus Christ. This might seem strange, as the gospel is about Jesus and his death on the cross. But there are reasons for Paul's speaking in this way. Suppose he had begun his sermon with the statement, 'Jesus Christ is the Son of God'. This is a perfectly good theological statement that we as Christians know to be true. The trouble is that his audience would not have had the capacity to understand what this meant. Someone in the crowd may well have shouted back, 'OK, but of which god is he the son?' Coming from their perspective, these people had no idea of who God was; therefore, anything which Paul might have said about Jesus would have made very little sense. Jesus and his death on the cross are meaningless without a knowledge of God, man in his relationship to God, the fall, and the incarnation. The Athenians knew nothing of this, and so Paul had to do some preparatory work before coming to the climax of his message, which was obviously God's answer in Christ.

In much the same way, we need to be careful about our assumptions. In a post-modern world where people do not go to church or have any consciousness of personal sin, even sound theological statements will not register because the foundation is not in place. Many of the evangelistic bible study booklets that I have used over the years are based on the assumption that the users will have a Judeo-Christian worldview. This is increasingly unlikely to be the case, especially in pioneer stages church planting. Many unchurched people do not have the faintest idea what the bible teaches about God and his world. That being the case, *John* 3:16 and other verses that we use in evangelism may not be enough. A better method of communicating the gospel might be to start by using the book of *Genesis* to build up a foundation upon which verses like *John* 3:16 can then make sense.

Having looked at Paul's example, we now return to the issue of pioneer church planting in order to mention two issues which are pertinent to this stage of the process. First, we need to recognise that those who engage in church planting often plough a lonely furrow. Moving out of an existing church, where you have regular contact with friends and a good support network, to go into a church planting situation can be a very lonely experience. Church planters quickly get the impression that they are very much on their own. This feeling is intensified when they do meet up with other Christians and discover that very few people actually understand the pressures that church planters can face.

Linked with loneliness is the realisation that church planters often lack quality fellowship. Of course, we should not pre-suppose that just because someone belongs to an existing church, they will necessarily enjoy quality fellowship. It does not always follow! However, in church planting there is a degree of isolation, especially in the early stages, simply because there is not a coherent congregation for the church planter to fellowship with. They consequently need to be self-starters who find the spiritual strength to go on, even in the absence of encouragement from fellow Christians.

Parent

The pioneer stage in church planting is followed by the parental stage. As the name suggests, this stage is where a few people have become converts and as a consequence the church planter has some spiritual children to care for. The bible makes it abundantly clear that when people first become Christians, they are spiritual infants who need to be taught and encouraged and who are also vulnerable to the attacks of the devil. The parental stage is therefore a vital one, for if the people who come to Christ are not cared for and established firmly in their faith, then the new church will have little chance of succeeding.

Experience has taught that new Christians need a lot of support and time to be invested in them. Herein lies a problem for church planters. In an established church, especially a large one, there are generally plenty of mature Christians to call upon to be involved in the care and discipling of a new Christian. In a church plant, these mature Christians are absent. It is therefore up to the church planter to do the job. What is more, in many existing churches, the service structure and church programme provide a great deal of support and input for new Christians. There might be bible study groups, prayer chains, mentor groups, men's and women's activities in addition to the main Sunday services. Each of these would welcome and embrace new Christians, helping them to grow. Church plants, however, often lack such a developed programme, so again the church planter has his work cut out for him and, given the length of time it often takes new Christian to mature, the pressure to be a good spiritual parent could continue for quite some time.

There are various ways in which this work load can be handled. If the fledgling church is being planted by a team rather than an individual, then there can be shared responsibility. Indeed, if the team can be added to, it is possible at the parent stage of a church plant, to bring into the team someone who is particularly gifted in discipleship of new Christians and this will release the others to get on with the job of evangelism. Often, for purely practical reasons, the focus of a church planting team can also change depending on what is happening at the time. For example, at a time when there are few new Christians and contacts are not being converted, the focus can be primarily of evangelism. If, as a result of this, several people become Christians, it is appropriate and sensible to slow down a little on the evangelism and have a period of consolidation where the primary work being done is that of discipleship. In reality, no team can do everything equally well all of the time. Changing the pace of activities is therefore inevitable at times, and should be seen as positive and strategic.

Thinking Parents

As the work grows and the new Christians commit to being part of this worshipping community, a number of practical issues have to be dealt with. For example, how soon should the church planters start breaking bread with the new Christians? Should this begin once there are 5 converts, or 10 or 15? Linked with this, at what point can this small outreach group call itself a church?

At a very basic level, the New Testament teaches that where two or three believers are gathered together with Christ as their central focus, according to *Matthew* 18:20, Jesus is there with them. His presence gives their gathering significance.[1] Consequently, we should avoid equating church with numbers because clearly a church can exist with only a small number of people. However, we still need to think about what constitutes a church. To assist us in this quest, we do well to think back to the time of the Reformation. When the Reformers took their churches out of Catholicism, the fact that the only church in existence up to that point was the Catholic Church and they were no longer Catholic, forced them to ask what makes a church a church?

The conclusion that the reformers came to was that four things defined church. First, there had to be a commitment to the Word of God as the authority for church life. Secondly, there would need to be the practice of the sacraments of baptism and the Lord's supper. Thirdly, there should be discipline, that is, a commitment by the members of the church to live in accordance with scripture and a mechanism in place to act when someone departed from this. Finally there should be brotherly love.

This list is very useful and is an appropriate set of criteria for church planting situations. If the fledgling group of Christians submit to scripture, agree to be accountable to their leaders and one another, practise the sacraments, and commit to being a community, we should accept that they are a church, however small they may be as a group. Formalising all of this may take a little bit of time, but not long. In the meantime, it would be important to allow new converts to participate in communion from the very start of their Christian lives. This is, first, because Jesus requested that all of him followers remember him in this way,

---

1   See chapter 4 for more detailed consideration of this point.

however young in the faith they may be, and, secondly, because participating in communion can be significant in spiritual growth and development.

The development of leadership is another important issue to which this book dedicates an entire chapter. Nevertheless, it is important to note here that Jesus' model of training a group of key men to be the first generation of leaders in the church is important. From the very beginning of a church plant, the planters should prayerfully be looking for potential candidates who can be trained in the role of leaders.

As the new church forms, it is important to work within a wide circle to facilitate the proper establishment of the church. For example, if there are other evangelical churches in the same city or town, it would be important to establish a relationship with them and keep them informed as to the development of the church plant. Often, an actual 'ceremony' can prove useful to give the new church proper recognition and it would be important to involve these other churches in this, so that the existence of this new expression of the body of Christ is fully recognised by all. Of course, there might not be other evangelical churches in the area, in which case it would be good to invite a church leader, perhaps from the sending church, to take part in the ceremony. All of this will consolidate the fledgling church and instill a much-needed sense of confidence and security.

Partner

The next church planting stage that needs to be worked through is known as the Partner stage. That is where the church planter ceases to be a parent with full control of the church and begins to delegate responsibility to others. It may be to be a permanent partner with others in leading the church, or the partner stage may be a prelude to the planter's moving out of the new church altogether. Chapter 14 looks in detail at this stage, but some things need to be stated here since they are important.

First, we need to note that it is not always the case that church planters delegate their responsibility to others or move away from the church once it is planted. At times, and for a variety of reasons, a planter may feel the need to stay and effectively become the 'pastor' figure of the new church. This is not necessarily a problem, so long as there is genuine shared leadership. What can be a problem is if the planter is simply not willing to let go or share the responsibility of leadership in the church. Sadly this happens. Sometimes church planters, once they get to this stage in the life of the new work, want to keep things the way they are. They don't want change and are not open to listen to the ideas of others. When others do things, the planter can be very critical and feel that no one can do things as well as he can. Just as biological parents find it difficult to let go of their children, so some church planters find it difficult to grant freedom to their spiritual children. This attitude is a significant problem because it will ultimately drive away anyone in the church with talent and initiative and will retard any leadership development in the church. If, however, the church planter is willing to share responsibility and involve others, his staying-on can actually become a real benefit in the long term.

Secondly, mention must be made of the issues that come into play as the church moves from Parent stage to Partner stage. The primary issue is leadership. Put bluntly, no devolving of authority can take place without there being people in the church who can carry responsibility. Finding such people is easier in some places than it is in others. For example, some churches are planted in areas of high socio-economic deprivation where few people have good jobs or management experience. As a consequence, the church ends up being full of people who are not decision makers and finding leadership becomes a problem. In such situation, often the first generation of leaders will be people who were converts while they were young and therefore enjoyed significant input and training from the church planter during their formative years. However it is done, leadership needs to be developed, as this shift from Parent to Partner will simply not happen without it. The planter must consequently give it high priority and be willing to allow the developing leaders the space to learn from their mistakes as well as their successes.

A second issue is the shape that the church takes. This may change significantly during this transition and for a couple of reasons. Firstly, it is inevitable that if the church planter trains up a new generation of leaders, then they will have their own ideas to bring to the church. The better the job the planter has done in training, the more significant the change is liable to be. Secondly, as the church matures and develops it may need to be run in a different way and this again heralds a change in shape and structure.

If the transition from Parent to Partner goes well, the end result will be a more confident and dynamic church that enjoys shared leadership and a real sense of local ownership. It will be a church that is liable to survive long after the original planter has disappeared off the scene.

Participant

The final stage in the church planting cycle is the participant stage. For reasons mentioned above, some church plants never actually get to this stage because the planter stays on and continues to be an important component in the life and possibly the leadership of the church. As stated, this is not necessarily a problem provided there is a genuine sharing of leadership and a sense of local ownership. However, in many situations the church will reach this stage, not least because the planter has gone on to plant another church elsewhere.

The Participant stage is really about relationship. If someone has poured his life into a group of local Christians, many of whom have come to faith because of his influence, there will be a real bond there. Wherever the planter goes geographically, he will always have friends in the church he has planted. It will be natural for him to go back and visit, especially when invited—and invitations will certainly come.

It is important to state, however, that when he goes back, he does so as a visitor. There is a real danger if the planter forgets his role of participation and tries once more to influence or change things in the church. He needs to remember that it is not his church, and never has been. Sometimes church planters who go back for a visit don't openly confront things that they don't like about the church, but their demeanour and attitude can be very undermining of the leadership. Indeed, if they are not careful they can end up gossiping and maligning the leadership in the presence of church members. This must never be done. They should always see the positive and always affirm the leadership. Sometimes their advice might be sought by the leaders. In that situation they are entitled to express themselves, and even vigorously, but only because their opinion has been sought. However, they should have no authority in the church and therefore function purely in an advisory capacity. Any stepping back into a position of leadership will always be a retrograde step for the church.

Conclusion

Church planting is a complex business and one that requires thought and effort. However, if done well, it is the most exciting thing to be part of. It is therefore worth taking the time to think about how it should be done properly. The following chart is a useful reminder of the various stages involved:

STAGE	PLANTER	LOCALS	DANGERS
PIONEER	Making contacts and evangelising at his own initiative.	No leadership initially but helping the planter and being groomed for future leadership.	The planter never makes a deep enough impact in the community.
PARENT	Sets up structures and functions in them all. Has a major voice but willing to allow his spiritual children to grow.	Leadership roles in the church but usually under the direction of the planter. Being trained for leadership now and in the future.	The planter becomes dictatorial and does not allow the locals to grow.
PARTNER	Becomes more directly accountable to fellow leaders. Has a voice but it is not always listened to. Affirming local leadership. Helping to handle material resources in partnership with local leadership.	Taking on equal responsibility in the leadership of the church which means in practice that the locals have more power than the planter, including over material resources.	The planter might struggle with the issue of devolution and therefore the relationship with local leaders sours due to tension.
PARTICIPANT	Always available to help, but only under the direction of local leaders.	In charge of the church, it's finances and vision. Also giving leadership to the planter when he visits.	The church planter feels he is not needed and therefore does not make himself available to the church thus robbing it of his services.

CHAPTER 7

Different approaches to church planting

Stephen McQuoid

In a previous chapter we looked at some of the models that are employed in church planting. They are various and each offers something useful and distinctive in terms of its methodology. However, there is further variety still to be explored, because in planting a church there is a number of structural approaches that can come into play. Frequently when people think about church planting, they have in the back of their minds the idea of a missionary, with wife and children in tow, going into a new area (with or without a pith helmet) and establishing a new fellowship. This does happen, and often with great success. But many more approaches are possible, especially when the church planting is within the same country.

Imagination is a hugely important thing. God has given us as human beings a great capacity for creativity and he expects this to be used for his glory. Ironically, when it comes to church life, Christians often lack imagination and even feel that creativity is a bad thing. We can have a traditional pattern of church as our default position, and are unwilling to try and imagine what could be as opposed to what is. This is a real problem and can seriously constrict what God wants to do in our world. Society is constantly changing, as are the issues we wrestle with. Moreover, each town, village, rural or urban area presents its own distinctives and challenges. No two existing churches are exactly alike;

neither are any given groups of church planters. All this adds to the mix of issues that require consideration in any particular church plant.

With all this in mind, it is worthwhile reflecting on the kind of approach that can be utilised in church planting. By approach, we mean the mechanism that is used to make the church plant actually happen. In his excellent little book on church planting, Stuart Murray helpfully notes some of the ways in which church planting can happen.[1] I will make reference to some of these in this chapter.

Mother/daughter

The first kind of approach, and perhaps the most popular, is the mother/daughter approach. Stated simply, this approach involves an existing church sending out a significant group of its members to begin a new church. It might be because a significant number of its church members live in a given geographic area or that the church has had a desire to do something significant in a particular geographical area. Sometimes this kind of church plant occurs simply because one of the house groups becomes very large and needs either to split or just become a new church. Whatever the reason, the church is planted because a group of people who already know each other well, by virtue of the fact that they come from the same church, now set up a new church in a different location.

Not every mother/daughter church plant looks the same or operates in the same way. For example, in some situations the mother church might hand-pick the group of people who go into the new situation to plant, while in other situations they will simply look for volunteers. Likewise the size of group that leaves the mother church will vary, not least depending on the size of the church in the first place. I know of one mother church that was very large and sent 100 people out to begin a new church, while another smaller mother church was only able to release 16 people. Time scales can also vary. In one situation, the mother church sent out a group and expected them to function independently from the start. However in another situation, when the planting group was sent out to begin a new church, the two churches continued for several years operating with one eldership/leadership team, so that the new church had been in existence for several years before becoming autonomous.

---

[1]   Stuart Murray, *Planting churches: a framework for practitioners*, Milton Keynes: Paternoster 2008, pp. 47-80.

There are no right and wrong answers when it comes to deciding on these things. Inevitably, there will be a lot of different factors that will guide the decisions that are made. The important thing is to have a rationale for whatever decisions are made and ensure that everyone involved knows the reason why things are done in the way they are. The situation also requires constant monitoring so that, as changes in circumstance occur, the church plant can adapt to them.

One issue that does need to be born in mind with this model of church plant is the source on initiative in the project. There are times when a church plant of this kind comes about through a strategic initiative of the leadership. A group of elders may have a vision for church planting and so the developing of a daughter church is an anticipated and planned for event. However, this is not always the case. I have known of situations where a group of people within a church feel the need to church plant and then bring the idea to the elders. There is no intrinsic problem with this and certainly initiative needs to be encouraged. What is essential, however, is that everyone knows who the initiators are and that the leadership of the mother church have a handle on how quickly moves are made towards church planting and what parameters are in place to guide the process.

There are several important advantages to utilising the mother/daughter approach to church planting. First, the new church can begin its life with an already mature group of Christians who know each other well and are aware of each other's gifts. This is a very significant advantage as it can remove the fragility that can potentially exist within a new church set up. In this sense, the mother/daughter approach is a fairly safe one to use. Secondly, given the solid relationship that the new church will have with the mother church, there can be mutual support long after the new church has been established. We should not suppose that the support will just go in one direction because often some of the most dynamic people leave the mother church to form the daughter one and they can continue to be an inspiration in both places. More often than not, the fact that a church plant has taken place will be a blessing to both places. Thirdly, with a viable group of people leaving the mother church in a deliberate and planned way, it is possible to think through a credible structure and apply it immediately upon establishing the new church, thus avoiding the rather painful 'trial and error' route of establishing church patterns. A fourth benefit is that it will often cause the minimum of disruption in the lives of the planters. If the context of such a plant is that there are a lot of church members in a particular geographical location, then those members will not have to move house, change schools and jobs or lose contact with their neighbours. They will continue all of those things while getting a new and more local church started. All in all, it is easy to see the benefits of the mother/daughter approach as it is a fairly uncomplicated way of doing a church plant.

It would only be right to point out that this approach to church planting nevertheless requires a little thought. The main reason for this is that, while the new church plant is able to be well planned and executed, if the needs of the mother church are not thought about, then the mother church can suffer. There is a real sense in which when a church plant of this nature takes place, all the focus and excitement is on the new plant, while life in the mother church is 'more of the same' minus some very good people. This should not discourage church planting, but when the plant is being planned, it is important to prepare those who stay in the mother church, as well as those who go to form the daughter church.

Parent by accident approach

A second approach could be termed the 'accidental approach'. In every way this approach mirrors the mother/daughter approach, except when it comes to motive. Churches inherently have problems and internal tensions. This is simply unavoidable. Most of the time these can be dealt with and they are able to maintain their unity and sense of purpose. Sometimes, however, the problems and differences are such that a church can end up having a split. This is the saddest thing that can happen to a church. It should not happen, there is no excuse, but we would be utterly naïve if we denied that sometimes church splits will happen whether we like it or not.

When such a situation is looming, there is only one positive way of dealing with it—church plant! This might sound like a bad reason for planting a church, but actually it is not. When churches split, it is not always because the people involved are bad people. Sometimes they are good, but life is complex and we all bring our human frailty into church life. If the situation is irreconcilable, or even if the situation prevents the church working with a full sense of unity, church planting is a positive way of moving forward and one which will allow the maintenance of good relationships between the different parties. The problem often is that we leave it too late. Rather than looking ahead and using church planting as a creative way forward, we stall and a damaging split then happens. It is much better to plant out and be spared all this damage.

Dispersion

A third approach to church planting which is less common, but still very effective, is the dispersion approach. This does the same thing as the mother / daughter approach, but the key difference is that the entire membership of the sending church gets involved in the church plant, or rather church plants. In other words, members of the one large church divide into smaller groups and end up forming several smaller churches.

There can be several reasons or factors that cause this dispersed approach to happen. One of the key factors is the issue of persecution. In Ethiopia where I grew up, there was a communist revolution that heralded a fresh wave of persecution against the church. Up until that point, the Christian church had enjoyed about 100 years of moderate growth and churches were becoming very visible, especially in the capital Addis Ababa. When the communists began their persecutions, this visibility proved to be a problem and all church buildings were confiscated, while churches themselves were infiltrated. As a response, most medium to large churches divided into much smaller groups which became churches in their own right. This not only proved problematic to the communists who were trying to keep tabs on all the churches, but also led to the most startling period of growth in the churches' history. In any given, area rather than two or three active churches, there were now ten or fifteen.

However, persecution is not the only factor in dispersed church plants. Housing developments are another reason. In large urban areas, it is not uncommon that large-scale development can greatly reduce or increase the population of a given area. This in turn leads to a great deal of migration on the part of church members. Some churches have found that the area around their church building changes dramatically. Perhaps at one time it was surrounded by thousands of houses, but now it is in the middle of an industrial estate, or even a derelict area. Likewise, the socio-economic or racial mix might change. The church building might have been in a predominantly white area in the 1960's, but now the area is almost entirely Asian, while the membership still comprises white people who drive some distance to church. In such circumstances, the dispersion of the church makes eminent sense. Forming several congregations can impact several new areas at the same time. It can also mean that a church can target several very different areas at the same time and utilise the mix within the congregation to good effect. I know of one church, for example, that was based in a town comprised of a mixture of Eastern Europeans, Asians and working class white British. The same ethnic diversity was also apparent in the constituent of the church. They divided into three groups, so that they could effectively reach the three communities. It worked, not least because they also used Polish and Urdu as the languages of choice in two of the churches.

Another reason for a dispersed model can be a change in the philosophy of the church. We should not always assume that big is beautiful. Sometimes, the sheer size of a church has led to a discontentment among the members, especially if they are becoming increasingly active in a church that is very centrally controlled. In such situations, there can be a longing for more say in the life of the church. Sometimes, this can lead to a split, but on occasions some churches have taken the bold step of dividing into smaller groups, so that this desire for involvement can be met. The net result has been the formation of several new congregations which have been able to give a genuine sense of ownership to the members.

There can even be economic or practical reasons for the dispersal of a large church. One particular church in London was facing the prospect of enormous repair bills on their fairly old and large church building. The building itself was not really fit for purpose as it only had one big room and so there was a limit to the flexibility. What is more the parking was non-existent, but the land the church was built on was very valuable. There was the possibility of knocking the building down and starting again, but costs for this were also prohibitive. The church leaders decided that it was not a good use of money to repair the building, as it would still be impractical for use. The bold decision they made was that they would form into half a dozen small groups who would meet in homes. This they did and have never looked back.

Adoption

A fourth approach to church planting can be described as adoption. This is potentially a dangerous approach, but can also prove fruitful. There are many small and struggling churches throughout the UK, and indeed wider afield in Europe. Due to their limited gift, vision and resources, they are not making much of an impact in their community. However, some are based in areas of high population density in large cities and others are the only real evangelical witness in their town. It would therefore be a real loss if these churches were to close. Once our church 'space' in a community is lost, we may never get it back again.

The adoption approach to church planting sees a larger and viable church adopting one of these struggling churches, encouraging it and building it up, and then re-launching it once more into the community. The adoptive parent need not necessarily be a church, indeed CPI as a church planting organisation had done this with some churches.

There is an inherent danger that needs to be thought about with this approach. If a church is in decline, there is usually a reason for the decline. If that reason is not dealt with, then no matter what resources are poured into the church, it will not work. If the people who were responsible for the decline do not allow change, then any attempt at replanting will be in vein. Usually, the best approach in such a situation is to require the existing leadership of the church to step aside and replace them with some new and visionary leaders. These new leaders might come from the larger church that is doing the adoption. There can also be a benefit in closing the church for a period of several weeks, to allow things to be put right and to facilitate a fresh start. This might be particularly important if there will also be a change of name and a significant change in the structure and nature of the activities, especially the services. It will mean that any association with the old and decaying church is dropped.

There will, of course, be situations where the church being adopted simply does not have the manpower to do anything substantial. In that case, the adoptive church will not just provide training and impetus; it will also have to supply people. That will mean members of the adopting church transferring their church membership permanently to the church being helped. This can often involve great personal sacrifice, as these people move out of a strong and vibrant church into one that is in trouble. However, the rewards can also be great if the church is enabled to live and prosper.

Planting at a distance

Yet another approach is to plant at a distance. This is where a church decides to plant out into an area that is some distance away. It could be in another town or right on the other side of a major city. The rationale for such a church plant is that the leaders of the existing church realise that there are parts of the country where no viable church exists and therefore a great need. This kind of big-picture kingdom-thinking is very good, but the challenge is, how do you plant a church in an area that is miles away?

Clearly, in this kind of a situation, it is not possible to simply send a sizable group of people from one church to start another. After all, none of them live anywhere near the location. It would involve moving house, changing jobs and relocating schools. This could not be done with a sizable group of people. Other complications also exist. Moving to another part of the country involves getting used to a different cultural setting and possibly a different socio-economic location. The adaptation that the church planters would be likely to need to make is much greater than if they were planting a church just a mile or two down the road. The only way that this could conceivably be done is if the church doing the planting sends out a small team (perhaps just two or three couples) and they move to the area, possibly giving all their time to the church plant, thus requiring financial support. In essence, planting the new church becomes their career.

This, of course, is a very risky strategy. Moving to a new location has obvious complications and, if the whole project fails, the church planters will find themselves in a very difficult situation. It is also difficult, at a distance, for the sending church to offer much in the way of support. The planters will consequently be very much on their own. As a consequence, few ever rise to the challenge. However, for those who do, the good news is that this kind of church planting greatly extends the reach of the church.

Collaborative church planting

Many existing churches never attempt a church plant because they feel that do not have the capacity to do so. This is understandable, but should not be a pre-determining factor in a decision about church planting. The real question is, do we have leadership and desire? If the answer is 'yes', then a way can be found to plant another church. One of the most obvious ones is to organise collaboration between several churches in order to achieve a church plant.

Collaboration sounds good on paper, but there are obvious barriers that can make this difficult. For example, the geographical location of the churches involved might make the practicalities of working together difficult. Theology, particularly ecclesiology, might also be a divisive issue. Even if all the churches involved are from the same denomination, it does not follow that they can automatically work together, less still if they come from different denominations. Debates can also rage as to who 'owns' the church plant and who provides leadership. This especially becomes the case when the churches have to put possibly varying amounts of money into the project. It is not always easy to work out who contributes what to the project. Some churches might be able to offer many personnel, others few, and this imbalance can cause tension. Despite the difficulties, however, collaborative church planting has much to offer.

To begin with, churches in a given city or county can work out where the 'gaps' are and strategically go about the business of planting churches where they are most needed. The end product could be that no part of a city could be termed as unreached. Secondly, each participating church need only send a small group of people to begin the church plant. Five churches each sending out half a dozen church planting volunteers could begin a new church of 30 people, but each contributes just a fraction of that amount and therefore the impact on the individual parent church is more manageable. Thirdly, this kind of collaboration leads to an increased sense of unity in the body of Christ and is consequently God-honouring and spiritually-uplifting.

Cell network

Another approach to church planting is to use a cell network. This approach allows for a cell group(s) to begin functioning like churches in their own right, but without losing a connection with each other. In other words, the goal is to have a number of congregations, or rather cell groups, which work with a degree of autonomy and yet form one church. In each of these groups, the members fellowship together, share communion, have a teaching programme and do evangelism. Yet they are also linked to other groups in some concrete way. It may be that they have one leadership team or eldership that oversees all the cell groups, or that the cell groups come together on regular occasions to celebrate their unity and fellowship. However they are structured, they enjoy both the intimacy of a small group and a sense of belonging to something bigger.

There are several reasons why cell networks appeal. First, they offer the best of both worlds. Members can enjoy the benefits of a small, close-knit and intimate group, while at the same time benefit from being part of something much larger. They might celebrate communion and enjoy teaching on a weekly basis with up to 20 people, but have a once a month corporate celebration with 500 people. Secondly, the cell groups are small enough to meet in a private home, so the expense of a purpose-built church building is spared. The big celebrations can take place in a rented venue. Thirdly, if the cell groups are closely linked together, it is possible to have one leadership team and to share resources and gifts. Fourthly, there are benefits specifically in the area of church planting. Given that the cell groups are small, it takes only a limited critical mass of people to make a cell group viable. In a more conventional 'gathered church', a congregation of 15 would be considered small and struggling. However, in a cell network, a group of 15 people would be considered healthy and viable. This approach consequently makes church planting a less daunting business and something that can successfully happen over a relatively short time.

One question that is often asked of a cell network is whether or not these groups can truly be regarded as actual churches, rather than just glorified house groups. The answer to this question is both theological and practical, and really depends on what these groups do. If they are too centrally controlled and limit their activities, then it would be difficult to see them as churches in their own right. However, if each group has a distinctive strategy (which can still be achieved even under a joint leadership team) and each celebrates communion, has a teaching programme, does evangelism and discipleship, and has an internal structure that ensures spiritual and moral fidelity, then there is no reason to doubt that it truly is a church.

There are a couple of reasons why a cell network can be a very attractive option for an existing church. First, it can enable the church to cope with its internal diversity. Different people look for different things from church. For some, the worship is all important, for others teaching is. Some people have charismatic leanings, while others will be cessationist. Such diversity can cause tension in the life of a church, but planting within a cell network can alleviate this. Secondly, a cell network can enable an existing church to reach out to different areas in the community. In many large cities and towns, there is a patchwork of communities comprised of a variety of socio-economic groupings. An affluent area might sit right next to an area of social deprivation. In theory, any church ought to be able to bridge the gap between these communities and bring them together in Christian fellowship. However, in practice, the gulf is often a significant one and a church might find it increasingly difficult to reach out into an area that is very different from areas where most of the membership comes from. A possible way forward would be to begin a cell church in the new area and shape it in such a way that it can reach out relevantly. Once a church has been established, it is possible to have joint times of fellowship with the other member cells and thus express Christian fellowship across a wide cultural divide. Likewise, the cultural divide might be one of religion and not social class. The existing church might be located near a predominantly Muslim community. Again, a cell church plant might enable the community to be reached.

Spontaneous Generation

The approaches to church panting mentioned so far tend to be planned and well organised. While this is good and exciting, we should never forget that sometimes church planting can just happen almost by accident. While this spontaneous planting of churches is unusual, it does happen successfully and is clearly seen in the New Testament in situations like the church at Antioch. Perhaps the best way to describe spontaneous generation is to tell actual stories of what has happened.

Several years ago, I took a GLO summer team to the Croat-Serb border to help some farmers rebuild their houses and barns in the aftermath of the war. I discovered literally dozens of small churches had sprung up with no contact with the outside world. The reason for this was that a Catholic priest from Zagreb had been expelled from his catholic church in the capital because, following a conversion experience, he began to preach against the Papacy and catholic traditions. He returned to his home town of Vucovar and began teaching the bible to anyone who would listen. Many did, and churches began to appear all over the area that had no denominational link. This was spontaneous generation, not deliberate planning.

Meanwhile, a friend of mine in the North of Scotland found himself living in an area of his town where there were no evangelical churches. He and his family drove across town to a church, but felt this was not a good long-term solution. They were good evangelists and having befriended several of their non-Christian neighbours, witnessed to them. Several of them became Christians and they all made the decision that rather than continuing to drive across town on a Sunday, they would just begin their own church in his house. Again church just happened.

During the 'troubles' in Northern Ireland, another friend who went to a church in a militantly-Protestant area, ran a business which employed several Catholics. He was a good evangelist and a caring employer. As a result, several of his employees became Christians. They did not feel comfortable going to his church and didn't even feel safe going to church in an area that was Protestant and tribal. The solution was to plant a new church, which they did and have never looked back.

While these examples represent the exception rather than the norm, we should be encouraged and trust that God is able to do the miraculous, spontaneously leading Christians to begin new churches that were unplanned.

Pioneer Planters

Another remarkable way in which churches get planted is through the work of pioneer planters. Sometimes these people are self-directed, independent workers, but more often than not they are people sent by a mission agency or organisation for the specific task of church planting. It is this approach to church planting that is generally used by CPI. Pioneer church planters are often very driven and gifted people. They are totally focussed on the task of planting their church and are not easily deterred. They have something that cannot be taught in a bible college and that is the sheer determination to succeed.

Pioneer planters come in all shapes and sizes. Some are jovial and fun, others are hard to work with. Some are perfectionists, others give the impression that they don't care how things are done, so long as something is done. What unites them is the common feeling that they were born to church-plant and they find the prospect a challenge rather than something to be feared.

There are two basic categories of pioneer church planters. First, there are the serial planters. People who will take a remarkably short time to plant a church, and will then move on to the next. Serial planters are less afraid than others of leaving a young church with inexperienced leaders to its own devices. Indeed, there is a natural impatience that drives them on to the next project, barely before the present one is stable. Then, there are founding pastor church planters. These people will plant one church and then stay with it for the long haul, going from church planter to church pastor with apparent ease. The serial planters need to be cautious that they don't move on to the next plant too quickly, thus leaving the last one vulnerable. The founding pastor church planters need to be careful that they don't become so emotionally involved with their church plant that they consider it to be their personal property. In both cases, however, they will achieve their goal of church planting come what may.

Mission Team

One final approach to church planting is to send a mission team to do the job. Again, this generally happens when a Christian organisation or mission send a team out to a location to plant a church. Sometimes, this team will comprise of both full-time church planters and people with regular jobs who will commit to being part of the team. There are several ways in which this mission team differs from the approaches mentioned above. First, the mission team is accountable to an organisation rather than a church. Secondly, it will comprise members who come from different churches not just one. Indeed, they might even come from different countries. Thirdly, they will probably have gone through a fairly rigorous application and training process, as is often the case with mission organisations. Fourthly, they will generally be full-time church planters as opposed to volunteers who have to earn a living. Fifthly, they are liable to be part of a national or pan-national strategy which the mission organisation is overseeing.

There are many advantages to this approach. For example, the mission team can be well trained, prepared and resourced for the task, given the abilities and reach of the organization that they represent. Also, small churches can participate in the exciting work of church planting by linking in with a mission organisation that is doing church planting. However, there are also risks because if the organisation does not provide the appropriate backup, the mission team can feel very isolated and lonely. Nevertheless, the flexibility that this approach offers is a great asset.

Conclusion

It should be obvious by now that church planting can happen in many different ways and utilising a whole variety of approaches. This does not mean that it is an easy task. It does, however, demonstrate that it is a possible task, indeed it is happening all over the country. For that reason, churches need to lose their fear of church planting and see it as an important way of growing the kingdom of God.

CHAPTER 8

Church planting models

James Hyde

Church models are not a bad thing. They provide a church planting team with a common language and framework of thought with which to engage with each other and with their community about the task. They provide church planters with points of reference, and anticipated or expected outcomes. Used well, they communicate efficiently and effectively the 'engine' driving a particular church plant. When we know our engine, we know not only the basics like which fuel and oil to use, and how often we need to maintain it, but also how to tweak it by adding performance-enhancing parts.

Models of Ministry

While some commentators talk of up to twenty-one different church models[1], in this chapter I have chosen to focus on only five models, as it seems to me these are sufficiently defined to be distinguished from others and from each other. Each has a specific 'engine' driving them. I have not, however, commented on the model which some term 'House Church' or 'Organic Church'. Compared to

---

1　Tom Cheyney, 'Twenty-One Church Planting Designs/Models for the Twenty-First Century' (article prepared for the Church Planting Village website of the North American Mission Board—see http://www.churchplantingvillage.net/churchplantingvillagepb.aspx?pageid=8589991245, item 1 (accessed on 11 November 2011)).

the five models below, it seems to me that it has a completely different driving force.[2]

The **Program-Driven Model** is defined according to the programmes which make up its 'engine' and remains the most common model. Yet over the past 20 years, other models have been successfully developed that have given a choice to church planters seeking to reach greater numbers. Most well-known are the **Seeker-Driven Model** and its close relation, the **Purpose-Driven Model**. While the seeker-driven model is defined by the 'engine' of a crowd attending a 'seeker service', its close relation is defined by the way in which it focusses on planting a church around what it observes are the five biblical purposes of the church. The **Relationship-Driven Model** strips down its 'engine' to personal relationships. It is not churches that evangelise people, but people who evangelise people. The language speaks of planting 'cells' rather than 'congregations'. While all churches seek to serve their community in some way, the **Ministry-Driven Model** focuses on 'servanthood evangelism'. This 'engine' uses various kinds of service to meet the practical needs of the surrounding community, such as Healing on the Streets, Christians Against Poverty, Debt Counselling Centres or Street Pastors.

There are limits to the analogy of an 'engine' driving a model. It should be evident that, while a church planter may seek to pursue one model, many congregations attempt to employ more than one model, or want to adapt a model so that it better suits their situation as they perceive it. However, the need is for congregations and church planters to identify prayerfully the 'engine' driving their church plant. 'The unthinking replication of existing churches betrays a misunderstanding both of the needs of our society and the potential of church planting.'[3]

A note about numbers

Before we look in more detail at the five different models of church planting, the context of churchgoing in the UK deserves a mention. Research by Tearfund, entitled *Churchgoing in the UK* (published in 2007), reported that 48% of

---

2   Frank Viola, *Finding Organic Church: A comprehensive guide to starting and sustaining organic Christian* communities, Colorado Spring, CO: David C Cook 2009: 'The difference between organic churches and non-organic churches is the difference between General Motors and a vegetable garden.' (p. 21)
3   Stuart B.Murray, *Church Planting: Laying Foundations*, Carlisle: Paternoster 1998, p. 136.

churchgoers attend a church of less than 100 members. At the other end of the scale, less than 2% of churchgoers attend a church of over 1000 members. While these figures might surprise some readers from some other countries, casual observation by UK residents supports the view that church descriptions such as small, large and mega-church need to be contextualised to UK conditions.[4] If you want to plant a very large church of over 500 members, 85% of UK churchgoers will have no idea how that would work. It should therefore be of no surprise that church-plants in the UK which have become very large were started by planters from overseas.

Definitions of size used in this chapter and the percentage of UK churchgoers attending such churches according to Tearfund's 2007 survey
(NB 8% answered: 'Don't know')

48%		21%	16%	5%	2%
Small	Average	Large	Larger	Very Large	Mega
<50	51-100	101-200	201-500	501-1000	>1000

These definitions are important to a discussion of church models because any church, whatever its model, must choose a methodology of outreach. Broadly speaking, it seems there are two approaches. Those who state that it is far easier to win and disciple a crowd than to motivate existing members support methods that attract large numbers (greater than 100). We might call this approach 'crowd to core'. The other approach supports individuals who work from the inside towards the outside, first training up small numbers (less than 50) before sending them out. We might call this 'core to crowd'.

Against this background, each of the five models is summarised below, including a brief overview of their structure and perceived effectiveness in the UK context.

The Program-Driven Model

Evangelism and discipleship are the twin 'engines' of program-driven churches. The emphasis is on doing these two things in efficient and measurable ways

---

[4] Following Tearfund's survey, we use the following definitions: Small <50; Average 51-100; Large 101-200; Larger 201-500; Very Large 501-1000; Mega-church >1000.

with high levels of organisation. Joel Rainey identifies four marks of a program-driven model.[5]

First, programmes are non-negotiable. Much of the reason for this lies in the past success of this model and the assumption that, if something has worked, there is no need to change it. Programmes are seen as essential parts of church life, and in planting a church on this model, the aim is to establish and develop these programmes as soon as it is financially and strategically possible.

Secondly, a committee-led church. Committees meet to administer and implement the various aspects of the church's ministry. This is the primary way the model secures strong congregational participation. In the early life of the church, committees are established to assume responsibility for every aspect of programming (missions committee, evangelism committee, pastoral committee, Lord's Table committee, music committee, fabric committee, children and youth work committee).

Thirdly, the model emphasises building-centred ministry. While proponents accept that a building with great facilities alone will not grow a church, a central, active location can be a tremendous tool for offering a full programme of activities throughout the week. The building fund often becomes the rallying call for program-driven church plants.

Finally, the church is assumed to be part of the 'institutional' framework in the community. The program-driven church often will not consider itself a 'proper' church until it has become numerically and financially able to perform the ministry needed in the community[6]. Proponents of program-driven church planting warn that many planters start with too few members to be effective in reaching and witnessing to their mission field. Some proponents of this model even go as far as to declare that they will only plant a church once they have a church building, 5 staff members, 50 committed lay workers and an opening bank balance of £50,000[7]. Such church plants are known to attract 200 people to their first public service and are therefore some of the UK's larger churches from the start.[8]

---

5   Joel Owens Rainey, *A Comparison of the Effectiveness of Selective Church Planting Models Measured by Conversion Growth and New Church Starts* (Ed.D. dissertation., Southern Baptist Theological Seminary 2005, viewable via the relevant link at http://www.newchurches.com/tools-resources/research/ (11.11.2011)), p. 38-42
6   Often youth and childrens work.
7   Nicky Gumbel, Keynote talk at the Vision to Action conference, Holy Trinity Brompton (HTB), London 2009.
8   HTB's church plant in Brighton, for example.

Rainey suggests that program-driven church is 'highly resilient, and thus able to survive and even thrive in a variety of settings.'[9] Busy families are attracted to a church that serves the whole family. One of the reasons for the popularity of this model is the perceived ease with which it is implemented. A great amount of information and training can be obtained on how to plant and develop a church of this style. A look around the local Christian bookshop reveals that this model of church has its own step-by-step plan and fully-indexed and cross-referenced guide. Another reason why this model is well established is because denominations lean naturally towards the program-driven model, as it resembles their own organisational structure.

In spite of the advantages, Rainey reminds us that program-driven churches can become inward-looking, stand-alone churches that are structured for maintaining their present attenders rather than reaching out. Church attenders in a town or city who go shopping for a program-driven church will find that on the 'local church aisle', there are churches who will work hard to attract consumers to their brand. In the UK context of declining church attendance, church planters who use this model may well find themselves accused of 'sheep stealing'. Also small churches, average-sized churches, and even large churches, can find themselves struggling to be program-driven. Quality and variety suffer because workers and resources are extremely limited. For example, what works in a larger church with highly-paid university graduates on London's Kensington High Street does not do so well in a rural village. In summary, it seems that the program-driven model of church planting 'thrives best in suburban areas and 'county seat' locations among middle-class conservative families who share an 'institutional' campus-centred vision of church'.[10]

The Seeker-Driven Model

This model also has twin engines. Rainey identifies two common characteristics. Strikingly, the seeker-driven model

> employs the main worship service exclusively as an evangelistic tool… Most of the time, creating this type of atmosphere means dichotomising between the "seeker service" and the "believers service." Bill Hybels of Willow Creek believes, for example, that "you cannot, maximally, in the

---
9   Rainey, *op. cit.*, p. 40.
10 Rainey, *op. cit.*, p. 42.

same service, meet the needs of both Christians and non-Christians"…
Therefore, elements of worship that are thought to be reserved for
believers, such as The Lord's Supper, are sequestered from the primary
service designed for seekers'.[11]

This may sound familiar to those who grew up with a Gospel Meeting separate from the Breaking of Bread Meeting. But its implementation in contemporary seeker-driven models produces mega-churches of over 1000 members, where instead of newssheets and hymn books being given to newcomers, ear plugs for loud music are handed out to those who look over 50![12]

The difference is the second engine of this model. Seeker-driven models plant from the 'crowd to core'. This model requires a large crowd to be mobilised, the larger the better. The model 'focuses its people's resources on bringing their lost friends to church from day one. Relational and "contagious" evangelism is the foundational core value of each and every seeker-based church'.[13] Unlike other models, a church planter who successfully implements a seeker-driven model will be happy that 50% of his large congregation (that is, of more than 100) are not yet followers of Christ, because it means members are inviting their friends. Churchgoers from the UK have little experience of churches with hundreds of people; only a third of UK churches have more than 200 members; therefore, it is not surprising that many seeker-driven church-plants in the UK are started by church planters who are not from these shores.[14]

Due to its twin engines of seeker service and attracting large numbers of those who are not traditional churchgoers, it is not surprising that seeker-driven churches tend to thrive in densely-populated cities, especially with young professionals, whether that is Sydney or London, Bradford or Edinburgh. For example, Hillsongs London held its first public service with up to 100 attenders in University Halls on Oxford Street. It now meets in the Dominion Theatre, Covent Garden. At its launch in September 1999, it was bigger than half of the churches in the UK, and by 2010 it claimed over 9,500 attenders at six identical seeker services.[15]

---

11   Rainey, *op. cit.*, p. 47.
12   For example, the Edge Church in Bristol hands out ear plugs.
13   Rainey, *op. cit.*, p. 48
14   For example, Hillsongs London, or the Edge Church Bristol.
15   As stated in the relevant Wikipedia article.

The Purpose-Driven Model

The engine that drives the purpose-driven model is a focus on organising around what Rick Warren describes as the five biblical purposes of church (worship, fellowship, discipleship, ministry, and evangelism). This concept was launched publicly in 1995 with his book, *The Purpose Driven Church*. Warren contends that this focus builds morale among staff and members, reduces frustration, and allows greater concentration and cooperation among the people of the church[16]. Rainey explains 'what sets this model apart from its seeker-driven cousin is that there is no dichotomy between the "seeker" service and the "believers" service.' The popularity of the purpose-driven approach can perhaps in part be explained by the fact that such a service that appeals to both seekers and believers. This looks a lot like the 'Family Service' that the majority of average-size UK churches seek to use.

What distinguishes the purpose-driven model from the programme-driven model is that this is not a twin-engine model but a five-engine model! The budget is divided between the five purposes, the preaching calendar is similarly divided, the small groups of the church identify with one of the purposes and it seems that even the crèche should follow the five purposes. For those church planters who enjoy tweaking 'engines', the purpose-driven model provides endless opportunity.

The strength of the purpose-driven model is founded on the principle that there is no single key to church planting. 'Blessed are the balanced; for they shall outlast everyone else.'

As to the appeal of this model, Warren's multi-million best-selling follow-up book, *The Purpose Driven Life*,[17] famously begins with the sentence, 'It's not about you.' This particular focus on purpose is self-evidently successful. A wide readership, both geographically and ethnically, is purchasing the book. The purpose-driven model appeals to both rural and urban seekers and believers, to both working class and professional class.

---

16   Rick Warren, *The purpose driven church: Growth without compromising your message and mission*, Grand Rapids, MI: Zondervan, 1995, p. 107.
17   Grand Rapids, Mich.: Zondervan 2002.

Relationship-Driven Model

Rainey summarises for us: 'The Relational church has programmes just as the Program-based church has relationships. What sets this particular model apart is the centrality of relational evangelism, and the emphasis of mutual care for and accountability to one another.'[18] There are many types of relationship-driven model. These include cell networks, missional churches, incarnational churches, and emerging churches. (These are not synonyms; there are distinctions between each.) The engine of this model is 'core to crowd'. It is diametrically opposite to the engine of the seeker-driven model. However, that this is the case is not always obvious. Consider the following from Leonard Sweet:

> What would it mean to decentralize something like worship? Worship must become a key component to every small, separate cell group that is free to worship in its own way while integrated into the larger church. Eighty-five percent of churches now offer cell-group opportunities, each one of which should include a worship component. At the same time, hyper-centralized worship services, where the whole body comes together for celebrations, become more important than ever.'[19]

While both the seeker-driven model and the relationship-driven model accommodate a large celebration worship service (of more than 100 people), the engine that drives the latter begins not with gathering a crowd, but with the core of the church building relationship with each other. In the UK context, it is often described as a 'fresh expression'.[20] Rainey observes that the primary rationale for the recent upsurge in relationship-driven church is the imposing presence of post-modernism and the continuing decline in the number of nominal churchgoers. The targets of the relationship-driven model are 'anti-institutional and non-institutional individuals...who have few preconceived notions of what church is supposed to be in a modern context.'[21] Rainey concludes, 'In short, the

---

18   Rainey, *op. cit.*, p. 55.
19   Leonard I. Sweet, *Postmodern pilgrims: First century passion for the 21st century world.* Nashville, TN: Broadman and Holman Publishers 2000, p. 121.
20   Fresh Expressions 'Encourages new forms of church for a fast changing world, working with Christians from a variety of denominations and traditions. Fresh Expressions website (.http://www.freshexpressions.org.uk/).
21   Rainey, *op. cit.*, p. 58.

Relational model appears to be the pre-eminent model for reaching the young urban post-modern.'[22]

However, relationship-driven church planters will also find knocking on their door those from tight-knit communities on the edges of mainstream, whether that be villages, market towns or ethnic groups. Most small UK churches (of less than 50 people) are relationship-driven, and activities often revolve around one or two families who do everything. Consequently, the model is widespread in the UK.

The relational church employs, budgets and plans around relationships and thus its engine runs differently than the previous 'institutional' church models. For example, relational churches are often organised geographically (all groups within a postcode) rather than generationally (crèche, children, youth, adults, seniors). Relationship-driven church plants do not need their own building, unlike the others who require space for their worship services. They will hire venues depending on the numbers expected, from coffee houses to school halls, and, if they build, they tend to have multiple rooms to cater for different sized groups.[23] Some very large relational churches in the UK (those with more than 500 attenders) are using the concept of 'clusters' or 'missional communities' and describe the church staff and central programmes as being a 'resource church' or 'minster church'.[24]

As a result of the emphasis on genuine relationship, Rainey points out that the relationship-driven church will take much longer to plant and consequently will require a longer period of initial funding. Relationships are not built with a bible study programme bought from the internet, nor at a loud and glitzy 60-minute worship service. Berquist states that those planting the church need to be free from expectations (their own and other people's) about numerical growth. While it is important to grow in numbers, real transformational growth may take longer. 'It also takes several generations of church reproduction for exponential growth to become significant.'[25] That said, for those who persevere, some relationship-driven churches count themselves in the thousands[26].

---

22 Rainey, *op. cit.*, p. 60.
23 For example, Grosvenor Church Barnstaple's conversion of a railway goods shed.
24 For example, St Thomas Church Philadelphia.
25 Linda Berquist, *Relational Based Church Planting*, Alpharetta GA: The North American Mission Board 2000, p. 29.
26 Elim Pentecostal London City Church reported in 2003, 11,000 people in 1800 cells. Source Kensington Temple London City Church website 2010 (www.kt.org).

Ministry-Driven Model

This method of church planting makes the aim of your church 'to produce disciples who do stuff, not disciples who only know stuff.'[27] Rainey points to a predominant example of this type of ministry in North America as Steve Sjogren's Vineyard Church in Cincinnati, Ohio and its emphasis on 'servant evangelism'. In the UK, we might look to Northern Ireland, Causeway Coast Vineyard Church's support of the 'Healing on the Streets' ministry, though many UK churches, both existing ones and those being planted, 'do stuff'.[28]

Sjogren began by implementing what he calls 'servant evangelism'. This is a way of sharing the good news of Christ with others in your community through simple, practical means that can be done by people in everyday situations—from washing cars through giving away soft drinks to cleaning up a neighbor's yard.'[29] Sjogren claims that 'in our skeptical age, it is absolutely essential to *show* God's love before we speak about it. People might remember the words you say for a few hours, but they are likely to remember your acts of generosity for months, years, and in many cases, the rest of their lives.' In contrast to the first four models, the engine of the ministry-driven model is a 'go and do' rather than a 'come and see' approach to reaching out.

In Coleraine, this saw Causeway Coast Vineyard services held in a pub after the first year of meeting in the church planter's house. Alan Scott, a Glaswegian and Kathryn Scott, his Ulster-born wife, were reported in a local paper as saying, 'It's just a venue. The church is the people who are the body of Christ.' 'We want to be distinctive and take away any cultural barriers that might stop people attending church. For example, some people think that the church is after their money. We counter that by giving away free things, so that people see that we're not there to take. We're there to show God's love practically, by giving.' This has varied from giving away food to cleaning the toilets of local businesses.[30]

Rainey points out that implementation of this church model is as diverse as the number of communities in which it is often employed. It is self evident that the people in a church plant can use their talents to serve the kingdom of God with the skills they use everyday in the workplace. Church planters can build networks with established caring systems like the police, schools, and

---

27   Steve Sjogren and Rob Lewin. *Community of kindness*. Ventura, CA: Regal Books 2003, p. 27.
28   See Causeway Coast Vineyard Website 2010 (www.causewaycoastvineyard.com/)
29   Sjogren and Lewin, *op. cit.*, p. 91.
30   Causeway Coast Vineyard Website 2010.

health centres and create ministry opportunities for congregational members. Many new Christians in church plants are not comfortable filling positions in a church structure, but will feel at home using their own skills as 'ministry' to the community. Other proponents of this model will plant churches that support 'Street Pastors'[31] or establish a debt-counselling service like Christians Against Poverty[32]. Some church planters may go on to build community centres, schools, libraries and health centres.

Rainey goes on to note that the difficulties in planting a church on this model are primarily related to time and money. Not surprisingly, assessing the needs of the community will uncover the increasing number of old people, the fragmentation of the family due to the economic necessity of both parents working and the subsequent needs for child care and family activities, not to mention the increasing inward migration of ethnic minorities to urban areas and continental Europeans to suburban towns. Consequently, church plants will take longer to become self sustaining, simply due to new attenders being the marginalised of society and relatively lacking in wealth and education. However, as these church plants start to meet the needs of the community, they may find themselves partnering with government-funded community organizations, thus adding to the resources of the church plant. Rainey concludes 'this reality puts the Ministry based model in the unique position of receiving funding for their often high-cost activities from sources perhaps not available to other models.'[33] Small- or average-sized church plants can produce more 'engine power' than many of the larger congregations in their locality.

What are you aiming at in planting a church?

Perhaps you are like Charlie Brown practising archery in the "Peanuts" cartoon. He pulls back his bow and shoots several arrows towards his garden fence. Charlie Brown then pulls out a piece of chalk and carefully draws a target around each arrow sticking in the fence. Lucy walks up and says 'What are you doing? That's not archery!' He replies, 'But this way, I never miss.'[34]

This brings us to some final points about church models. First, let's choose our arrows carefully, prayerfully selecting a church model that meet the needs

---

31 See Street Pastors website (www.streetpastors.co.uk).
32 See Christians against Poverty website (www.capuk.org).
33 Rainey, p. 55.
34 Charles Schulz's classic comic strip, *Peanuts,* started in 1950.

of our community and the potential that planting a new church offers to our communities. Church planters must take time to know their communities well.

Secondly, perhaps we should consider that some arrows suit certain church planters better than others. The gifting and personality of church planters will influence the choice of what drives the church. A planter who likes to get things done may feel frustrated with making voluminous grant applications to funders in a ministry-driven plant. A planter who likes to wake up in the morning and say, 'I wonder what will happen today', will struggle with the coordination and diary planning required in a purpose-driven plant. A planter with teaching gifts will find his collection of 40-minute sermons of limited value to the eight people sitting in his living room in a relationship-driven model. A planter who is pastoral may feel overwhelmed with the hundreds of new faces at a seeker-driven service. The committees of a program-driven model can all too easily sideline the planter with a prophetic edge. If we get this wrong, no matter how well the church plants are doing numerically, there will never be a consensus that the church is accomplishing what it should. However, church planters who draw others into a team will find their gifts are complemented by others. Church planters must know what their primary gifting is, and the giftings of their team.

Finally, let's ask for a clearer vision of God's target in our communities. A church planter's objective is to bring a clear presentation of Christ and the gospel to greater numbers of people. We must not let our focus drift from God's target and onto our chosen model. We cannot draw targets around our own finely-crafted arrows and claim success for our chosen church planting model. The target of our church planting models has been set for us. Planting a church should never be a 'hit or miss' affair.

CHAPTER 9

Thinking about starting points

David Buchan

What happens if you throw a stone into a pond? There is a point of entry with a splash followed by a series of mini waves as the effect ripples from the centre out. This is the epicentre, in terms of physics, the 'focus'; the point at which there is the most energy released that moves outward in a dynamic way. In the same way, whatever emanates from our presence within a community comes from within each believing person—the Kingdom of God generating ripples that seek to make an impact on those around us.

Where is the starting point in church planting? It is in who we are *before* the church plant begins because *being* must always take precedence over *doing*.

Inner conviction

There must be an inner conviction about many things, and especially about the gospel. It is God's remedy for a world tainted by a *maladie* that reveals itself through the all too recognisable features of our broken world: misuse of substances, people and the environment. We need to be convinced that in fact, it's not supposed to be like this! We can choose to accept things as the way they are and conform, or we can challenge the order of things.

We need a conviction that there is a Creator God who is there, who does care and who wants to do something about his World. We need to be convinced that there is a loving heavenly Father who has already intervened into this world's affairs. He has stepped into time and space seeking to reconcile people to himself and restore their lives. This is the truth of *incarnation*: God's fingerprints and footprints already leading the way into our communities.

Now, of course, I am aware that our secular, non-God-friendly and allergic-to-all-religious-terms reader will have suffered a stroke by now. Only recently a life-long community activist in Easterhouse, one of Glasgow's largest housing Schemes, reacted strongly to one church's mission plans to distribute bibles to gang members. He declared that 'God hasn't been here once in the 60 years since we were built'. I'm not sure where the gentleman has been living for his 60 years, as there are and have been many Christians living and involved in the area, whether through direct church-based actions or through other community projects.

This myopia is typical of many hostile towards 'religion' in general and Christianity in particular. One of the early convictions impressed upon me was that God seemed to be alive and well on planet earth and already at work in the community long before we arrived and keen to continue long after our departure!

Another inner conviction must surely be that people can come into contact with this God and receive love and forgiveness from him: in essence have their basic human needs met by the Maker himself. I remember summing this up for a French journalist curious about why a Scottish couple was living in France. He had heard a nurse at the local hospital for elderly speak enthusiastically about us taking a group of children to play their musical instruments and sing Christmas songs, so he made an appointment to speak to us. He then asked the safer question about how Christmas was celebrated in Scotland, and what we missed by being in a different culture. After sharing the delights of Christmas crackers and the benefits of quality family time with him, he then felt brave enough to enquire what message a Pastor might like to convey about the 'real meaning of Christmas'. The subsequent half-page article with photo insert included the following:

> If our basic need was information, God would have sent an Educator. If our basic need was technology, God would have sent a Technician. If our basic need was money God would have sent a Financial Advisor. If our basic need was chocolate (a seasonal adaptation) God would have sent a *Chocolatier* (a chocolate maker). However our basic need is forgiveness, so God sent a Saviour.

The inner conviction that people can be changed, that lives and situations can be transformed is a central one. I remember meeting Harry in the centre of Glasgow one day. A year before he had been one of 12 residents of an alcohol rehabilitation centre. I particularly recall that, out of all the men from all walks of life (including a consultant psychiatrist), Harry was the only one who took seriously the prayer and bible sessions. Meeting him here one year on, he openly shared his appreciation of the staff, declared his faith and emphasised that only God helped him to change.

I also remember visiting churches in England as bible students with GLO (now Tilsley College). In one I met a couple at a church meal who shared humbly and enthusiastically about how they had been married, separated and divorced, due in part to the wife's addiction to prescription drugs which aggravated other difficulties in their relationship. However, through the concern and acceptance shown by this church, she had found healing and help. Her partner had independently met another Christian, who had helped him to find faith, and to be reconciled with his former wife, and they were now planning to be remarried within six months!

In the same way I am forever grateful to real Christians who have lived the Christian life in a dynamic relevant way and encouraged me to do the same, essentially 'seeking first the Kingdom of God and His right way of living.' This has greatly influenced me together with the conviction that the presence of God's people in a community can and should make a difference. Kingdom principles of living should be seen and felt consciously or unconsciously and it is this presence that authenticates any proclamation of the message.

One example of this happened during our time in Viewpark. I can still remember poor Dougie's face as he tried to hide his shock when he realised that he had been 'taken in' by my enquiry. He was on his way to the local shop to buy his almost daily bottle of *Buckfast*, courtesy of those wine-making monks at Buckfast Abbey, when I asked him if he had heard of the New Wine on the market, called 'Living Waters'. He admitted that he hadn't and wondered if it was any good. Of course, I had to admit that I personally felt that it was as it had reached the parts that other wines couldn't reach and was very satisfying. He did grin sheepishly and hurried off! Incidentally we once visited the peaceful tranquillity of Buckfast Abbey while on holiday in Devon and were pleasantly surprised to learn that the monks also make 'home-made honey' which I've never seen exported as widely as the liquid nectar appreciated by the fortified wine lovers of Scotland!

Poor 'Nusky' was another one taken by surprise. I was out late walking a dog entrusted to us for the weekend and witnessed his group chase a boy from a rival area. This boy had walked his girlfriend home and was in the wrong place at the wrong time and ran into the girl's house to seek refuge from the 'Viewpark Young Team' who proceeded to kick at the door. Running up to Nusky, I challenged him in the street that this wasn't right and surprised him by announcing that there was a new 'rule' coming to Viewpark, one where God ruled and people would be respected! He did not contradict me and quietly said 'Aye, alright Davy' before escaping down the road.

Invited

Have you been invited to help within the community? This invitation is vital—it must be one that comes from *within* the community. It can be from any source. It might be a struggling church who wishes to be relevant to the needs around them. It could be other activists looking for volunteers to help with community projects. It could be the authorities wishing to promote community engagement and inter-agency cooperation. Whatever the source, each invitation should be considered prayerfully. Of course there will be issues of autonomy, but no project should be imposed on the community. It should be seen as something *good* for the community, with plenty of *feel good* factors because it responds to previously identified issues (e.g. young people hanging around, the need for parenting skills, cleaning-up the environment).

For the team in Viewpark, it had been a mixture of all these things at different moments. Naturally, the first overt invitation came through the church, but it was particularly satisfying to learn that several Christians from different backgrounds had been praying for Christians to come and live in the area.

Visits to all the existing clergy were positive, although it is fair to say that one or two were perhaps cautious and cooler in their welcome. The Pastor of the Church of the Nazarene felt we could spend all of our time in the lower area of the Scheme and still have more than enough to do. Most of the clergy understood that we were not trying to 'sheep-steal' but were attempting to reach those outwith conventional folds and essentially non-church attenders, in order to influence the area for good.

It was in visiting the local Information and Advice Centre that we were to receive our biggest welcome. The Manager quickly introduced us to Mary Theresa, one of their volunteers and a Christian. With a smile she gave each of us a big hug, then asked if we knew what the letters V/P stood for. She had to explain that this was short-form for 'Viewpark', but really it stood for 'Very Important People'—both the GLO team but especially the people we were called to reach!

Identification

We need to decide what our commitment to people is: are we content to simply drive in, 'do' an activity, then drive away or are we prepared to be there for the 'long haul'?

This involves no longer waiting for 'them' to come to 'us' or simply inviting 'them' to turn up to 'our' meetings. Instead through patient identification with them, their concerns and issues become ours; their desire for change becomes ours too. We become engaged in the process.

Of course, the most profound and meaningful way of doing this is the one that our Lord chose when he 'became flesh and dwelt among us'. The fact that the God of the Universe was prepared to come to meet and mix with folk from all walks of life has never ceased to amaze me. The implications for us seemed so powerful and greatly influenced the Viewpark version of cross-cultural mission, as the launch title for the project 'Bridging the gap' implied. The image of building bridges acknowledged two things: the tendency of churches to drift apart from the community they are part of and therefore need to reconnect with, but also the task of going to the people where they are. This should not be confused with the misperceived notion of building bridges to bring people to church but rather being the church where they are.

It therefore cannot be overstated enough—for maximum impact to be achieved, you need to live in the Estate you're trying to reach.

Incarnation

The theological *raison d'être* and the kingpin that holds everything together is of course incarnation. Pip Wilson already defined it in his book *Gutter Feelings* when he stated that: 'Incarnation in the youth club, among young people, is presence without oppression. That is what we strive to live out'.[1]

---

1 Pip Wilson, *Gutter Feelings: Christian youth work in the inner city*, Basingstoke: Marshall Pickering 1985, p. 128.

Surely this is what the apostle Paul meant when he emphasised the importance of people before projects, declaring: 'We loved you so much that we were delighted to share with you not only the gospel of God but our lives as well, because you had become so dear to us' (*1 Thessalonians* 2:8).

There has been a mistaken historical tendency to place the emphasis on *words,* usually interpreted as preaching. We have created difficulties and dilemmas and debated about the 'social gospel' which have been unhelpful. There is no compromise, nor is there only one method of reaching people or sharing the Good News. This is well expressed in what was attributed to St. Francis of Assisi when he sent his followers out on mission, encouraging them to 'preach the gospel and, if necessary, use words'—a wonderful idea which always infuriates those hooked on preaching the word, rather than living it! In fact as Pip Wilson goes on to say:

> ...and the result, we have come to realise is not the message. The medium is the message. The individual and team life as youth workers must demonstrate Jesus' reign within us. What we do must match what we say. We are not proclaiming a concept, 'four gospel laws' or whatever, but a kingdom where God reigns and others are welcome—very welcome indeed![2]

Investigative learning

This stage is so crucial and will help to shape the direction you need to go in. It involves listening and learning. What are the perceived needs of the community? What are local people talking about? What has been written and documented already: community profiles, social policies, etc. Check out the local library; speak to long-serving activists, teachers, and elderly citizens.

Keep an ear to the ground—what or who is being celebrated, e.g., a long-serving volunteer at the local information and advice centre? Which person has been behind organising summer play programmes and local galas? What are their perceptions? How do they view the church, the possible role and involvement of Christians, or simply other people with a heart for their community?

What are other Christians already doing? Who prays in house groups in the area? Who do people go to with their spiritual concerns? Often when we want

---

[2] Wilson, *Gutter Feelings*, p. 128.

to plough ahead with our programme, we fail to see what God might have been doing before we turned up.

Involvement

From finding out what's already happening, we will be surprised by how much we can already be part of. One local radio station organised a River Clean-up Day and looked for community groups to enlist. This turned out to be a fun, if messy, way to show practical concern for the community.

Although we were quick to organise a children's holiday club within a month of moving into the Scheme, our involvement with young people took slightly longer. The opportunity presented itself in another God-given way. Two parents, Jeanette and Jean, were already running a youth club for what seemed a wide age range—13 to 22 years of age. They needed help and we were glad to offer it, but soon learned that after several years of running it on their own, they needed a break.

With the prospect of no youth club provision looming, we agreed to take on the task, renaming it 'The King's Club' and re-organising it and dividing the age-groups into two nights. We felt we should also put our stamp on it by introducing a 5-10 minute 'God slot' in what became known as 'Centre-Spot'. Persevering with that proved to be a challenge! We later found that smaller discovery groups in a different venue and night worked better.

Another breakthrough came when we met a group of concerned parents who wanted help to think through long-term solutions to the problems associated with bored youngsters hanging about on the streets. Jeanette and Jean helped form an action group which formulated an application for government funds called 'Urban Aid', to build a purpose-built youth project with staff employed to address the problems, educate the youth and provide positive activities promoting responsibility and fulfilment. Christians volunteered to help, give advice and a lot of time to this project, making a conscious decision to let this project run independently and not to push for a 'Christian' centre which would have been viewed with suspicion. It was also satisfying that Jeanette and Jean later came on board with spiritual things.

Several young people responded in a positive way to the message and their parents were happy with the perceived change in their attitudes and behaviour. This was the case with Jean's son, John, who was only aged 10 at the time, but it was when Jean saw the real change in her husband, Ian, that she finally committed herself to the Lord at a Billy Graham rally held in the stadium belonging to *Glasgow Celtic*, affectionately know as 'Paradise' by its supporters! John responded to encouragement to grow in faith and has served as a Youth and Community Pastor for many years. He later spoke about how he was impacted by the genuine care and commitment he saw from the resident GLO team. His friend, Debbie, also made a commitment at an early age and continued faithfully, using her gifts as a music teacher within Liberty Community Church. There is little space to speak of others like Helen, Elizabeth, Shona and Elsie who also continue in the walk of faith.

However, sadly not everyone was enthusiastic about their children showing an interest in Christian things. One lad received a beating on return home from a bible Discovery Group, as his alcoholic father told him he wanted no 'F....ing Christians' in his house. Within a few years this same lad, at the age of 16 years, was to be implicated in the beating and murder of a local man by a group of lads.

Intensity

All of us wish to make an impact, to perhaps find significance in whatever we do.

However it seems to me that it is not really *where* you go that matters, or necessarily *what* you do when you get there.

What seems to count is *the way in which you do it*—your manner, your motives, in essence, who you are. Because who you are is the unique, indelible trace you will leave when you are gone. It is not simply about community involvement but rather about the quality of that involvement with real people, their hopes and dreams.

A church worker once told me that, despite his efforts to share the Christian faith in a town over 14 years, he only ever saw one man come to faith in Christ. The new convert left soon after to work in another town.

The worker, clearly gifted in bible teaching, found himself in a role he felt uncomfortable with, that of evangelism and church planting, yet had been counselled to persevere. As a result he felt fairly ineffective in the town he was trying to reach, yet he came to derive much of his significance through regular teaching slots in other churches or conferences that regularly took him away from the community he was trying to reach. It became clear to everyone but him that low involvement equalled low impact.

Unfortunately he found that he had to justify his existence and his 'lack of results' by complaining that the town folks were unresponsive—the soil was 'too hard' or the people were not interested, due to the influence over the years of an atheistic, post-modern outlook. One couldn't really make an impact here.

The moral of the story? It's not the length of time we spend in a town, a community or a village; it's the intensity of our presence there.

CHAPTER 10

Cross-cultural church-planting in the UK

Andy Gibson

I remember with reasonable clarity the classes on foreign mission that I sat through at bible college—particularly those which stressed the importance of a missionaries understanding issues of culture and language. We were told that it was crucial to understand the way that people in a foreign country lived, why they lived that way, how they thought, and how different that was to the way we lived and thought. I filed that information away in my mind under the section 'interesting, but not particularly relevant to me.' I have no recollection of anyone raising the need for me to understand the culture of the place that I would end up working in, as I was not going to be going abroad. I was going to work in the UK, England in fact, and as I was English, culture wasn't an issue. Or was it?

If a person travels abroad to work as a missionary in some form or other, the first thing they normally do is learn the language. It would be a very unwise missionary who did not learn to communicate with the people they were trying to reach with the gospel! How could they tell them about Jesus, if they were unable to communicate effectively? For many missionaries this involves a great deal of sacrifice in money and time, as they either attend a language school, or toil away learning the new language in their spare time. Some missionaries are able to pick up the new language quickly, but others find it very difficult and have had to slog away for as long as their missionary careers last so as to be able to communicate effectively with the people they are seeking to reach.

A wise missionary would also find out about the way people think in their new location, seeking to understand what makes the local people tick. They will read up on the history of the area, seeking to understand the context into which they are going to be working. They will find out about the local customs, the sporting traditions, and the culinary habits of the people they will be working amongst. And, to be able to reach these people, they will have to abandon much of their own way of life, and adapt to the new culture—speaking the new language, eating different food, dressing differently, and following the normal pattern of living that exists amongst the people whom they have been called to win for Christ.

All of these aspects of missionary life are understood and accepted as normal. We have all sat in missionary meetings and heard tales about differences in culture, and looked at slides of people whose lives bear no relation to our own. We clearly understand the need for significant adaptation if a person is to reach the lost in foreign countries. Whilst all this is understood and acknowledged in terms of foreign mission, it is far less understood, acknowledged, or even discussed, when it comes to reaching people within our own country.

Cultural differences

My wife and I, who are both English, spent eight years working full-time in a church plant in England. We learnt a great deal from lots of different people and situations during that period of time, but one of them was just how important it is to understand the cultural differences that exist between peoples within the United Kingdom, and the need to be prepared and equipped for them.

What do we mean by the word 'culture'? Wikipedia's volunteer writer offers among his definitions of culture the following: 'The set of shared attitudes, values, goals, and practices that characterizes an institution, organization or group.'[1] The Collins English Dictionary defines culture as 'the customs, rituals, and values shared by the members of an organization that have to be accepted by new members.' We could say that culture in this context is simply: 'the way people do things.'

---

1   http://en.wikipedia.org/wiki/Culture (accessed on 13.9.11).

It is important to be aware of cultural differences in Christian work of any context, but it is especially important to have a clear grasp and understanding of the particular culture of the people in the location that you are seeking to plant a new church. The term 'cross-cultural' does not apply just to someone from the UK reaching lost people in North Africa; it also applies to someone from the south east England seeking to reach lost people in the north east of England. It doesn't refer just to people from the UK reaching lost people in India; it also applies to a university graduate reaching people who left school at sixteen and dropped out of education. It doesn't refer just to people from the UK reaching lost people in South America; it also refers to someone who has been brought up in an inner city council estate reaching people who live in the leafy middle class suburbs.

We tend to think that everyone in the UK has the same culture. After all, we all speak the same language, don't we? We've all had the same education, haven't we? We all eat the same food, don't we? We all watch the same TV, don't we? Actually, no! Take language for instance. Not everyone of the approximately sixty million people who live in the UK, speaks English as their first language. We have always had people who speak Welsh and Scots Gaelic as their first language, but the waves of immigration in the second half of the twentieth century have meant that we have sizeable groups of people for whom English is still either a foreign language or a second language. Most of our major cities have significant populations of people who originate from other countries, speaking languages ranging from Urdu, to Russian, to Somalian. The challenges of communicating effectively with people who either don't speak English or struggle to speak English are obvious.

Then, take education as another issue. Aside from people who have recently arrived in the UK, who will obviously have received a different education from those of us who have grown up in the UK, there are also great differences in the education that people will have received, even if they have lived in the UK all their lives. A person who has dropped out of education, or has left school at sixteen with no qualifications, will have clearly received a radically-different educational experience from someone who has gone on to be awarded A levels and a degree (and, in an increasing number of cases, postgraduate qualifications).

We tend to gloss over such differences, but the reality is that the typical graduate will live differently, think differently and even act differently from the typical person who left school at sixteen with no qualifications.

Real-Life Cultural Differences

So what do these cultural differences look like in reality, and what has it got to do with church planting, or Christian ministry? Perhaps the best way for me to describe them and illustrate from is my own experience. My parents are Christians; my dad was a middle ranking Customs Officer; and we lived in a nice street in West London. We then moved to semi-rural Hampshire, and lived in a four-bed detached house on a very nice estate. I didn't enjoy school and was glad to leave at sixteen, to join HM Customs & Excise and follow in my father's footsteps. My wife had a similar upbringing but, being smarter than I am, decided to go on and complete further education. When my wife and I were led by the Lord to work full-time with a church plant in our mid- twenties, we bought an ex-council house on the estate where the church was being planted. So what cultural differences did we discover? Actually, there were many, and some of them greatly affected the way we operated and worked.

To begin with, I befriended one man in our street with whom we had come into contact through door-to-door work and through the church's children's work. He was invited to join a football team that our church had started, and this enabled me to spend some time with him. I made a point of finding other opportunities to be with him so as to build the friendship. Ultimately, I wanted to be able to share the gospel with him. My prayer was that someday I could lead him to the Lord.

My wife and I hoped that perhaps he and his wife would come round for an evening and eat a meal with us, so that we might develop a relationship with them as a couple and with their whole family. That is, after all, how we as a couple tend to socialise with other people. It is the way we do things, and it is the way we are comfortable doing things—it is part of our culture. However, it soon became clear that this was not going to happen, because it was not part of their culture. Our suggestion of an evening meal at our house, which would have consisted of a nice meal, bottle of wine, and hopefully fun conversation was politely turned down. Instead, two options were suggested to us. The first was that I spend the evening with him and watch a pornographic film and drink a few cans of beer. The second was that we would accompany them to the bingo. Neither of these suggestions hugely appealed to us for obvious reasons. The bottom line was that, even without the obvious no-go areas, such as a pornographic film, and despite our best efforts to bridge the gap, we inhabited radically different worlds, even though we lived in the same street. We had more in common with a couple from Eastern Europe who lived opposite us and spoke little English, than we did with the English couple, who, despite sharing our nationality and language, had a very different culture from us.

So what were we to do? How were we to build a friendship with this couple when the things we liked doing were so radically different, and some of the things on offer from them were completely out of the question for us? It's important to remember that over 90% of people come to faith in Christ through a friendship with another Christian. They might make a profession of faith in a meeting or at an event of some sort, but all the research shows that the key thing was the relationship. This of course is entirely biblical—God is a relational God, and Jesus spent much of his time eating with people and building relationships with them. We were unable to progress our relationship with this couple, and although we remained on good terms with them, that was as far as it went. We lived in different cultures that were difficult to marry.

A second example will further emphasize the point. When we first began to work on the estate, we would visit church contacts and people we were proactively trying to befriend, with a view to inviting them to special events that the church was putting on. We would often visit several weeks in advance of an event, on the assumption that, as we had diaries that were filling up, sometimes for things that were eighteen months in advance, so must other people. We soon discovered that most people on the estate did not possess a diary and had no idea what they were doing in two days' time, let alone in two weeks time! The result was that despite being invited and often being genuinely interested in the events on offer, their lifestyles were such that they forgot about the event, because they were not used to planning ahead. We had to learn to adapt and visit people just a few days ahead of an event, and even then often phone as a reminder on the day itself.

A third example is worth noting. I grew up without a TV. A weekly trip to the library was part of family life and I would read four books a week until the time I started work. I read nothing like that amount of literature now, simply because my lifestyle does not permit it, but so much of who and what I am still revolves around reading and digesting information. So, when one lady was saved and we began meeting with her on a weekly basis to work through a discipleship course, we suddenly had to re-think the whole way we communicated biblical truth with her. The course required the ability to read bible verses and answer simple comprehension questions along the lines of: 'in verse 5, who does Jesus say that he is…?' The problem was that she could barely read, and not only that, she was unable to perform simple comprehension exercises. I suddenly realised how difficult understanding even the NIV was for someone who had left school with poor literacy skills. The reality was that we lived in different cultures—I inhabited a reading culture and she lived in a TV culture. For us to effectively disciple her was going to be as great a challenge as discipling someone from another country who spoke English only badly.

The examples I have given are real and difficult to manage, but not impossible. The reason I share them is to illustrate the reality that working in the UK can be as cross-cultural as being a missionary in a foreign country. We have many different sub-cultures in this country. There are significant ethnic groups in the UK, whose culture is very different to the traditional British culture and whose first language is not English. In addition, there are native Welsh and Scots Gaelic language communities. There are significant differences in regional cultures within the UK. When you add to this the sub-cultures that have been illustrated above, it is easy to see how complex church planting can be, even if we never leave the UK.

The specific examples I have given stem from my own experience of working in a deprived council estate in an English city. I would, however, have had to take just as much account of the cultural differences that would exist if I was involved in planting a church on an estate full of people who were all university graduates and working in executive positions. I left school at sixteen and can often feel out of my depth in a room full of people who have been educated to a much higher level than myself. If I was teaching a group of new Christians who had the benefits of a rich and extensive further education, I would have to alter my approach and deal with their particular perspectives, and this would be just as challenging as working with someone who couldn't read.

Relationships

Relationships are key! As we have already seen, most people come to faith in Christ through a relationship with a Christian. If I was looking to plant a church in a particular place, I would need to ask the question: 'am I able to connect with the kind of people who live there and am I capable of building an authentic relationship with them, so that I might be able to meaningfully share the gospel with them and disciple them?' If the answer is 'no', or even if I have significant doubts, then I would have to ask serious questions as to whether I was the right person to be involved in that church plant.

Research suggests that the people who we are most likely to reach are those who are most like ourselves. There are exceptions to every rule including this one; some Christians are able to step outside of their own culture and lifestyle and reach people who are very different from themselves. However, such a move requires a significant effort and goes well beyond our comfort zone. If we are going to cross a cultural divide, then it is vitally important that we begin by being aware of the divide, understand it, and take steps to adjust ourselves to it.

I try to study other churches and church plants to see what I can learn from them. When it comes to church plants, what I have noticed is that those that seem to have made the most impact are the ones whose leaders and pioneers had researched the area, the people, and the culture into which they planted. As a result of this, they not only knew what to expect, but had taken steps to adjust personally, as well as structurally within the church, so as to take account of the culture of the people that they were seeking to reach.

Research

If you were moving to a foreign country to plant a church and you were wise, you would not merely replicate the exact model of your home church. Instead, you would take the principles of church structure taught in the New Testament and then apply them within the cultural setting where you were working. This same principle must also apply to church plants within the UK.

For instance, I know of one church plant that was started in an area of high unemployment and long term deprivation. Due to the unemployment levels, most people on the estate had become late-night people, people whose mornings were spent in bed as there was no job to get up for. In order to relate to the local populace, the church plant held their main service on a Sunday evening, not the morning, to fit in with this local habit. Of course, there was no biblical reason why not, indeed in *Acts* many churches met in the evening. The governing question was, when on a Sunday or on another day are we likely to get the greatest number of people?

Rick Warren explains the concept:

> Once you've collected all the information on your community, I encourage you to create a composite profile of the typical unchurched person your church wants to reach. Combining the characteristics of your area into a single, mythical person who will make it easier for members of your church to understand who your target is. If you've

done a good job at collecting information, your members should recognize this mythical person as their next door neighbour.

At Saddleback, we've named our composite profile 'Saddleback Sam.' Most of our members would have no problem describing Sam."

Saddleback Sam is the typical unchurched man who lives in our area. His age is late thirties or early forties. He has a college degree and may have an advanced degree. He is married to Saddleback Samantha, and they have two kids, Steve and Sally.

Health and fitness are high priorities for Sam and his family. You can usually see Sam jogging each morning, and Samantha attends an aerobics class three times a week at the Family Fitness Centre. Both of them like to listen to contemporary pop and country music, especially when they are working out.[2]

Rick Warren goes on to describe Saddleback Sam's social life, career, attitude towards religion and spiritual matters, his dress code, and his financial habits. I believe it is essential that we do this. When we understand who the typical person in our community is, we can see, first, whether individually we are able to cross the cultural divide in question, and, then, we can begin to set up and structure our church, and our evangelistic methods, so as to relate to this cultural identity.

Incarnation

If we are planting a church that is seeking to reach a geographical area, then I believe that it is essential that the church planters and core team move into the neighbourhood. When we look at the bible, we see the Lord Jesus Christ demonstrating this to us in his supreme model. *John* 1:1 says 'The Word became flesh and made his dwelling among us' (NIV). The Message paraphrase puts it this way: 'The Word became flesh and blood and moved into the neighbourhood.' If we are to follow the example of our Saviour, then we too need to move into the neighbourhood and become one of the locals. As we have already seen, relationships are key to reaching lost people, and it is very hard to establish and develop relationships with people if we drive into an area for a church service or event and then drive away again.

---

[2] Rick Warren, *The Purpose Driven Church: Growth without compromising your message or mission*, Grand Rapids, Michigan: Zondervan 1995, pp. 169-170.

The need to move into the neighbourhood and identify with people is even more important if the planters and core team live in affluent areas and are planting into needy and deprived areas. It is not impossible, but it is very difficult to connect with people and be taken seriously if we drive into an area of deprivation and poverty in a BMW, tell people how much Jesus loves them and how much we love them, and then drive off again to our own nice, safe, and prosperous neighbourhood.

This is a reality that 'The Message' in Manchester has understood and taken to heart in its Eden partnerships—see www.message.org.uk and www.eden-network.org . 'The Message' insists that the people joining its church planting teams move into the area where the church plant is focused and become part of the community. This enables the church planters to gain and win the trust of the local people and the right to be heard. The Message website, talking about the Eden partnerships, states:

> Eden's mandate is to go to the most challenging urban areas and share God's life-changing love in words and actions. Eden teams choose to live in these communities, sharing the problems of those growing up there and helping them with their needs. To date, The Message has planted thirteen Eden partnerships, involving around 300 people becoming 'downwardly mobile' and moving into Greater Manchester's statistically toughest communities.

Moving into a neighbourhood is not as straight forward as it sounds. If you live in a nice, safe, and prosperous community, then it will take a great deal of sacrifice to sell up and move into a council house in a deprived area. The challenge becomes even greater if you have children. I might mean uprooting them from a good school and sending them to a poor school, knowing that such a step may seriously affect your children's happiness, education and future. These are issues that we need to think through seriously and prayerfully before taking action. Some couples take the attitude that if God has called them to such a move, then he will provide for and protect their children. Other couples take the attitude that although God has called them, he has not called their children; so although they live in the neighbourhood, they will take their children to a school out of the area. Other couples will decide to wait until their children have left home before making such a move. I don't think there is a right or wrong approach in this area; the important thing is that we fully understand the implications of whatever steps we take and are prepared for them.

We must also bring some balance to this argument. It is very fashionable to plant in socially-needy areas, and of course there is a strong biblical mandate to help the poor and to reach them with the gospel. However, we must not think that all church planting must be about what the Message website describes as "becoming 'downwardly mobile'". We must realise that people in well-off areas may not have the social and economic needs of an inner city area, but they still need the gospel and are just as eternally lost without it! We need churches to be planted in all sorts of areas and communities, rich and poor. If we do plant in economically well off areas, then we need to think through the cultural issues, just as much as we do when planting in a socially needy area. The key questions to be asked are: what is the culture of the planters? And, what is the culture of the location the plant will be taking place in? These two questions will help prevent a mismatch between the planters and the location, and will help the planters prepare properly for their task.

When planting in a well-off area, there is a range of issues that require reflection. If you seek to plant in an area where the average house is a four-bedroom 'executive' house, then the likelihood is that the average Christian worker or missionary will struggle to afford such a place. Then, there is the cultural divide that comes from mixing with and trying to reach a high-income community (they will certainly be getting paid a lot more than the planter!). For instance, their pastimes may be financially out of reach for the planter, so he might find it difficult to join in and build relationships.

One last thing we must not forget is that in many locations in the UK differing cultures can run into each other within just a few streets. It is quite common to cross a road and move from an area populated by one ethnic group and into an area populated by another ethnic group. Or as you cross that road, you move from a council estate into an 'executive' estate. So, even as you look at one area to plant in, it might actually have several different cultures co-existing side by side. This will mean that a 'one size fits all' approach to your plant may not be appropriate.

Summary

So, what can we conclude? Basically this: when planting a new church, great time and effort must be given to understanding your own culture, understanding the culture of the people in the location that you are planting, and understanding the differences. When you have devoted sufficient time and energy into researching and understanding these issues, the questions to then ask are: is my own culture sufficiently similar to the new culture to enable me to fit in? And: if there are significant differences between my culture and the new culture, am I able to sufficiently adapt to the new culture? If the new culture is dissimilar to your own and you are unable to adapt sufficiently to it, then perhaps this can be taken as an indication that someone else should plant the church and you should find somewhere that is more suited to your own culture.

The way forward

How do you go about defining your own culture? Some basic questions should help you understand what you do and how you do it. You should ask yourself: what education have I had? What jobs have I held? Where did I grow up? What do I do in my spare time? What do I like to watch on TV? What books do I like to read? What movies do I watch? What newspaper do I read? Where would I go on a day off? What food do I like? Where would I go on holiday? Answering these questions (and you may think of more) will help in getting a good understanding of your own culture.

How do you go about defining the culture of an area? One tool is to use a census. The latest census information can be retrieved from the Office of National Statistics website (www.statistics.gov.uk). There you can find all sorts of information that will help you understand the make-up of your target area. A web search looking at your target area will bring up all sorts of other useful websites and you should pay special attention to those that portray the history of the area. It is helpful to know why things are the way they are. A simple walk through your target area will very quickly help you grasp what it is like to live in an area—what are the houses like? What cars are outside the houses? What sort of shops exist? A simple tool is to ask the local newsagent what are the best selling newspapers? When I began to take notice of this, I quickly realised that in the newsagent in my street, only three copies of broadsheet newspapers where sold, and I bought one of them. Look around at the catering establishments— are there any pubs, and if so, what are they like inside and, apart from drinking, what are the people doing? Are there any cafés, coffee shops, fast food outlets or restaurants and, if so, what are they like? What are the menus and prices? Are they places that you would be comfortable in or able to go to?

If you are able to get access to the local police, you can ask them what the issues are in the local community. Meetings with other key people such the local councillor, MP, health visitors, and school head teachers can all be very helpful in understanding the culture of the area, and the needs and issues that face it. Should you decide that you can adapt to the new culture and go ahead and plant, this research information will then of course be very helpful in deciding how to reach the people in your target area.

CHAPTER 11

Building an authentic community

Martin Erwin

⁴²They devoted themselves to the apostles' teaching and to the fellowship, to the breaking of bread and to prayer. ⁴³Everyone was filled with awe, and many wonders and miraculous signs were done by the apostles. ⁴⁴All the believers were together and had everything in common. ⁴⁵Selling their possessions and goods, they gave to anyone as he had need. ⁴⁶Every day they continued to meet together in the temple courts. They broke bread in their homes and ate together with glad and sincere hearts, ⁴⁷praising God and enjoying the favour of all the people. And the Lord added to their number daily those who were being saved. (*Acts* 2: 42-47)

It just sounds so idyllic doesn't it? 'They were together and had everything in common…' That is how we want the church to be, isn't it?

The truth is that these verses, while providing both historical context and a helpful model of church life, actually depict the first days of a brand new church—in this case THE brand new church.

Many of us have taught from these verses, and indeed, we used them at the very beginning to help us establish some principles for Challenge Community Church in Hereford. However, what we failed to do was to recognize that these verses defined the 'mood' of the early days of church life and, given time, growth, and human nature, things change.

It is the same church in *Acts* 6 where we read (v. 1), 'In those days when the number of disciples was increasing, the Grecian Jews among them complained against the Hebraic Jews because their widows were being overlooked in the daily distribution of food.'

Many local churches struggle to grow, and even to survive. There are of course various reasons for this, including doctrinal differences, cultural challenges, age-profile and church location. All of these need to be addressed if a church or church plant is to grow and flourish.

However, one of greatest reasons why many church plants fail is the fact that the church consists of individuals. We all bring to the local church our own needs and expectations. It has often been said that more churches split over personality issues than doctrinal ones. Whether this holds true in reality or not is not really at issue—in truth it strikes a chord with many of us.

These human frailties are magnified in a church plant. Often expectations are heightened, which in itself is a positive and exciting aspect of being involved in a new church. Over the years, new churches have been planted directly because of frustration or disappointment in existing churches that suffer from low expectations, and which often seem to have settled for maintenance rather than mission. In the early days, the church planter will often attract people who are tired of being stuck in a rut. The 'lure' of the new has a romance and excitement attached to it, and often the church planter will be a 'charismatic' and enthusiastic leader and attractive to many believers.

If you have been involved in church planting, or are considering launching out, you must recognize, therefore, that early growth is almost certain, but carries inherent dangers.

Two questions to be considered then are 'how do we guard against false hopes crushing or destroying the new church?' and, secondly, 'how do we harness and focus the energy and excitement of the early days?'

'How do we guard against false hopes crushing or destroying the new church?'

The Scout movement has a simple motto—'Be Prepared.' In reality, to be forewarned is to be forearmed.

When we began Challenge Community Church (CCC) in September 1996, we had fresh, innocent excitement. None of us (8 adults) had been involved in church planting before. We had received neither formal, nor informal training, knew very few other church plants and certainly, hardly any within the Brethren movement. We had a simple vision—to reach the 'South Wye' housing estates of Hereford with the gospel, and to establish a living local church at the heart of the community.

With only 8 of us, and 9 when my fiancée, Rachel became my wife in 1997, decisions were easy to make. Although we had recognised two elders, myself and Louis Clifton, any major ideas or plans could be discussed with everyone at our weekly home group. In the early days, involving everyone in decision making was a great experience for all. Unity was easy—it was the church's honeymoon after all!

However, as we grew to a dozen, then 15, then 20, that model became unworkable, even dangerous. In one church meeting where we were chatting through an apparently simple change, things became quite heated as one member suggested that the elders were clearly 'out of touch,' and hadn't thought the issue through properly. I was livid, but managed to keep my feelings hidden. My response waited for a late evening phone call, and I showed less grace than the original unhelpful comment!

After apologies and time that particular relationship healed, but a sharp leadership lesson had been learnt. Leadership structures were refashioned, and basic protocols established and growth continued.

'How do we harness and focus the energy and excitement of the early days?'

Given the right opportunity, almost everyone involved in the church plant can have a raft of good ideas. These will range from reasons for the new church's existence, projects that it should embark on, the centrality of evangelism, or worship, the need for a building (or not!). On and on it goes, and the danger is that the work can too quickly become very fragmented, with those engaged in the work becoming stretched and ultimately 'burnt out'—the fate of many church planters, and the highest single reason why church plants fail.

Therefore, it is vital that the church planters establish clarity regarding key issues from very early on. Those areas include:

- The vision
- Church doctrine and practices
- Leadership structures

Other secondary issues need to be sorted early on too, including relationships with other churches, particularly the parent church (where one exists).

Uniting around the Vision…

In so many ways, this is absolutely key. I will say more about this later but, for the moment, let me underline the need for the leaders to be clear about the vision. As the church grows, so will demands on resources, time and people. A clear vision about who we are, why we are here and what our purpose is as a church is essential.

When CCC began in 1996, the work inherited, indeed was built upon the children's outreach that had been run so successfully for many years by our parent church, Barton Christian Fellowship. However, after about a year or so of continuing to run a successful Sunday school, with occasionally well-attended Family services interspersed at key junctures in the year, it became apparent that the small dedicated group of adults who were the 'church' would be unable to effectively grow numerically or spiritually. We eventually took the difficult decision to close the Sunday school!

That drastic action may not be necessary for every church plant, but for us it was essential. Our focus on Sundays moved to worship and teaching, with a style more suited to adults, families and the culture we were seeking to reach. We didn't give up on children though! We approached a local primary school and began a mid-week after school club. 40-50 children still regularly attend that programme each week, double the size of the work we closed.

As a result, our Sunday programme began to attract adults and families, and growth began in earnest.

It wasn't a painless decision. One of our key members disagreed with the decision from day one, and eventually drifted away from the work. Clarity about your vision is fundamental, may be painful, but will ultimately be fruitful.

Uniting around Doctrine and Practice…

In a world as religiously and culturally diverse as Britain today, it is simply not good enough to 'presume' that all of those who join you will adhere to matters of doctrine as you do. With regard to new converts, most will have little or no concept of the fundamentals of the Christian faith, never mind some of the 'secondary' issues that we may espouse.

When running a holiday bible club at a local church, this was brought forcefully home to me when in the quiz a child answered the question "Who was the 'Mary' mentioned in the story?" with the answer "Jesus' girlfriend." It wasn't the apparent absurdity of the answer, but the lack of response on the part of the other children that struck me. No point getting upset with the child—in all likelihood their parents may have given a less intelligent response! The reality is that the residual biblical knowledge in our society only exists with those over 60, and even then it is minimal.

Even Christians who will join your church from other fellowships may have very different outlooks on issues of doctrine and practice, even if their churchmanship has been similar to yours.

Write it down

As a result and in response to the diverse culture in which we live, we committed early on to produce a 'Statement of Faith' and a 'Statement of Practices.'

For us, the Statement of Faith had to simply express the centrality of the Gospel, and the fundamental tenets of the faith that marked us. Rather than re-invent the wheel, after some consideration we adopted the Evangelical Alliance Statement of Faith. There are other similar statements but, for us, it met a need which perhaps didn't exist in earlier generations, particularly in the Brethren circles with which we were associated.

That first statement effectively identifies us as 'evangelical.' However, what about the secondary issues and practices which we hold as a result of biblical conviction, but would not be held by all churches in our city, or indeed, all evangelicals? Issues such as believer's baptism, the place of communion, the role of women, baptism of the Holy Spirit and the place of spiritual gifts.

A small group of us met, and thrashed these issues out. What did the Bible teach about such things? As objectively and openly as possible, we came to the view we held on these issues—how we understood the scriptures, how they applied in our culture and context, and how these practices would be held and taught.

This was a good exercise! It allowed us to re-examine some of the inherited traits of our tradition, and once again hold them up in the light of scripture. As a result, we changed our views on some and reaffirmed our commitment to others.

Those two statements are not taught as 'catechisms' or recited by rote in the church. However, both are reproduced in print, on our website, and are taught in the 'member's class' which forms part of the discipleship course for new believers, and as a 'stand alone' class for those seeking to join us on moving from another church or area.

Uniting around Leadership Structures…

As our fellowship has grown, so our leadership structure has adapted. Again, it is dangerous to presume that we know what the New Testament teaches on leadership because our tradition holds a particular view. The church I was brought up in had an 'oversight' but no deacons. I moved to study at the GLO Training for Service Course (now Tilsley College) and discovered that the church I fellowshipped with had deacons too. When I moved to England, my new home fellowship elected their deacons for a 3 year term! They couldn't all be right—or could they?

It quickly becomes clear on even a cursory reading of the growth of the church throughout the New Testament, that not all the churches had the same leadership structures. There are clear principles given regarding qualifications for elders and deacons. Interestingly, these are given so that churches that don't have them can appoint them. In other words, churches were planted and functioned for a time with no established elders. Others, as in Jerusalem (perhaps uniquely), had a council, whilst Antioch seemed to be led by a gifted team of prophets and teachers.

We have sought to maintain a biblical pattern of church leadership. That pattern seems to allow us the flexibility to adapt to growth, threats and opportunities, as we seek to live out the life of a local church.

Leadership is key. It is investigated more fully elsewhere in this book, but here let me simply say, that your leadership structures must be simple, clear and effective if you are to build an authentic community.

Shared L.O.V.E.

Alright. So you are safe-guarding against overly diverse expectations, harnessing the energy of a new church, and uniting around vision, doctrine and leadership. That must guarantee that you will become an authentic church community—right? Wrong!

Perhaps, a few years ago, I might have felt that was enough. We've ticked all the boxes, so now let's pray and get on with the work and 'hey presto' all will be well.

When I became a full-time evangelist in my early 20's, I had enthusiasm, gifting, a calling, and the recognition of key leaders. What more is necessary? Experience.

A while ago, I was listening to a round table discussion on preaching involving John Piper, Mark Driscoll and a couple of other Christian leaders. Their discussion turned to the question "What makes a good preacher great?" The answer was as simple as it was profound—Life. Piper underlined that it is rare for a guy in his 20's to have experienced the joys, sorrows, hurts and successes of an older man. 'When you have stood at a few more graves, welcomed some more children, cried a few more tears, and walked a few more miles, as long as you keep in step with the Spirit, you will discover a depth and quality in your ministry that could not have existed without the experience that life has brought you.'

I have begun to discover this in my own life too. After I had begun to recover from M.E. a few years ago, I was speaking at a church house-party. It was a fellowship where I was well known and had regularly preached in the past. During a coffee break, a man I knew approached me and asked if I had noticed any difference in my preaching since my illness. To be honest, after six months off and having suffered the depression and anxiety of an 'unknown' illness, I was just glad to be preaching again.

'Well,' he said, 'For your encouragement, there is a new sensitivity in your preaching. Thank you!'

I believe that this growing experience is apparent in the life of a new church too. I have been perturbed at times by the stories of 'overnight' success that are often held up to church planters. On digging a little, I discover that most of these were not 'overnight' at all, but perhaps 15-20 years in the making, including false starts, false dawns, and embarrassing mistakes.

This sharing of life together I have simplified into the Acronym L.O.V.E.:

> Shared **L**ives, shared **O**penness, shared **V**ision, and shared **E**xperiences.

Shared Lives

In our world, so much about our friendships is really superficial. This is true in our experience of 'fellowship' too. The 'Hi, how are you,' welcome is most usually followed by the 'I'm fine thanks, how are you,' response. We are encouraged to stay after the service to 'enjoy fellowship over a cup of tea' together.

How do we raise fellowship, sharing lives, beyond this minimal experience? The primary answer is that we do it 'deliberately.' The self-serving and materialistic nature of our society sadly permeates our churches too. We must respond to this challenge by teaching and modelling what shared lives look like. If it is true that 'it is no longer I who live, but Christ who lives in me,' and that 'I have died to myself' (*Gal.* 2: 19, 20), then a genuine expression of New Testament community needs to model what that looks like.

The establishment of home groups is a good place to start. For us, as the church grows, for the elders to provide pastoral care on the personal level that people may expect, is an impossible task. However, as people connect regularly in a home, sharing the scriptures and their lives, a beautiful thing begins to happen. They are touched by one another's trials, and share the joys of one another's successes. People genuinely begin to 'bear one another's burdens' (*Gal.* 6: 2), and the fellowship grows to a deeper level, living out the commands of Christ.

Our evangelism, too, becomes marked by a sharing of life with lost people. The 'Storehouse' ministry began to meet the grocery needs of families left with bare cupboards for various reasons. That work has grown, and now connects with our church Family Worker, who is partly funded by two local schools, and the Christians against Poverty worker, who brings the gospel to broken homes, as she helps people to respond to the brokenness of their own debt.

Shared lives are vital if we are to demonstrate the gospel by our community life

Shared Openness

By openness, I mean flexibility, responsiveness, spiritual sensitivity to need, opportunity and the Holy Spirit's leading. Many works of God, over time, can become ponderous and unresponsive. As someone has said 'Yesterday's movements are today's monuments and museums.'

The church in *Acts* displayed this openness on various occasions. In *Acts* 6, the apostles respond to the complaint of the Hellenistic Jews regarding the unfair distribution of food and appointed 'the seven' to oversee this ministry successfully; Philip the evangelist responded to the Spirit of God as he went to Samaria, then to the Ethiopian eunuch, and then on again; Peter responded to the vision, and took the gospel to the home of Cornelius; the church leaders at Antioch responded to the call to release Paul and Barnabas to a new mission; Paul responded to the vision of the man from Macedonia—'come and help us.' On and on it goes…

More established and traditional churches can become 'bogged down' with their own history, architecture, age or culture. A flexible, open, responding culture should permeate the new church. We must be careful not to see any ministry or work as permanent or sacrosanct to the detriment of our sensitivity to the leading of the Holy Spirit.

The new church has the benefit that no one can say 'we tried that here once and it didn't work!' Beware, however, that day will come sooner than you think! When it does, the leaders need to be ready to say 'with God's help, we can surely do this,' as Joshua and Caleb did standing on the verge of the Promised Land.

This open culture creates a 'can do' attitude! Why? Because we have a 'can do' God. One who wants to do incredibly more than we ask or imagine.

Shared Vision

Earlier, we took a brief look at the importance of uniting around the vision. But how do you come to determine the vision, to know what it is and then to establish a genuine community, set on pursuing it?

Early on, as a group, before our official launch as a church plant we met each week for bible study. The primary theme of those studies was to seek to establish in our thinking on what a real church looked like. What does a church do? What is vital and what is optional? What can be determined by culture regarding the 'how' of being a church.

Of great help to us was Rick Warren's book, *The Purpose Driven Church*. I know that it has been a tremendous asset to other UK church plants too. In it, Warren identifies 'the great commandment,' and the 'great commission' as the central focus for all we should do.

The Great Commandment

'[34] Hearing that Jesus had silenced the Sadducees, the Pharisees got together. [35] One of them, an expert in the law, tested him with this question: [36] Teacher, which is the greatest commandment in the Law? [37] Jesus replied: 'Love the Lord your God with all your heart and with all your soul and with all your mind.' [38] This is the first and greatest commandment. [39] And the second is like it: 'Love your neighbour as yourself.' [40] All the Law and the Prophets hang on these two commandments.' (*Mt.* 22: 34-40)

The Great Commission

[18] Then Jesus came to them and said, All authority in heaven and on earth has been given to me. [19] Therefore go and make disciples of all nations, baptising them in the name of the Father and of the Son and of the Holy Spirit, [20] and teaching them to obey everything I have commanded you. And surely I am with you always, to the very end of the age.' (*Mt.* 28: 18-20)

I highly recommend Rick Warren's book as essential reading for anyone seeking to church-plant today. The recognition of five purposes—evangelism, worship, fellowship, discipleship and service—greatly helped us in bringing balance into the early days of the new church. For a time, our leadership team was structured around these purposes which gave extra focus to agendas, discussions and planning.

Beyond that, we established a mission statement. For us that is simply 'to bring people to Jesus and equip them for service in His world.' It is not extravagant, magical or even necessary. However, it focuses the mind, states simply why we are here, and is short enough to be memorable. If you are going to have a mission statement, keep it short.

More recently we have expressed our vision (how we will achieve the mission statement) in this way:

We will do this by…Serving Together…
- God in Worship
- One another in Fellowship
- Our community in Gospel acts of Love
- Our world in Mission

On top of this, one of our Sunday morning services each autumn is called 'Vision Sunday.' This is the opportunity to restate, define, emphasise and introduce important aspects of the vision.

In some ways you could probably take what I or others have written and run with it. However, that will miss the point! The exercise of actually discerning what God is calling YOU to do is essential.

At CCC, on a 24-hour elders' retreat in 2007, we were at a very low ebb. The church had shrunk over a period of 3 or 4 years, enthusiasm was waning and we were losing key members due to geographic relocation, including Andy and Claire Gibson who had been so central to the work since 1999. Added to that, the building project toward which we had prayed, saved, planned and spent was on the verge of 'going down the swanny!' It was a key moment in the life of the church, now 11 years old.

On that retreat, we sensed God say two words to us. 'Kingdom' and 'Family.' The outworking of those prophetic words to us has formed the shape and implementation of our vision and mission. They were key to us, not purely from a biblical point of view, but uniquely to us culturally.

Ask God to reveal the unique calling and vision that he has for your local church. Then pursue it for all you're worth!

Shared Experiences

A post-modern view states that 'it's about the journey.' As an evangelical, I think the destination is pretty important! I mean, you don't want to have a great time travelling, only to find out you've ended up in completely the wrong place! Having said that, the journey shapes you, and it should.

We have rejoiced with those who rejoice and mourned with those who mourn. We have celebrated the birth of new believers and shed tears as they have been baptised. We have held the hands of those with life-threatening illnesses, and known the gratitude of the healed, and the pain of the lost. We have supported those walking up the aisle, and picked up the pieces of broken lives and broken homes. Children have grown up with us, some to serve the Lord and others to serve themselves. Pain, grief, tears, happiness, hard work and celebration have marked the journey thus far, and we have only just begun.

However, those shared experiences mould us, shape us and join us together. We aren't there yet, and neither are you, but by God's grace, we will be the authentic community that He has always intended for us to be. As Bill Hybels has often said, 'The local church is the hope of the world.' May our churches and church plants represent that authentic community towards which we are called.

Chapter 12

Discipling new converts

Andy Gibson

Just before the Lord Jesus ascended to heaven, he gave what is known as 'The Great Commission.' In this commission to his disciples and therefore to us today, he said we were to 'go and make disciples of all nations… teaching them to obey everything I have commanded you.' (*Mt.* 28: 19&20 NIV). Jesus didn't ask us to make converts, he asked us to make disciples. Disciples, will of course have to be converts, but Jesus was asking for much more. If we look throughout the gospels, Jesus repeatedly called people not primarily to convert, but to follow and obey his teaching. So Jesus' commission to us incorporates the idea of people being converted, but more than that, to see their conversion as part of a larger package of becoming one of his disciples. We must be careful that we don't see 'discipleship' as either a 'second stage' in the Christian life following conversion, or even as an 'optional extra' for those who want to take their faith more seriously. The reality is that when Jesus talked about discipleship, he saw conversion as merely the first step in the process of being one of his disciples. Being a disciple of Jesus is really about believing in him, following him, learning from him, and becoming like him.

Before we can look in detail at discipling new Christians and the importance of this, it is vital that we understand what a disciple is. The word 'disciple' is used over two hundred and sixty times in the gospels, either by Jesus or to describe his followers. The Collins English dictionary defines 'disciple' as 'follower, one who takes another as teacher and model.' The English word 'disciple' translates the Greek word *mathetes*, which literally means 'a learner'. As we examine the gospel records, we discover that the primary route to following and learning from Jesus was by being with him. A personal relationship is therefore at the very heart of Christian discipleship, and that relationship is with none other than the Son of God himself. Peter Maiden, in his book *Discipleship*, writes

> Jesus' call to discipleship is not an invitation to participate in a programme or even to share in a cause but to be with a Person, so that he can make us into the people he wants us to be. The call to discipleship is the call to relationship, a relationship that will gradually make us all that God intended us to be.[1]

I want to make it absolutely clear that I believe in 'conversions' and I believe in preaching and calling people to conversion. However, as we have already seen, being a disciple involves much more than the first step of conversion. There is always a danger that we can push people towards 'praying the prayer' or 'making a commitment', when they are not actually ready to be a disciple of Jesus. I know that in one sense no-one is ready to become a disciple of Jesus—we come as we are and allow his grace and love to change us as the Holy Spirit fills us. But we have to be careful that we don't encourage a climate where people respond to our gospel presentations in a one-sided way. By that I mean, we have to remember that we are calling people to repentance (*Lk.* 24: 27) and obedience (*Jn.* 14: 23), as well as to enjoy the benefits of forgiveness and eternal life.

We must acknowledge that there is huge pressure, often self-inflicted, when planting a new church, to see numerical growth. We have all read the books of American church planters who saw their churches grow from four to four thousand in a matter of weeks, and we are obviously keen for similar success. However, we must be careful that in our desire for numerical growth, and in our quest to keep people coming along to our new church, that we don't shy away from presenting to new converts the radical demands for discipleship that Jesus makes. It is important that we acknowledge this pressure. When your new church only numbers twenty people, and you know that if you attempt to disciple the latest six converts and call them to obedience to Christ and in doing so you will lose five of them because they are simply not prepared to walk the path that Christ calls them to walk, there will be a huge temptation to soften the teachings of Jesus and the apostles, so as to not lose people. It is always very difficult to watch people turn away from following Jesus, but this is especially so

---

1   Peter Maiden, *Discipleship*, Milton Keynes: Authentic Media 2007, p.15.

when you are numerically weak. So, we must be aware of the pressures upon us to see numerical growth, and we must be aware that as we begin to disciple new believers, we may not see all of them go on in their faith.

Sadly, it is true that both in church planting and in existing churches, we have often been very poor at making disciples. People are saved and then often left to fend for themselves, frequently receiving little further input. These new converts are thrown in at the deep end of church life, having little idea of what to do, how to behave, what is going on, and what Jesus expects of them in life. We then wonder why these same people sometimes drift away, or never really make the progress we were expecting them to. It is true that some people are 'self starters' and will take the initiative to learn for themselves and will take responsibility for their own growth. But such people are generally the exceptions rather than the rule. This is why Jesus commanded us to make disciples—it is our responsibility, and we need to take seriously the task of helping people to obey everything that Jesus commanded. It is also important to understand that 'discipleship' is not a six-week course, or something that happens only to new Christians. Every believer is intended to be a disciple and this is intended to continue until we meet Jesus face to face (1 *Jn.* 3: 2).

When a person is saved in our culture, they will increasingly have little or no knowledge of the bible, Christian doctrine, or church life. Most new converts will have never read a bible, attended a church service, and will have no idea what the Lord's Supper is about or why we baptise. More important, they will have little or no knowledge of the teachings of Jesus that he has commanded us to obey, or of the person of Jesus that they are meant to imitate. This was brought home forcibly to me very recently when working with a recently-saved 23-year old girl, who had never attended any kind of church in her life! Despite being very intelligent and well educated, and even having spent the last ten years in the USA (the most religious country in the western world), she knew absolutely nothing about the Christian faith. All of this means that when a person is saved, we have a lot of work to do!

The first thing that I do when a person professes faith in Christ is to give them a bible—after all most people don't own one. The most sensible thing to do here is to give them the same version that is normally used during Sunday services, although if it is a young person, someone who struggles to read, or a person who has a low level of education, a simpler version might be wise. You should not assume that the new believer will know what to do with their bible or how to find their way around it. It is a good idea to show them how to find the different books and how to find specific chapters and verses.

Alongside a bible, I give every new believer a set of daily bible reading notes, especially designed for new Christians. There is a number of organisations that produce such notes: they typically last for thirty days and deal with the basics of the Christian faith. The benefit of these notes is that they encourage the discipline of daily bible reading and prayer. It is important to remember that, once the thirty days comes to an end, the new believer needs to be moved on to regular daily reading notes. The most sensible course of action is to consistently use notes produced by the same organization, as this helps the person to feel comfortable with the style and format, and brings a sense of continuity.

Depending on the person being discipled, it may be appropriate to get them into reading the bible systematically as well. So in addition to their new daily readings, they could read a chapter a day. This gets them further used to reading the biblical text and becoming familiar with it.

The question of daily bible reading and daily prayer should be revisited regularly when working through a discipleship course for new Christians. Most discipleship courses have a whole session on the bible, its contents, and how to read it. Typically, there are also sections on how to pray and when to pray. The structure of most discipleship courses also provides the opportunity to encourage the new convert to pray and read their bible.

There are two identifiable aspects of discipleship. The first is the gaining of practical knowledge and the second is the development of Christ-like character. These two are distinct, yet bound together. If you think about Jesus' disciples, their training included both developing their knowledge of Christ and developing their character into Christ-like-ness. If you take the average new believer today, they will have little or no biblical knowledge. The method that I have followed is to equip the new believer with practical knowledge, while continually exposing them to the person, words, and works of Jesus in order for them to grow more like him.

But discipleship is not a course, it is a way of life. That said, a course can be a very helpful tool in the early days of discipling a new believer. There are a number of courses available, I have developed my own course which I call, *Following Jesus*, and it contains one session on each of the following topics: 'Becoming Like Jesus' (what is a disciple?), 'Discovering Jesus', 'I Was Made In God's Image' (creation, fall, sin, salvation), 'Prayer & Fasting', 'The Bible' (why read it, how to read it, reliability, contents), 'The Holy Spirit', 'Baptism', 'Wired

To Worship', 'The Lord's Supper', 'Sharing My Faith', 'When Jesus comes again', 'God's Family' (how to interact with other Christians), 'Gifts From God', 'Using my Resources', 'What is the Church and how do I belong?' and 'Serving God'. The idea is that within a week or two of having made a commitment, the new believer meets with a leader, either one-on-one or in a group, and begins a one session per week course which will introduce them to the basics of the Christian life in the early months of their faith. Using tools like this helps the leader to be sure the person has genuinely understood the implications of their decision to become a Christian. They are also a great vehicle for confronting the person with baptism and church membership.

When working with any new Christian, it is important to assess their educational level and their ability to read, write, and perform basic comprehension tasks. Most bible study methods, and most discipleship courses, presume the person can read verses of scripture, examine them, and then ask simple questions of the text. While most new believers will be able to handle this, it may not always be the case. I remember one individual that my wife and I discipled who could barely read and who was certainly unable to ask questions of the text. We had to completely alter our approach, use a much simpler translation; the style of our discipleship classes with her was much more instructional from us to her, rather than getting her to arrive at her own conclusions from the text. There is no simple solution to this problem. Suffice it to say that it is an issue to be aware of, and if you are planting a church in an area that has low literacy rates, you may need to alter your approach completely, and you might find it helpful to get some training on teaching young people and adults with low literacy skills.

I believe that it is the responsibility of church leaders, and those doing the discipling, actively and strongly to encourage the new Christian to get baptised. After all, in the Great Commission Jesus demanded that, as we make disciples, we also baptise them (*Mt.* 28: 19). Clearly, we are to take the initiative and present to the new Christian the importance of baptism. Baptism is not presented in the bible as a 'stage 2', after 'stage 1' (conversion), nor is it presented as something you do when you get 'really committed.' The biblical pattern was that the individual is baptised as soon as they are saved (*Mk.* 16: 15, 16; & *Acts* 2: 38-41; & 8: 12 & 36-38). It is the evidence that a person has really committed themselves to Christ. Experience also teaches us that, from and emotional and psychological point of view, baptism is of enormous significance to the individual concerned.

Having said this, as baptism is an alien concept for most new believers, it is worth requiring them to work through some kind of baptismal class, to ensure they have grasped why they should be baptised and what they are doing (and what they are not doing) in being baptised. This can be incorporated into a wider discipleship class.

Individual local churches have differing approaches to church membership. Some choose not to have a formal membership, while others have a very clear membership and a structured route into membership. It is my conviction that the latter is certainly preferable. Having a formal membership brings a genuine sense of accountability as well as a sense of belonging to church life. It will emphasize the importance of the local church and encourage members not to take the issue of their involvement and relationship with the church lightly. The question of church membership can also be included in a discipleship programme. In covering the topic, it is important to enable the new believer to fully understand how the particular church functions. This would include matters such as the leadership structure of the church, its financial arrangements, and the rationale for its activities. This also enables the leaders to present very clearly what the expectations are of church members. There is no point in complaining about people's involvement (or lack of involvement) in their local church, if the expectations of the leaders have never been explained to the new Christian or new member.

Using a 'discipleship course' also helps in the task of developing Christ-like behaviour in the new believer. A good discipleship class should have practical application points throughout, and give opportunities to discuss behaviour and attitudes. Those running the class should never be the servant of the resource material; it should be the other way round. Time should be allowed to deal with questions that come up, covering them adequately before moving on. Discernment is needed to identify the particular challenges that each new Christian will face as they try and live a Christ-like life. A good question to ask is, 'What do you think following Jesus might mean for you?' The answer to this question will be varied. For some, an implication could be that they have to stop binge drinking; others might need to sort out a complicated relationship; and others still might have to pay particular attention to their language. Asking the right question will allow the new believer to identify for themselves areas of character development or spiritual growth that are needed in their life

At this point, we need further reflection on the question of lifestyle. In our post-modern, post-Christian society, we will inevitably have people coming to faith who have a great deal of baggage. As spiritual parents, we cannot ignore this baggage, as it will be a major hindrance to long-term spiritual growth. There are two types of baggage that we will face, moral baggage and emotional baggage.

Moral baggage

Given the disappearance of the Judeo-Christian worldview from today's society, it is hardly surprising that so many new believers struggle with moral baggage. Indeed, so far has our society gone down a pathway of moral relativism that many people struggle even to recognise what sin is, let alone to try and deal with it. This presents us with a huge challenge if our discipleship programme is to be successful. However we run our discipleship classes, this challenge needs to be faced. There is a number of guiding principles that we need to bear in mind.

Don't run

First, we need to determine that we will not run away from the topic. Sadly, this often happens, because churches do not find it comfortable to deal with messy situations. Nevertheless, we need to understand that any serious evangelism will bring mess with it, and in church planting this will especially be the case. The choice is simple, either you confront such issues or the church plant will never work.

Biblical standards

Secondly, while dealing with these messy situations, ensure you maintain biblical standards. This is self-evident, because if we drop our standards in order to have an easy life, we lose the whole purpose of discipleship, which is to produce Christ-likeness in the lives of new believers. Maintaining standards can lead to an inherent tension in the church planting situation. It could mean that you preach something from the pulpit that is not as yet being lived out in the lives of the new believers. For example, you could be preaching about the importance of marriage, while having new believers in the congregation who are co-habiting. This is simply one of the complications of effective church planting. The starting point, however, is to strive for biblical faithfulness.

A Christ-like attitude

We need to be Christ-like in dealing with people. During his ministry Jesus not only rubbed shoulders with people whose lives were in an intractable moral mess; he also lovingly dealt with their problems, as they made their first few steps towards faith (*Jn.* 8). His grace and courage should be our template.

Remember they are babies

We also need to bear in mind new Christians are spiritual babies (*1 Pet.* 2: 2). It is unreasonable to expect a baby to drive a car, hold down job, or work out their income tax. This kind of activity can only be done with a measure of maturity. Parents therefore do not let their children make big decisions for themselves until they are capable of doing so. All new Christians are spiritual babies. We need to be patient with them and recognise their lack of spiritual maturity.

The wider picture

Each person should also be seen as an individual in their own right. We should never generalize, but rather think of the wider context of the person's situation. Some lives are very chaotic and complex, and we should not think that there will always be easy solutions.

Acute and chronic problems

There is also a need to separate acute problems from chronic ones. Suppose, for example, the young person whom you are discipling goes to a party and gets very drunk. This could be a one-off incident that should be handled in a very different way from when someone has a serious and habitual drink problem and regularly slips up. Practical wisdom and discernment are a must.

Emotional baggage

As well as moral baggage there is emotional baggage. We live in a society where work pressures, family crises, marital breakdown, abuse and bereavement have left many people wounded and hurting. A significant proportion of people who become Christians will carry some of these hurts with them into their newfound faith.

Churches stagger under the weight of all the emotional baggage. This baggage is often roughly treated by Christian leaders who are intolerant of the needs of those to whom they minister. Again several things need to be born in mind.

Don't minimise problems

In some cases, people present problems that to the casual observer seem insignificant; however, they are important to them and this need to be remembered.

Be prepared for the long haul

People are not machines that can be fixed quickly. We are highly complex beings and our emotional makeup is full of complexity. Some people have the capacity to bounce back after problems and keep going; others simply cannot. The work of pastoral care is long-term.

Treat every person with sensitivity
Without sensitivity, the emotional baggage that our church members carry will get more acute rather than lessen. Churches should be havens where emotionally-damaged people feel safe and have the confidence to deal with the issues that haunt them.

Look to God for healing
It is also vital that we recognise God's role in our pastoral care. In his omniscience, God knows exactly what circumstances have caused the damage and the remedy that will bring healing. We need to prayerfully involve God in our discipleship.

Beware of being swallowed by the monster of dependence
From a practical point of view, it is important to bear in mind that, although the church needs to care for people who are hurting, wisdom is also needed in deciding just what level of help to give and how it should be given. The situation should be avoided in which a person with emotional baggage becomes so wrapped up in themselves that they begin to find security in their problems and do not want to move on and deal with them. In such situations, a person can become so time consuming the church planter will have little time to do anything else.

• •

As the process of discipling is worked through it is important to be realistic and patient. The person leading the course should regularly re-visit the issues, challenging and encouraging the new believer as to what progress they are making and what steps they need to take or might need help in taking. This enables a level of accountability to develop, which, if followed up, can develop and continue way beyond any discipleship course. Living for Christ is difficult, even for a mature Christian. Clearly, new believers have an even greater challenge. They should be given all the support they need and this will inevitably involve a significant investment of time and energy.

In the early days of a typical UK church plant, there might be a steady trickle of new believers, and initially it may be feasible for one person to do all the discipling if they make it a priority. However, if the trickle continues, it won't be long before the person doing the discipling has his or her week full and has no time to do anything else. There are three options at this stage. Option one is to continue as you are doing and watch everything grind to a halt. Clearly, this is not a good option. Option two is to recruit more people to do the discipling. This is a good idea as it is always good to have more people involved, but may not be practical if there is only one person working full time for the church and everyone else is heavily committed in other areas of church life. Option three is to try to group together new believers where possible, so that instead of meeting with individuals one-on-one, you meet with them in a group. One advantage of this is that you might be able to meet with up to ten or twelve people at a time in a home, and so make very good use of your limited and precious time. Another advantage is that some new Christians will find one-on-one study a little intimidating and might find the dynamic of learning in a group much easier. One disadvantage of group-based discipleship is that an individual may not want to, or be able to, share on a deeper level in front of others and so issues in that person's life might be missed or neglected. It can also mean that there is less accountability between the new believer and the person doing the discipling.

Running a discipleship group involving several people is generally easiest off the back of an evangelistic effort such as a Christianity Explored course or an Alpha course. If you have four or five people who have been saved through such a course, you can then start a discipleship course as soon as the evangelistic course is finished. There will be continuity and a natural cohesion already in place. However, if you have people coming to faith one at a time through Sunday services, or through doing something like Christianity Explored one-on-one, then it is best if at all possible to begin discipling them on their own. The alternative is that you wait until you have enough people for a group, but this may take a long time, and in the mean time the new believer is left without any input, which would not be good and could cause them real problems.

One of our aims when working with new Christians, and especially when planting a new church, is to get the new believer to move away from dependency on one person. There is the risk that, as a new Christian meets with a leader for discipleship, they begin to rely too heavily on the leader and fail to develop their own relationship with the Lord, thus undermining the very purpose of their being discipled. One way of helping to prevent this is to encourage the new believer to join a home group as soon as possible. This enables the new Christian to begin to develop relationships with other believers, so that they can be encouraged and built up (*Heb*. 10: 24, 25). Don't wait until they have finished the discipleship course—get them connected with an appropriate home group straightaway if possible. Another reason for seeking to integrate the new believer into a home group is that it is not possible for the church planter or discipleship group leader to keep meeting with every new Christian on a permanent basis.

If you are running a discipleship course and have a group of eight new Christians, when they have finished the course, it might be possible for this group to form a new home group, rather than split them up and send them to different existing home groups. This is a great way to grow the number of home groups that you have! You might want to consider appointing an existing church member to lead the home group, or you might be able to appoint one of the group as the leader, or at the very least as the host.

It is clear from scripture that every believer is a disciple and should be discipled. It is also clear, as has already been stated, that discipleship is not just a course, but a whole-life issue. Having said that, as a church leader and planter, you will have to make decisions about what you do with your time, and whom you invest your time in. While it is important to ensure that all new believers get a firm grounding and receive clear instruction in their new faith (this can be done with a discipleship course), we do have to be wise about whom we invest in. Our model for discipleship is surely the Lord Jesus himself, and we see that although he had hundreds of disciples, he also had a smaller group of seventy-two (*Lk.* 10: 1), and an even smaller group of just twelve. It was these twelve that he chose to invest most of his time in. Beyond this, we see him focusing even more closely on just three men—Peter, James and John (*Mt.* 17: 1). We must learn from the example of Jesus and wisely seek out those new believers that we believe would value and would benefit from extra input. When working with new Christians, it soon becomes evident who is hungry and wants to grow and learn more, and who is less keen. It is also likely that it is from this group of believers, who receive a greater investment of time, that future leaders will be identified.

Discipleship is not an optional extra or a 'stage two' of the Christian life following on from conversion. Discipleship should be an ongoing process by which we are all learning from Jesus, following Jesus, obeying Jesus, and becoming like Jesus. When we have the privilege of leading people to faith in the Lord Jesus Christ, we must remember that this is only the start, and that we have a duty and a responsibility to disciple them. Discipling people can be one of the most rewarding things you can do. I can think of a number of people that I have had the privilege of discipling and it is so encouraging to see the journey they have been on, and the progress they have made. However, sadly, it can also be discouraging, as we can pour a lot of our time and effort into people, only to see them fall away, often refusing to surrender to the demands of the Lord upon their life. Such casualties are painful to bear, but are part of the cost of investing ourselves in people's lives.

We shall see some turn back, but we shall also see many press on. As we plant and lead churches, a clear and structured discipleship strategy is important, to ensure that we are obedient to the call of Christ in the Great Commission, and to ensure that the new believers entrusted to us grow, develop, and reach their potential in Christ.

CHAPTER 13

The challenges of a building

Giles Arnold

As with all aspects of church planting, the decision to take on a building must be considered very prayerfully. There are many challenges involving church buildings, some more practical and others more subjective. Consider first whether you actually want or need a building! Many new churches choose to operate without a building because of the questions associated with 'ownership' of a building, that is, responsibility for it, whether it is purchased or rented.

Before deciding to acquire a building, it is wise to consider the following points.

First, it can be very difficult to overcome the close association in people's minds (both within the church and outside) between the church congregation and the church building. This is not helped by the use of the word 'church' in English to describe both the congregation and the building in which the congregation meets. One simple way of disassociating the two is by not having a building at all!

Secondly, what does the building say about the church? Even if we are able to disassociate the congregation from the building used by the congregation, the building will often be the first impression that non-believers have of the church. It will often speak volumes about the people who meet in it. We should surely want this impression to be very welcoming and positive.

Thirdly, are you confident that the building will not begin to dominate the church agenda. Too often, churches begin to view their ministry in terms of what the building can be used for. Any church should ensure that their building fits the church's vision, rather than the other way round. In addition, 'ownership' of a building (whether purchased or rented) will bring with it costly maintenance and statutory obligations, and the church must be careful not to allow these obligations to dominate or limit the vision.

There are of course huge, mainly practical, advantages in having a permanent building to operate from. It can be very helpful to have a building which advertises the church's presence and from which the community can be reached. A building will be a central point at which to hold meetings at the church's convenience, rather than at the convenience of the school or other church or organisation whose building you 'borrow'. All equipment can be stored at the building, and chairs and equipment do not have to be set up and packed away each week. And the various activities can leave posters and art work displayed each week.

Once you are sure that the Lord is leading you to a building there are several challenges to consider.

1. The challenge of the building's fitting the vision

Vision

As noted above, churches too often view their ministry in terms of what the building can be used for. Although we have to be practical with the resources God has given us, this is often the wrong way to look at the building. The basic activities of church do not change, in terms of worship, teaching and outreach. But the God-given vision of each church differs from the next. If you already have a building which does not fit with the vision, can it be adapted, altered or extended so that it does fit the vision? If not, should you be looking for another building?

If you do not already have a building and are looking to buy or rent one, bear in mind that its use and capacity must submit to the vision that you have as a church. Before employing an architect to draw up plans for a new building, the church needs to be clear about what it needs the building for, now and in the future. You need to consider what resources and facilities will be required to meet the vision that God has given you. This includes outside space (play and sports and amenity (e.g., garden) areas and car parking), meeting and worship rooms, kitchen, WCs, lobby area, offices, storage and other specialist rooms. Think through relationship of rooms to each other, shared access, temporary partitions and possible second storeys. Consider disabled access. Think 'outside the box', such as making use of development opportunities within the property.

Before employing an architect, it is also worth considering the options for the possible layout of the new property or altering an existing property. Sketch diagrams can be drawn up of different rooms and their uses, showing the relationship between other parts of the building, the flow of people and flexibility of space. General rules of thumb are that 25 square metres is required per parking space and one square metre per seat in the worship area. It is worth at this stage setting out priorities, with those matters that are core, those that are important but which it may be possible to delay, and those that are peripheral (i.e., luxuries or 'like to do but not vital').

If you are considering the conversion or adaptation of an existing building, there is a number of key areas that need to be considered, including:

- The flow of traffic and people through the building, ensuring that, where possible, this is intuitive, does not create bottlenecks, allows a number of activities to take place at the same time and does not waste space.
- Space should be used flexibly, allowing for expansion and division of rooms where necessary, shared use of communal facilities such as kitchens and WCs, and construction of the space so that it can be used for multiple purposes.
- Adequate well-located storage should be provided. A general rule of thumb is to double the amount of space that you think you may need!

Architects and other professionals

The next stage is normally to employ an architect, and possibly a quantity surveyor, to carry out a feasibility study on various options, which must include costings. It is important to select an architect who is sympathetic with the work of the church, as the architect may also be required to project-manage the building works and apply for planning consent. It is also important that the architect has experience in the area of the work required (e.g., modern buildings or listed buildings). Most architects are prepared to have an initial meeting with the client free of charge and should then be asked to set out their fee structure and the extent of the work to be covered by them. It is important to see examples of past work; ideally, recommendations or references from other churches; and confirmation that they have adequate professional indemnity insurance. It is important that the architect is given a clear brief, explaining both the church's vision and the facilities that are required. The more clarity there is before committing to a project the better; misunderstanding and lack of communication can lead to all sorts of extra expenses. It is important to avoid changing, and adding to, a scheme as the work goes along, as this is a recipe for disproportionate extra cost. Written contracts should be drawn up.

If the building project is complicated it may be best to use a planning consultant, who should be prepared to work in conjunction with the architect. The planning consultant would help with the consultation with the local planning authority and deal with any complex issues in obtaining planning consent. For larger projects, it is important to consult not only with the planners, but also with local councillors, neighbours, community representatives and others who would be affected, as well as keeping the church informed of progress.

Funding

Having drawn up and costed the options, the next stage is to consider where the capital funding is to come from. This is likely to be from a number of sources, including the church's building fund, pledged gifts from the church, grant funding from other bodies, capital from the sale of other properties and/or a mortgage/loan to be raised on the property (or other properties). A shortfall in the funding required may result in having to reduce or phase the project, or having to seek additional funds. It is also worth bearing in mind that costs are likely to increase, as there may be a delay between designing and starting the project. It may therefore be prudent to allow for a 10-20% increase.

2. The challenge of what people see in a building

Welcoming

If your building is the first thing that people see of you what do you want to convey about yourselves? A large, centuries-old, crumbling building with seemingly-impregnable solid-oak doors, dated furnishings, lack of proper heating and damp musty smell of decay, speaks of something that is out-of-date, inaccessible, unwelcoming and irrelevant. This message is a barrier to be overcome if people from outside the church are to be attracted into the building.

One pastor of a growing church, when offered a traditional looking church building to rent commented 'no, thank you—it looks too much like a church building'! By contrast, a new and growing church looking for suitable premises chose to rent a retail showroom, with a modern entrance, flexible layout and light and open rooms, not to mention the car parking, rather than a traditional chapel with its inherent damp, inflexible layout and unwelcoming appearance, even though it was necessary to obtain planning consent for change of use of the showroom. But if you already have a traditional and/or unappealing building, all is not lost! Alterations can be made (even if it is L isted, though this does give rise to constraints) as referred to above, and ultimately we have a big God whose purposes are not thwarted!

We do, however, want the building to be welcoming. This is achieved by clear signposting, proper lighting, lots of glass exposing the entrance (which gives the impression of openness and inclusivity), an attractive design (at least at the front of the building), and adequate welcoming and meeting space.

Location

The location of the building is important. Ideally, the building should be located in the centre of the community that you are trying to reach, so that there is identification with the community and the building is visible and accessible. It is also important to have a base from which to impact the community and in which various community-orientated activities can be run. In an un-churched society, frequently the last thing people will go into is a building that is used for worship. Initial contact with people will be through community-linked activities, such as mums and tots, life training, senior citizens' lunch clubs and U3A[1]. However, a building located outside the centre of the community is not an insurmountable problem. After all, in today's society, many people are happy to travel by car and therefore, unless the building is far away, this will not be a problem. In such situations, suitable parking at the property or nearby is necessary. It is also good to ascertain how accessible the building is by public transport or by bicycle.

3. The challenge of whether to buy or rent

To buy or to rent?

In the past, churches in particular have assumed that any properties used by the church would be purchased. Many churches and charities today are choosing to rent rather than buy. You will need to weigh up the options and seek financial advice. Consider the availability of capital and regular annual income. If there is sufficient capital available, it may be preferable to purchase the property. If there is regular income, but no capital, this may push you towards renting. However,

---

[1] University of the Third Age.

the option of taking a mortgage may still be available. Consider flexibility and whether there is a temporary need for the property or a long-term need. Will the type of accommodation needed in the future vary from the present need (e.g., will the church outgrow the building in the next few years?)? Consider how the proposed building fits in with the existing buildings and how they complement the mission of the church.

As a charity, the church will almost certainly require a formal valuation and professional advice, to show that you are making a sound and reasonable decision, and have not paid more than you need to for the property. By renting a building rather than purchasing it, you will have the flexibility of moving to another building as and when the church outgrows the existing building. To purchase a building will ensure that you are not 'wasting' money on rent and will give you a capital asset against which you can raise a mortgage or which you can sell if you need to move to another property. If you rent a building and spend a lot of money on it, by extending it and/or adding new facilities or a new roof for example, when you leave the building and move on, that expenditure will be lost to you, but will be to the benefit of the landlord. Under the rules relating to compensation for tenant's improvements when a lease is surrendered or reaches its end, you may find the amount of compensation is low compared to what you spent.

The property that you currently have, or are looking at, may be too large for your present use. It does, however, allow for future growth, and parts of the property could be let to others either to raise income (for ministry or for the paying of a mortgage) or for an associated ministry.

Letting arrangements

If you are allowing others to use space within the building, you need to take care that you have the appropriate agreement in place. For occasional use with non-exclusive occupation, and for perhaps only a few hours per week, a hiring agreement would be suitable. This sets the letting on a formal basis, ensures that each party understands the basis of the letting, and deals with specific matters such as insurance (users should have their own public liability insurance), contact details, and fire and security procedures.

For regular bookings, particularly if they offer exclusive occupation (even if this is only for part of the building), consideration should be given as to whether the letting is to be within the Landlord and Tenant Act 1954. This Act gives the tenant an automatic right to renew the tenancy or lease, and normally applies to any length of occupation over 12 months and to any tenancy granted for more than six months. It is possible to contract out of this part of the Act, but appropriate notices need to be served before the tenancy starts. Care needs to be taken with short-terms lettings that are extended to over six months, since the security of tenure protection for a tenant will apply if the tenant is in occupation for more than twelve months; hence you are in danger of granting more security to the occupier than you had intended. In every letting, care also needs to be taken in dealing with improvements (work carried out by the tenant other than repairs) as consent by the landlord (even informally given) will entitle the tenant to compensation in respect of his improvement costs. I recommend that for more regular users a lease is drawn up, clearly setting out the intentions of the parties in detailed terms. These terms should include:

- The exact area included in the letting, and rights such as access, storage and parking
- Length of lease (and any early-break arrangements)
- Rent (amount and when payable) and any rent-free period or rent rebates (possibly resulting from tenants' improvements)
- Rent review(s) and basis of review (e.g., RPI or market rent)
- The type of use of the premises that is authorised under the lease
- Arrangements for sub-letting or assigning of the lease, both for part of the property or for the whole of the property
- Insurance (who should pay and what would be covered)
- Repair responsibilities
- Services, access and special arrangements;
- Alterations or improvements to the property;
- Costs (e.g., for drawing up the lease or for serving notices during the lease).

Appropriate professional advice should be sought at an early stage.
The level of rent must be a market rent if the tenant is not working for the charity, is not part of the work of the charity (i.e., the activity does not fall within the charitable objects of the church), or is not a charity with similar objects to your church or charity. Leases for seven years or longer now need to be registered with the Land Registry as an interest in the property and certain prescribed information must be provided. Consider whether your charity's governing documents (trust deed or memorandum and articles if a charitable company) allow you to

lease out or accept the type of use proposed. Consider whether the proposed use will require planning consent for change of use.

If purchase of the property was zero-rated for VAT purposes (as a result of being used for a relevant charitable purpose), it must remain in non-business use for a period of 10 years after purchase—so care needs to be taken when letting surplus premises: the costs of having to repay VAT could be significant. Specialist VAT advice should be taken before committing to any purchase or lease.

Leasing a property

If you choose to lease a property rather than purchase it, there is a number of questions that need to be considered. These are set out in the appendix to this chapter and are matters of importance to both landlords in granting leases and tenants in accepting leases. It is important to seek professional advice at an early stage.

Mortgage

When purchasing a property, you may need to raise a mortgage for church and community buildings. Specialist lenders are often required, who will understand the arrangements and risks, and may offer more competitive rates than high street lenders. If the church owns residential as well as church properties, you may be able to raise a mortgage more easily on the residential property and at a better rate in order to fund work on the church building. You need to ensure that the arrangement is properly constructed and allowed by the charity's governing documents. You are required under the Charities Act to seek independent professional advice on taking out a mortgage. Criteria will vary for each lender, but as a rule of thumb lenders will only lend 70% of the final *value* of the building after the building works have been completed—that value is likely to be less than the building costs! The lender will often carry out an affordability calculation under which the church will have to show, for example, that it has uncommitted income (i.e., income not required for other purposes) that is 1.5 times greater than the cost of the mortgage. The lender will take into account the established income of the church and commitments from members of the church for increased giving in the future. This needs to be committed giving, rather than hoped-for giving.

Lenders will usually want to see the last three years' accounts and a business plan, along with details of the church structure, leadership, trusteeship and history. Lenders may want to see evidence that the borrowers have the required deposit and funds to cover the quite significant associated fees for purchase. In some circumstances, they may require guarantees from the trustees. The lender will require a survey of the property, to assess the condition and suitability as security for the loan, and will want to ensure that the correct planning consents have been obtained. Thought needs to be given to the term of the loan, as the main leader/borrower may be older, which could be a factor taken into consideration by the lender.

4. The challenge of tackling the legal questions

When buying a church or non-church building, there are different legal and statutory questions to be aware of.

Ownership

You may think that ownership itself will not be an issue. However, there are many situations, particularly in respect of existing church buildings, where ownership is unclear. Sometimes, this results from the fact that the building is held under a charitable trust set up so many years ago and the original trustees are no longer alive; yet the legal ownership of the property does not appear to have been properly passed down to the current trustees. Tied in with this is the question of whether the title to the land has been registered with the Land Registry. Registration often makes it easier to identify the owners and reduces the necessity to locate the original legal documents by which the land was purchased. If the ownership is unclear, the title unregistered and documents missing, establishing ownership can be a major headache. It is not necessarily an insoluble problem, but early legal advice should be sought.

Having established the ownership, and either obtained the Land Registry entries for the property or the original conveyances and transfers, it should be possible to work out whether the boundaries and access to the property as indicated in the documents are in line with existing arrangements on the ground. If the legal documents indicate something other than the current physical boundaries or access, there are likely to be disputes over these in the future. Sometimes, the church uses land it does not own or other third parties use land owned by the church. These situations need to be investigated and if necessary resolved.

It is often advisable that the property should be owned in the name of a company on behalf of the church rather than in the names of individual trustees on behalf of the church. This has two advantages. First, unless it is deliberately wound up, a company does not cease to exist as long as the correct returns are made to Companies House. Therefore, the Land Registry entries do not need to be changed every time the identity of any of the managing trustees changes. Secondly, any liability for rent, mortgage or other covenants, such as repairs, are limited to the value of the assets of the company, whereas trustees would normally have unlimited liability for all debts relating to the property—hence their own personal assets may be put at risk.

Whether you are purchasing a church or non-church building you should investigate the deeds and/or Land Registry documents so as to be aware of any restrictions relating to the property.

Trust Deed Restrictions

The use of existing church buildings will often be governed by the trust deed under which the property is held. Restrictions are as varied as the necessity to 'break bread every Lord's Day', that women cannot participate audibly in services and prohibition on using drums and trumpets in the property. Most trust deeds of church premises require the occupying church to adhere to certain doctrines, as well as practices, and they often set out procedures for management of the premises, including sales, lettings and mortgages. You need to be familiar with these. The Charity Commission are often willing to adapt old trust deeds to suit modern interpretation or custom, but will not generally adjudicate over matters of doctrine.

You need also to check in the trust deed on the minimum number of trustees required and how they are appointed. It is important to establish this in order to ensure the existing trustees are in a position to gift or sell the property—indeed, if the number of trustees falls below the required minimum, commonly the only action the remaining trustees may take is to bring the number up to the minimum.

When a new trustee is appointed, this must be notified to the Land Registry. If the land was previously unregistered, the appointment triggers compulsory registration. The Land Registry charges a fee to change the register every time there is a new trustee. Hence, it may be wise to appoint the Official Custodian or an appropriate organisation as trustee or to incorporate the charity as described above, in order to avoid this necessity and the attendant legal costs of ensuring that the notification is done as it should be.

Restrictive Covenants

The deeds and/or Land Registry documents will also reveal whether there are any restrictive covenants placed on the land by previous owners, often restricting the use of the property to church use and prohibiting certain other varied uses such as selling alcohol, using the property for residential purposes, or even dying cloth or tanning leather! Some of these restrictive covenants may not now be enforceable, partly because the original owner (Covenantee) does not now own any nearby land which might be affected by those activities, thereby making the covenant void, or because the covenant does not bind successors in title. Again, legal advice is essential on the covenants. Your advisors should be able to assess whether it is worth trying to have them removed, which can be a lengthy and expensive process, or, more usually, they will arrange for (inexpensive) indemnity insurance to cover the possibility that someone might try to enforce the covenants against you. A covenant restricting the use to church use can have the effect of reducing the value of the property; this can be an advantage when purchasing the building for church use, but may also be a disadvantage later when selling the property.

Under-values

With respect to values, care needs to be taken where if a property is to be sold or let by one charity to another, for a sum less than the market value. The Charity Commission will only allow such a transfer where the two charities have similar purposes/objects or the charity selling the property has a power to gift the property. If there is no power to gift (the power to 'dispose' is not enough to allow the selling charity to give the property away), the Charity Commission may allow a gift if the selling charity could sell at full value, but has the power then to give any proceeds of sale to various causes, including the purchasing charity. The Charity Commission takes the view that short-cutting such a process by gifting the property directly to the new charity is possible. It is advisable to check with them. Every case should be looked at carefully and, as with any property disposal, trustees are expected to take professional advice on value, particularly where the disposal should be at market value.

Planning Use

As well as restrictions on use in the legal documents relating to the property, there will often be planning restrictions on the use of a building. If the property is already a church building, then it can continue to be used as such. If, however, it is currently used for other uses outside of the D1 Use Class (defined as non-residential institutions, such as places of worship, church halls, clinics, health centres, day nurseries, museums, libraries and non-residential education & training centres), then planning consent would be required for change of use to church use. Whether the planners would grant consent for change of use depends on a number of factors, particularly the location of the building (they are usually cautious about church use within residential areas due to the inherent noise factors), whether there is adequate parking and access to the building, and whether it would be a loss of property which in principle generates employment. Each local authority has different planning policies for church and community buildings and these need to be investigated (for example, in the Local Plan if there is one or the Local Planning Framework) and the proposed change of use discussed with the planning authority. They will often give advice prior to an application being made without charging, but some authorities will charge for the privilege of a pre-application enquiry.

When a church occupies a building, there is an increased likelihood of the premises being used for mixed purposes; for instance the church may run a soup kitchen or host conferences. Many of these activities would be regarded as an ancillary use in church premises. Hence, it would be helpful to try to identify possible future uses of the premises before abandoning existing authorised uses. It may be that only part of the building will be used as a place of worship.

Another point to bear in mind is that if the property's use changes, it is important to inform the local authority and valuation office of the change of use, so that the rates can be adjusted. If the building is to be used as a place of worship, I recommend that an application is made to the local authority for it to be a Registered Place of Worship, as this will automatically be exempt from business rates.

Disability Access
The Disability Discrimination Acts require those responsible for a building open to the public to make 'reasonable adjustments' to the physical features of that building so as to overcome physical barriers to access. Quite apart from the legal requirements to make the property more accessible, we as Christians should want to give disabled people (and those affected by disability, such as family members of disabled people) the same opportunity to hear the gospel, and to participate fully in the church's life, as anyone else. Under the law, we are to make reasonable adjustments to physical features or provide reasonable alternative methods to enable a disabled person to take part in church activities. This may mean the provision of ramps, lifts, an accessible toilet (for wheelchair access), a loop induction system, improved lighting and proper signage.

The Act turns on the term, 'reasonable'. When considering what would be reasonable, we need to take into account the resources available, the practical effect of any changes, the possible disruption to church activities, resources already spent on providing access, and the availability of finance or other assistance. The standards of physical accessibility to buildings given in approved Document M of the Building Regulations are considered to be a reasonable standard to achieve and therefore are the benchmark for what is deemed accessible. If an access audit has not already been done, that is recommended. This will involve going through the whole building and grounds, to identify the often-unsuspected barriers imposed on people with disabilities and suggesting ways of overcoming them. Some examples of points to review are as follows:

- *Car park*—Ensuring there are no hazards or obstructions to visually impaired people, that the surface is suitable and that disabled parking spaces are provided near the entrance.
- *Physical access to and within the building*—Provision of hand rails to steps, ramps, ensuring that access doors are sufficiently wide to allow wheelchairs to pass, removing obstacles (at low level or not easily visible), marking the edge of steps, and providing suitable handles to doors.
- *Toilets*—Provision of accessible unisex WCs, ensuring that doors are of adequate width and that the WCs are at the same floor level (i.e., without intervening steps) as, and close to, main meeting areas.
- *Seating*—Provision of spaces for wheelchairs, and chairs with arms to help people with arthritis, for example.
- *Lighting*—Of access ways, and for book and lip-reading.
- *PA system*—Loop induction system or infra-red system, and taping of meetings for people confined to home.
- *Books and projector screens*—Provision of large print (sans serif typeface at 16pt) and Braille books, and OHP acetates and projected slides using at least 30pt type.
- *Noticeboard and publicity*—Use of upper and lowercase, contrasting colours for print material (e.g., black on white or black on pale yellow) on matt paper; provision of clear, sufficiently-large signage.
- *Website*—Number of typefaces to be kept to a minimum; white and pale pastel colours for backgrounds; and sans serif typeface, not too small.

Other Regulations

There are other regulations that need to be considered for church buildings. These include the asbestos regulations, which require an Asbestos Management Plan to be drawn up for any non-residential building. The previous owners of the property should be able to provide an Asbestos Management Plan, as it has been required from May 2004. If no such plan exists, or it cannot be provided, the church will have to put one in place.

The fire regulations require a Fire Risk Assessment to be carried out by the users of the building. The Fire Service will sometimes help with Fire Risk Assessments, but as they are the policing body for these, they often now refuse to help.

Food hygiene regulations require that there is in place a documented food safety management system for 'food operations'. Environmental Health Services at your local authority will advise on this and are often more lenient with charities.

If the church, or anyone hiring any part of it, provides alcohol during functions on a regular basis, there will need to be a Premises Licence and the sale of alcohol will need to be supervised by someone with a personal licence. This is administered by the local authority for the area. The Licensing Act 2003 allows for authorisation of temporary licensable activities, e.g., a wedding reception or a church fete, by notice given by the premises user to the local authority, but this is strictly limited in extent and advice should be sought from the local authority in good time before the proposed event.

Insurance

One final legal issue to tackle is insurance, as this will be required for a building, the contents and the activities of the church. This should also cover, where appropriate, property owner's liability, public liability, and employer's liability. In view of the liability of trustees, and in particular the unlimited liability of trustees of unincorporated trusts, the trustees should consider taking out trustee indemnity insurance, although it is not mandatory.

5. The challenge of running a building

The initial and ongoing maintenance costs and commitments must be considered before responsibility is taken for any building.

Condition Survey

The physical condition of an existing building should be surveyed professionally before it is taken on, especially if there has been no regular maintenance. If there is any doubt about the structural integrity of the building (e.g., signs of cracking or movement), then a structural survey should also be arranged. It is also recommended that the electrical and gas systems, and boiler and plumbing, are checked by qualified people, as these could give rise to major unknown expenditures.

Although church buildings are exempt from the building regulations for insulating roofs, and on-let properties do not require Energy Performance Certificates, it is worth investigating the energy performance of the building, if only because of the potential energy costs of heating it or the possible discomfort to users. In simple terms, this would involve checking whether the windows are double glazed, the extent of insulation in the roof space, thickness of walls and thermal values of the floor. Improving the energy performance of the property should reduce costs for future heating, though, in financial terms, it is desirable to balance the cost of improvements against likely future savings and the benefits of being warmer.

Generally, before proceeding with acquisition, it is important to form a good idea of the works that will be required to put the building in good order, as well as any works that would be required to alter the building or improve it for your own use. In deciding whether the building can be afforded, these costs will need to be added to the cost of purchasing or renting the building.

Routine Maintenance

Why are some church buildings beautifully maintained and others appear to be badly neglected? Sometimes, it is due to the financial support of the church and resources available. However, often it is because simple and cost-effective maintenance routines have not been carried out, resulting in damage to the property which can only be repaired at major cost. In order to avoid this, a maintenance programme should be adopted, which will require three things:

1. One or more persons to be given responsibility for preparing the programme and overseeing its implementation.
2. Regular and routine checks on the state of the property. This would include monthly walks around the property to pick up any immediate works required; two or three inspections of gutters and gullies over the autumn and winter, to ensure that they are working correctly and not full of debris; and annual servicing of boilers and septic tanks. It is also good practice to have a five-yearly inspection by someone outside the church with relevant experience in property maintenance. The electrical should also be checked at least every five years.
3. An adequate budget to cover basic maintenance and ongoing repairs (e.g., external decoration of woodwork every four years).

Appendix
Questions relating to a potential lease

1. **Landlord**—who is the landlord? Are there any superior landlords and is their consent to the proposed sub-letting and/or alterations required?
2. **Premises**—What is included in the lease? If it is for only part of a building, are there communal areas (e.g., lobbies, WCs, kitchens, lifts and car parks)? What rights are there over these communal areas, and who is responsible for them? Are there car parking spaces allocated specifically to the premises to be let? If the lease relates only to part of the building, who is occupying the remainder of the building, and how will this affect the lease and use?
3. **Term**—when will the lease start (this is not necessarily the date on which the lease is legally agreed)? How long will it be—what does the landlord want, and what does the tenant want? Is there a possible compromise position?
4. **Break**—depending on the length of the lease, is it appropriate to have a break clause to allow the tenant to terminate the lease early? Is the tenant happy to have this at a specific point during the term of the lease, or is it preferable to have it on a rolling basis (e.g., after two years, the tenant will be able to give six months' notice at any time)?
5. **Security of Tenure**—will the lease be within the Landlord and Tenant Act 1954 or will it exclude Part II of the Act (which would effectively mean the tenant could not automatically apply for a new lease)? Exclusion from the 1954 Act weakens the tenant's bargaining position on rent and other terms in any new lease.
6. **Rent**—what is the rent proposed and what rent does the tenant wish to pay? How often is the rent payable (i.e., monthly or quarterly)? Is this in advance or in arrears? Does the landlord want to charge VAT on the rent? If premises are being used for charitable purposes (carefully defined by legislation), VAT cannot be charged on the rent, providing this is made clear to the landlord from the beginning. Is there to be a rent-free period, to allow for fitting out or accommodation work or repairs that need to be done, or for some other reason?
7. **Rent Review**—is there to be a rent review during the term of the lease? Normally, this is on a third or fifth anniversary. Should the new rent be a market rent, or is it upwards only, or perhaps tied to the change in the RPI in the intervening period (your view of this may depend on how you think

property rents are going to change in the future compared to the RPI)? It may be possible to agree future rents now.
8. **Use**—what is the present use of the premises? If it is not D1 Use Class (i.e., place of worship, community use or non-residential education or training centre), then planning consent will be required for change of use. Who will be obtaining the consent and what will happen in the meantime (i.e., will there be an agreement to lease, which would trigger the lease once the planning consent has been obtained?)? Is the landlord aware of the proposed use and willing to give formal consent to it, if necessary? Remember that a wide authorised use in the tenancy could have the effect of increasing the rent that the landlord requires now or on a rent review.
9. **Alienation**—normally, the landlord tries to limit the ability of the tenant to assign (transfer) the lease to someone else, or to sub-let either the whole premises or part of it. What does the tenant require? If it is only to be able to hire out rooms, then this can be allowed within the lease. Will the landlord's consent be needed to assign the lease to new trustees of the church? The church should try to avoid being liable to give an Authorised Guarantee Agreement on an assignment, especially if the assignee is not a similar charity, as benefiting a different charity or a commercial assignee may be outside its powers. If the lease is taken in the trustees' personal names, then they should try to specifically limit their liability to the assets of the trust, so that their personal assets are not put at risk.
10. **Insurance**—does the landlord wish to insure the building or will he require the tenant to do so? If the landlord is paying for the insurance and the tenant is only occupying part of the building, how is the insurance re-charged to the tenant (i.e., will the proportion be based on floor area)?
11. **Repairs**—what repairs are the landlord and tenant responsible for respectively? If the tenant is only occupying part of the building, is the landlord responsible for repairs to the outside of the building (i.e., roof, rainwater goods, walls and possibly windows and doors) and, if so, how will he recharge the cost to the tenant? Make sure that someone, whether it be the landlord or tenant, is responsible to maintain every part of the building. Is the building in good condition and are there likely to be major works during the lease, the cost of which will fall on the tenant. What state are the premises in? If the premises are in poor condition, will the tenant require the landlord to put them in good condition at the beginning of the lease, or will the landlord expect the tenant to do so (for which, perhaps, a rent

rebate will be granted), or will the tenant accept the premises in their current condition, but not be required to return them in any better condition at the end of the lease? It may be necessary for an agreed schedule of condition (with photographs) to be prepared to establish the current condition of the premises at the outset so that there is agreed documentary evidence that can be referred to if there is disagreement at a later stage.

12. **Service Charge**—Is the landlord responsible for the repairs to communal areas, for items such as fire alarm systems, lift maintenance, electricity, gas, water and sewerage etc, and how are the costs to be recharged to the tenant? Normally this is by way of a service charge. If so, how is it to be calculated and is the basis fair to the tenant? How is this charged—when the landlord incurs the cost, or on a quarterly or annual basis, or on a fixed figure?

13. **Improvements**—Is the landlord expecting to carry out any improvements to the premises and, if so, what? Does the tenant wish to carry out any improvements and, if so, on what basis will these be treated (i.e., will the landlord give a rent rebate to purchase them, or will he compensate for them at the end of the lease)?

14. **Disability Discrimination Act**—Is the building accessible for disabled people and, if not, what will be required to make it so? Who will be dealing with, and paying for, these works?

15. **Asbestos**—The 2002 and 2006 Asbestos Regulations required a survey and management plan for asbestos in all non-residential buildings. Has the landlord carried out this survey? The tenant should ask for a copy of the survey and the management plan.

16. **Costs**—Does the landlord expect the tenant to pay the landlord's letting and legal costs, or will each party bear their own costs?

17. **Subject to contract**—Any correspondence should be marked 'subject to contract' to avoid commitment to specific terms while they are still under negotiation.

CHAPTER 14

Developing and appointing leaders

Roger Chilvers

There can be no doubt that leadership is one of the key elements of succesful church planting. If there is no effective leadership, there will be no church planting. It is one of the most acute challenges that we face, both generally in church life and perhaps specifically in the starting and establishment of new churches.

It is a sad fact that many areas of the population, new housing estates, inner city areas, rural communities and even some larger towns have no living, witnessing church, simply because large thriving churches, sometimes within a few miles have no vision for planting a new church, despite the large amount of research that shows that church planting is the single most effective means of evangelism.

Usually, the reason that those churches have no plans for planting is that they lack leadership which has a passion for the wider community and the vision for planting. It is significant that, when asked why there are no plans for planting a new church, the response so often is, 'We do not have the people, and/or experience and/or maturity etc.' However, this is really an excuse and a poor one at that. The question that should be asked is, 'What are your plans/training programmes/investment in time and money etc. to provide the experience/maturity/partnership with other like-minded fellowships, which will enable you to provide the people that you lack who can plant churches? It is perhaps for this reason that looking east, to places like China, is an enormous challenge, as there the peppering of whole countries with new churches has led to a radical move forward in the spread of the gospel.

Every aspect of church planting demands leadership, not only in the new church once it has started, but in getting to the point of deciding to plant a new church in the first place and even in bringing the possibility of church planting onto the agenda in the potential parent church.

The need for leadership in a new church planting process

The styles of possible church plants vary considerably, and so do the reasons for planting. Sometimes, a mature church outgrows its buildings and facilities and therefore needs to plant; other times a church decides that current structures require a complete new start; or an expanding church sees the start of church in a new area as the means of fulfilling its mission mandate. Perhaps a new fellowship might even be seen as the best way to meet the spiritual needs of widely differing cultural or social community. In each of these situations, there will be a particular need for leadership. This need may be divided into three groups or phases each of which has its challenges and requirements if it is to be successful.

1. First, there are leaders needed to act as the initiators, to be the cause that brings about the new work. For this, the leadership style will, in all probability, be strongly entrepreneurial. This phase is, therefore, likely to be led by those that can see both the need and the way forward to the vision of a new church.

2. Secondly, there is the element of leadership that is required to organise and set the fledgling new work on a pathway of growth and development. This aspect of leadership will be most successful if it is led by people who clearly understand what the New Testament means by 'church', how church should operate and how a church can be brought to maturity.

3. Thirdly, running alongside these phases, there are the often forgotten leaders who are required to handle the re-motivating and encouraging of the sending church which will feel noticeably deprived, once the church plant begins. These leaders need to ensure growth in the sending church as well as offer support to the new work.

Leaders that initiate

This may not be the hardest area of leadership, but if the anticipated church plant is from an existing healthy and growing church, someone is needed to lead the thinking and vision for a new work. Without intentionality nothing happens!

The reality is, more often than not, there will be some for whom the whole idea of sending a group off to plant a new church will be controversial. Good leadership is essential to counter this and bring about the action needed. Even the idea of planting a new church can be seen as a threat to a mature group. The church has, in all probability, got used to the feeling of success, both numerically and in the programming and initiatives that they are able to maintain. Consequently, the feel good factor is high and few are willing to risk losing that! The feeling can often be, 'we have taken so long to get to the position of health and relative strength that is would be wrong to put this at risk by planting a new church with little guarantee of success. And in any case, where will we get the finance and the new workers from to make up for those who will go to start something new?' The problem is that existing work, with its strength and multiple opportunities for service, is seen to be the ideal model for what a church and its programme should be and it is difficult for some to see that being replicated.

To overcome this requires considerable leadership skill. Sadly, experience shows that often, respected leaders in the existing work, whose significant efforts are largely responsible for the growth, are among the most reluctant to plant and are defensive of their 'success'. Their passion for the existing work becomes an Achilles heel with regard to the church plant.

The leader(s) needed to overcome this are the groundbreakers—seen in their entrepreneurial gifts. Such people are likely to have a very clear picture in their minds of what they want to see happen, and will have huge enthusiasm to pursue such a vision. They are often difficult to live with, but are the people who, if not used, will either defect to another camp or will degenerate into being trouble-makers, leading the old guard to say things like, 'There you are, I told you they were not the right people to lead a new work'.

Yet such leaders are needed. They are shameless about the vision and full of faith that such a project can and should be undertaken. For them, the past is past and the only thing that matters is what happens tomorrow. They are not easily discouraged, even when there are problems to overcome. In fact, their confidence is contagious and, before long, a group will begin to form around them to share the enthusiasm. Because for them the whole idea of church planting is a God-given vision, they even see 'enthusiasm' in line with its original meaning of 'in God' (*en theos*)!

The danger of such visionary leaders is that they are likely to have blank areas in their thinking. There will be things that they either have not thought about or areas where their thinking is inadequate. For example, theoretically they may agree with teams, but in practice it is difficult for them to function as part of or submit to such a team. These are dangerous people in a church and it takes considerable maturity and grace on the part of all for them to find their right role. But it is unlikely that there will be a church planted without one or two people with such gifts. These are the people, like Peter, who brashly and boldly initiate but who, in so doing, sometimes get things wrong and are likely to unwittingly upset people. They are the Samsons, whose strength is used to break new ground and give birth to new vision.

Leaders that develop the work

Though it is the initiators who give a lead to the vision, they are rarely the best people to develop the work, once the first steps have been taken—at least, not without the considerable help of others. In practice, this means that, from the earliest development of the idea of church planting, consideration should be given to getting others around the initiators who will be able to guide and develop the framework, in order to bring to maturity a long-term development. If they are not found, the new work is unlikely to last. These leaders do not usually get much recognition. After all, they probably didn't start the new church, but they are exceedingly important. The reason that there is a significant failure rate of new churches is largely because of leadership problems. When this phase is not taken seriously enough and the fragile plant, with barely enough of a root structure to find nourishment, is left solely in the hands of the initiators, they will either burn themselves out or burn others in seeking to make progress. After all, initiators are by nature likely to find the 'steady-state' phase difficult on their own and will by nature and gifting quickly find other initiatives in which to be involved, even if they are still part of the newly-formed church.

The developmental or steady-state leaders in a church planting situation are likely to have an almost unconscious ability to recognise what is best for the church. They ask the questions, 'Is this the time for consolidation or new developments? Can the new church sustain all the good ideas that people bring to the surface in discussion? How will we make sure the pastoral work is adequately handled? How do you maintain the initial sudden growth phase which usually accompanies a new plant and that brings in a range of new untaught people with pastoral problems and yet at the same time meet the need of those mature believers who are financing and maintaining the new work?'

The issues are usually ones of insight, discernment and assessment. A new church seems regularly to be at the cross roads, with multiple choices for the way forward, and the development leaders will need to enable the church to make the right choices with the big picture in mind. If such choices were left to the entrepreneur, he would, in all probability, simply select the path that would add more people or more ministries. Size and spread is always likely to be his choice (which is why he can always tell you how many people attend each meeting!); whereas the long-term, big-picture choices will take into account the development of maturity, handling of pastoral issues and exhaustion, questions that do not easily fit into simple numerical considerations. The developmental leader will readily understand the image of a tent and God's instruction in *Isaiah* 54: 2 that to 'enlarge the place of your tent' and to 'lengthen the cords', you must 'strengthen your stakes'.

Leaders that shepherd

This aspect of leadership is critical in two areas; that of the new church and that of the planting church. Both will have special needs as a new church is planted.

It has sometimes rightly been said that new people come to a church on the strength of its programme and teaching, but they remain on the strength of its pastoral/shepherding care. Of course, these are not watertight compartments; there is a strong overlap so that the teaching may well make a strong contribution to the pastoral care of the church. But it is certainly true that if the leadership focuses entirely on programme issues (numbers, structures, teaching, music, technology, leadership of meetings etc.), these eventually will lead to the church becoming a less-than-satisfying spectator activity in which the individual will merely be a seat-filler. Pastoral concern that gives consideration to the shepherding and leading of people is essential.

However, there are two aspects of this 'shepherding'. Pastoral issues certainly focus on people's needs and concerns, but another aspect of being 'shepherds of God's flock' (1 Peter 5:2) is that of confrontation when necessary and direction-setting for the individual as well as the church. Sadly, this has sometimes been abused and has led to what has been referred to as intrusive 'shepherding', in which the shepherd (pastor-leader) takes control of the individual in an unhealthy and overbearing way. But the important role of gently giving direction and guidance to individuals when necessary, without 'lording it over them' (*1 Pet.* 5: 3) is much needed, especially in the early months and years of church planting when new believers have had little, if any, example to follow from mature believers. They simply have not seen how Christians live. It is this that Paul refers to when he tells Timothy 'Set an example for (of) the believers in speech, in life, in love, in faith, and in purity.' (*1 Tim.* 4: 11). It is important to note that these are things that he is to 'command and teach'. In today's culture, it is increasingly an issue, especially in counselling, of how to give such instruction and guidance without overriding the 'rights' and viewpoint of the individual.

So the leader who has this shepherding responsibility is one who loves, nurtures, encourages, supports, corrects and directs, yet has the ability to do so without overriding the will of the individual. Instead, he helps to shape it. Such a person is essential when it comes to developing teams, committees and groups that are needed to plan things. Almost by definition, a new church is going to have a lot of immaturity to deal with, and it is easy for factions to develop in which special shepherd care is the only thing that will keep it from collapsing in disaster. Interestingly, it should be borne in mind that it is often not the new Christians who show most immaturity, but long-standing believers (who should know better) that have come either from the planting church or, more likely, from other places to join and 'help' this new work. It has been said that the light always attracts a few bugs and new churches almost always do! They cause trouble, sometimes from the best of motives, simply because, in their 'maturity' (so they think), they are the ones who feel most strongly about the way they think things ought to be done.

The other major area of shepherd leadership that is needed in the context of church planting is in the church that has done the planting. The loss to the parent church of a group of what are often the best and most able workers to start a new church is seen at first as a wonderful step forward ('what a privilege to have a part in planting a new church'), but this can quickly degenerate into an unspoken resentment. 'Who is going to do all the work and so take their place?' 'Why should we be called on to give money to support this fledgling work which is draining away our success—reduced numbers, smaller financial resource, more limited programme etc?' Wise pastoral care to handle these often-hidden feelings in a gentle and firm way, which can re-envision the parent church, is a big responsibility which needs to be addressed quickly. In most cases, it is best that this is under way before the new church is started.

Every newly-planted church has its own particular leadership needs to enable it to grow into maturity. More than that, it is likely that any church will find growth difficult, if not impossible, unless those entrusted with leadership are able to discern both the God-given direction for the church, and how to communicate it to the fellowship in a way that facilitates the actions that need to be taken. In practice, this not only applies to new church plants, but to any church wanting to grow, and failure to achieve this is certainly one of the primary reasons that some churches easily stagnate and eventually decline.

The recognition of those with leadership gifts, and the appointing of them to senior leadership in a church through whatever means, is therefore a crucial issue. It is both right and natural to look for orthodoxy and maturity when calling new individuals to join a leadership team or body of elders. But they are not the only qualities. Orthodoxy (right doctrine) must be accompanied by a less-thought-about, though no less essential, element—orthopraxy (right action). In fact, it comes as a shock to many to realise that the various lists of qualities for elders found in the New Testament are almost entirely to do with behaviour rather than belief. It is true that Paul emphasises the importance of teaching, 'what is in accord with sound doctrine' (*Tit.* 2: 1). Presumably, this is at least one of the reasons why he indicates that an overseer 'must not be a recent convert' (*1 Tim.* 3:6), although he does not say what is meant by a 'recent convert'. It seems likely that, in the case of the New Testament, most would not have had many years' experience of walking the Christian pathway. But the overall context and verses that enlarge on the qualities that are required for leaders (elders) revealingly almost entirely focus on behaviour (orthopraxy) rather than belief (orthodoxy).

Many churches have suffered a slow decline at the hands of well-meaning, well-taught, mature, kind and godly men, simply because as individuals and as a leadership team they were hardly ever seen to be at the forefront of developing a sense of vision and a passionate desire for growth. Nor were they seen to lead the way in developing evangelistic projects and well-thought-through programmes for expansion. For some unexplained reason in these situations, evangelism is primarily seen to be the responsibility of younger people. As a young person, I once attended a teaching programme led by a very well-known bible teacher, who perceptively said, 'Young people, if you want to know how important the prayer meeting is, watch the elders. If you want to know how important personal evangelism is in your church, watch the elders. If you want to know how important church planting is, watch the elders'. In saying that, surely he was doing no more than echoing Peter who called leaders to be 'examples to the flock' (*1 Pet.* 5: 3). Sadly, one of the essential issues of local church life, that of developing strategies for growth through people being converted and bringing them into maturity, is rarely seen as one of the elders primary responsibilities, as if evangelism was the responsibility of the younger half of the church. As a consequence working this out in a visionary way, developing and articulating where church should be going and how to get there, is simply left to others, usually a few enthusiasts, if it is done at all.

Developing and implementing a vision for growth

So how are a vision for growth and its implementation to be thought-through in a local church context?

1. The senior leadership (group of elders/oversight) develops a vision 'for' the church

This is the result of much prayerful research and discussion. It is very much a spiritual exercise impacted greatly by local and cultural issues. *Acts* 6: 4 relates to this. Questions to be asked include:

- What do we see as the key issues that we as a church are likely to have over the next (say) two years?
- What are the issues in growth, pastoral work, maturing of believers, provision of opportunities to practice etc?
- What do we need in finance, time allocation, training/teaching programmes, specialist/expertise help, etc. to bring this vision to fruition?

2. The vision is expanded into structures and programmes by departmental leaders, so that it is rooted in the church.

The elders share what is felt to be the God-given vision or way forward with the other church leaders, giving them the authority and responsibility to develop the necessary programmes in the various aspects of church life for which they are responsible.

3. The vision is then taken up by the church membership and it then gets worked out in the whole of church life

What started as a spiritual exercise of the leadership becomes the vision of the whole church, not just as a theoretical excercise captured in a vision statement, but as a working and practical driving force in the church. The vision therefore gets worked out at the grass roots as well as amongst the leaders.

Appointing leadership in a new church

Leaders are not identified by the things said or done, but by those that follow. Someone may have the title of leader, or any other title implying it, but if no one listens and follows when the call goes out to move forward, then he is not a leader, at least not at that point. It is followers who determine leadership. The extraordinary leadership of Jesus in calling his disciples is an illustration of this. Jesus said 'Follow me' and '*immediately*' they left their nets and followed him' (*Mt.* 4: 18-22). In church life the same principle applies. It is a sobering exercise to look at the local church and ask, who are the members following? Now, of course, this in no way implies that the leaders are always right, or whether they are ever right for that matter. But if people are following someone, that person is a leader, whatever title, or none, others may have given him.

However, this tells us that leadership and leadership gifts are not of themselves reliable guides to what is needed. The history of the church is littered with many who clearly have been extraordinary leaders, but who have proved disastrous for the church, and it may well be that this has been one of the reasons that there has been a resistance to identifying and deploying leadership gifts in many local churches. In Brethren churches, for example, the list of those who clearly were leaders, but were given no room for the exercise of their abilities and gifts and therefore reluctantly left to find fruitful ministries elsewhere, is both long and marked with many distinguished names!

It is because leadership can be exercised well or badly that the New Testament is clear about what the qualities of elders (leaders) should be. Whether you view the lists in *1 Timothy* 3: 1-7, *Titus* 1: 6-9 or *1 Peter* 5: 1-4 as a check-list of minimum requirements for recognition as an elder, or whether they are to be thought of as areas towards which elders should be seen to be striving, these are surely the heart of the character of an elder. They certainly define the type of leadership that the New Testament calls for, and taking them seriously will save recognised leaders from exploiting their role in the church.

But how does the recognition, appointment and exercise of leadership work out in the church-planting situation? Some check points may help.

1. Do not be in too much of a hurry

When the church plant is beginning to get under way and assumes an independent life, do not be in too much of a hurry to establish a group of elders/leaders. This is especially important if the new church has a high percentage of newcomers, whether people converted from the neighbourhood, or other individuals that have joined the fledgling work from elsewhere.

If there is an exciting group of new Christians who have been converted in the initial days of evangelism and planting, there may well be one or two who possess what may be leadership gifts, but the biblical injunction concerning not appointing recent converts to the role of overseer applies (*1 Tim.* 3:6). When Paul gave that instruction to Timothy, he added that the reason behind it was the risk of conceit; presumably a feeling of self-importance. It is so easy for a new person who is relatively unschooled in Christian teaching and active church life, to demonstrate many of the qualities that leadership needs, especially in the first flush of enthusiasm that of comes to new believers. But at that time such potential leaders may well not understand the doctrinal, pastoral and interpersonal pressures of normal church life and the firm gentleness with which these issues need to be handled. It is all too easy for someone in such a situation to be given authority in the church and destroy work, simply because they have not had time to mature in the things of God. In addition, the church itself, being new, has not had time to settle in character, structure and programme, and a strong leader could easily lead the whole fellowship in an unhelpful direction.

In practice, this means that the church-planting leader, the individual or group that has started the church, may well have to take a strong personal lead for some time before appointing others. The role of this person or group is likely to take a far more authoritative role than they may normally be comfortable demonstrating. This is probably essential in two ways.

First, it is important to establish the new church by providing structure and framework as it gets to grips with understanding what a church is from a New Testament perspective. This will show itself in several areas in establishing the foundations of Christian teaching: 'This is what we are' and 'This is what we do'. There is a risk that, in so doing, the leader will almost certainly become recognised as 'in charge' of everything, but that might be the price that is necessary in the very early days. The spiritual maturity of the planting leader is so important at this point, because the temptations to enjoy the recognition of the crowd can be great.

Secondly, both the young church and the individuals in it are especially vulnerable in the early days. Paul's concern for the church at Ephesus was that, 'savage wolves will come in among you and will not spare the flock' (*Acts* 20: 29). It is the role of the mature leader(s) to guard the flock and defend it by standing between the wolves and the sheep. The attack may be in any of a number of areas, including doctrinal, moral or pastoral issues. But when it happens, it is not the time for new and untaught leaders to be in control, for the attack can be overwhelming and exhausting.

So in all these things it is probably wise not to be too hasty in recognising and appointing new leadership.

2. Do not be too reluctant

If it is unwise to be too hasty, it is certainly unwise to be too slow in appointing new leaders. If the need to build and protect the new church is high in the early days, there are also dangers in being too slow for several reasons:

First, the church can easily become dependent on the initial leader and will look upon him as the oracle in all things, whose word becomes law! He is always right, or so the church begins to think. This frequently happens and the wise leaders will both recognise it as a problem and will guard against it.

Secondly, the initial leader can become so revered that no one could be good enough to take a leadership role alongside him. It is particularly difficult then to move on. In this situation, it is not so much that he becomes seen as the oracle who leads and directs everything, but even when he recognises the danger and how unhelpful it can be and decides to gradually take a lesser role, everyone is very conscious of him sitting in the back seat, so that he might as well be at the front! Some leaders have stayed in place so long that when eventually change does happen, the work collapses because the church has become seen as 'his' work.

In thinking this through, it is worth mentioning that it may be very unhelpful to long-term growth and maturity if leaders are always selected from among those who have come from other churches. Sometimes the sour fruit of such thinking can be more easily seen on the mission field where, on occasions, missionaries have replaced themselves, not with indigenous leaders, but with other missionaries from the home land. We think of this as unacceptable, yet exactly the same mindset can apply in church planting in the home country.

Thirdly, when appointing other leaders is thought necessary, if the initiating leader has been in place too long, any potential other leaders will compare themselves with him and are likely to feel an inordinate sense of inadequacy and refuse to accept leadership recognition. The same thing also applies in mature churches of many years standing where groups of elders have grown old along with the work, so that now the possibility of recognising new gifts of leadership becomes ever more difficult and will only happen through a disastrous and unsettling crisis.

3. Exercise spiritual insight and sensitivity

There are no rules as to when appointing new leaders should happen, so insight and sensitivity are needed. However, there are issues to consider:

First, it is likely that the workload will become too much for one person to handle. This may occur quickly or over a longer period of time. This is not so much to do with the number of things that need to be done, though that is a factor to take into account as a new church grows and becomes established, but the emotional and spiritual pressures that come from handling questions of immaturity and inexperience. Many of these matters need to be shared and talked over with others of like mind to prevent the individual leader from sinking under their weight.

Secondly, if there is only one leader, what happens when he is away or ill? Experience shows that for some reason (we have a cunning enemy!) major issues so often arise when the leader is away. It is for this reason that there is a danger of breakdown that comes from exhaustion, if the issue of shared leadership is not addressed.

Thirdly, appointing new leadership is not an instant decision. There is a pathway of action that will take some time to take the church along to the point of appointing new leaders. The whole process usually takes far longer than anticipated, with frequent corrections along the way. In going through that process, there are inevitably backward steps and corrections needed, as well as steps of progress. When the need for additional leaders becomes urgent, the danger is to short-cut the process (see below) by appointing someone to a senior leadership position too quickly; this can so easily lead to regrets later.

3. Teaching the church

The church, small and relatively weak though it may be, needs to go through a process of understanding. This will include a teaching programme that will deal with several elements:

- Why there is a need for establishing a new framework for leaders—teaching the principle of joint leadership and clarity in knowing the leaders' role and responsibilities.
- The New Testament teaching about leaders (elders/deacons)—teaching what the bible says and what it means.
- The cultural issues that relate to that particular church—teaching about the impact of family issues, age issues etc.
- The equality of seeing everyone as important—teaching that assures the whole church that all have gifts to exercise, though they differ from person to person. This may be especially important for those that would like to be leaders but are inappropriate.

In most situations, it is helpful to not only deal with these issues in a special teaching programme(s) but, having done so, to provide the notes for people to take home. This will give opportunity for individuals to read through what has been covered. It also allows those not able to attend the session(s) to receive the material. In some non-reading situations alternative (DVD/CDs) may be preferred.

4. Get the church praying

Over the period of a few weeks this needs to include special prayer, asking God to both provide and lead the church in identifying those whom the Holy Spirit has in mind for this important role. *Acts* 13: 1-3 provides a New Testament pattern for this.

Of course, the need for the appointment of new or additional leaders is because the church is new and, in most cases, immature. It should not be overlooked that this process will in itself be a major teaching experience for the church, as church members will learn how to handle decision-making as believers, i.e., seeing the need, examining the scriptures, fasting and praying together etc.

5. Allow the church to speak

At this point there are no firm instructions given to us. Perhaps the nearest New Testament instruction is that Paul appointed elders in each place where a new fellowship was started. But listening to the church, small and spiritually immature though it may be, is wise for several reasons:

First, individuals may know things about potential candidates that the initial leadership do not know, which may be relevant to the issue, and which should be taken into account in order to save much trouble later.

Secondly, they need to feel that the initial leaders are not merely imposing people on them by putting them in positions of authority.

Thirdly, in appointing people, the church members will eventually need to follow. Consequently the person being appointed needs to have the support of the church.

For many, the idea of selecting leadership in any form of election scheme is ill-advised. In Brethren churches, the terminology used is frequently that appropriate people are 'recognised' as having the abilities and gifts and only when that is so are they invited to join the leadership. This 'recognition' is often that given by existing leaders. While this may work well in established churches, it often is difficult to work out in newly-planted fellowships. Paul's 'appointing' of leaders/elders (*Acts* 14: 23) is certainly one way in which this could be handled, although there would be a reluctance on the part of some to take the role of Paul in doing this. A practical way in which this can be successfully handled is in a meeting of the church, following the teaching and prayer. Everyone is given paper and asked to write the names of all of those they feel have both the gifts and abilities and who, in their opinion, God has enabled for such a task. These are then collected and handled by the leaders of the meeting. Experience shows that in most cases a real consensus emerges. When the names have been prayed over by the leaders, oneness of heart is sought before announcing the names of the two or three thought to be most appropriate. In extreme cases, this process avoids the possibility of a strong but unsuitable character being invited, and at the same time is a means of involving the church in this important task.

6. Allow a period of evaluation

In a new church situation, such leaders may not have a strong understanding of what is involved in leadership. It is often wise therefore, to allow them to share with the existing leaders before they are finally invited to be recognised as leaders in the church. This will probably involve attending leaders' meetings (elders meetings) and undertaking some responsibilities. Some will find this immensely encouraging and strengthening as they take up the responsibility; for others it may provide a clarification which leads them to say, 'I do not think this is for me'. In the secular world, this time of evaluation is looked on as a probationary period and is a two-sided thing. Newcomers develop a greater understanding of the task, and the church and initial leaders will be able more carefully to assess their suitability. In so doing, it would be possible to go back and re-evaluate without causing serious damage. However, using the word 'probationary' may not be the most helpful, as it implies a trial and assessment, instead of a calling and partnership.

7. Appointing appropriate individuals

Once appropriate individuals have been identified following prayer, they can then be brought before the church and set apart for the task with hands laid on them, praying for them in their responsible work (*Acts* 13: 1-3).

It is worth noting that, if the immaturity of the church means that there are not many mature believers to choose from, it may be unwise to appoint more than one or two new leaders at any one time. Taking time in the process will at least allow a settling-down period, and may save the heartache of trying to establish a large group of new leaders/elders all at once.

8. Provide constant support

New leaders will usually benefit from some level of mentoring and guidance in the early days of exercising a new leadership role. In some situations, a training period through church leadership courses could helpfully precede appointment. This is especially important if the persons concerned are relatively new believers. Most people in that position will greatly welcome such support.

Finally, in the process of appointing leaders, it is worth noting that fear is one of the biggest and most important factors that can prevent significant growth. Understandably we do not want to make a mistake. But it can so easily be the result of lack of faith. Lack of faith on the part of the planting church (e.g., 'How will we carry on without those we sent to plant a new work?'); lack of faith in those that have taken a lead getting the new work under way (e.g., 'Are those we are seeking to recognise as leaders sufficiently mature?'); lack of faith in those who are being asked to accept responsibility (e.g., 'Could I do the job, after all, I am a relatively new Christian myself?').

In each of these areas, a proper understanding of the nature of the local church will help. It is not our church at all. The church is the focus of the highest expression of love that could ever be seen and we ought to recognise that, if Jesus' love for the church could bring people to himself, his love in the church can enable it to function as the delight of his heart. Providing we do all we can to see the New Testament principles worked out in establishing proper leadership, we can surely trust him to see the church function with appropriate leaders in a way that glorifies him as we seek to make disciples of all nations.

CHAPTER 15

Why size matters

Stephen McQuoid

It is often said that size matters. That is the case with many things in life, and it is certainly the case when it comes to church. In church, size matters, not because big churches are better than small churches, or medium sized better than mega churches, but simply because how a church is run, the activities that take place, the way in which services are conducted, will be dependent on numerous factors, including the size of the church. Churches of every size can be both good and bad. There is nothing wrong with being small or very large. House churches with 20 members can be as relatively powerful and productive as a church of 500. It is important, however, to recognise that size makes a big difference to a church, and consequently it will need to adapt and shape itself accordingly.

One good example of this issue concerns how worship is organised. Many churches embrace a variety of worship styles depending on what services they are conducting. In some churches, when it comes to communion, they have a service which is entirely devoted to this kind of worship experience. Again, often the communion service will take the form of 'open worship', that is, worship which is spontaneous as opposed to being led from the front. This kind of communion service depends entirely on people being willing to participate audibly by praying, sharing, reading the bible or asking for a song to be sung, and on others being able to hear them and benefit from what is being shared. In this kind of a service, size is extremely important.

If the church is very small, perhaps less than 15 people, there might not be many willing to participate. Indeed by the law of averages, in such a small church, few will be sufficiently gifted to open the bible and inspire others to worship. In such situations, there will need to be someone there who can really 'carry' the service, otherwise it might feel lifeless. If the church is very large, for example more than 150 attending, this kind of communion service might not work all that well for a different reason. In such a large crowd, participating is a very daunting thing and most will not feel up to it, and those who do must ensure that their voices carry, which adds to the pressure on those participating.

I can remember as a young Christian attending communion services of this kind and in churches of this size. The gracious members of the church warmly encouraged me and all the young people to take part in the service, but it was terrifying. The sheer number of people present made my heart pound when I prayed. The fact that a number of very mature and eloquent Christians were taking part contributed to my feelings of inadequacy. Even the size of the room can be a barrier to being heard. I know of one large church that insists on this kind of open worship despite over 200 people regularly attending the communion service, which takes place in a cavernous church building. Rather predictably, only a few experienced and confident people participate, the vast majority, which equates to about 90% of the congregation, don't. The building is so big that mikes are set up at strategic locations so that participants can utilise them and be heard, but the very fact that they have to get up out of their seats and make their way towards one of these mikes disrupts the service and deters all but the most brave or foolhardy. The result can be rather stultifying to what should be a very powerful worship experience. In such situations, size is a problem and it might be better to celebrate communion in smaller groups.

All of this relates to church planting. In general, church plants grow and keep growing. As they do so, they need to adapt what they do to accommodate the difference in size that occurs. This may mean a wholesale reshaping of all their services and a change of location from temporary accommodation (like a house) to a permanent location (like a community centre or a building owned by the church).

In a church plant, however, there is also another dynamic that runs alongside the size issue. Whenever a church planting work begins, ownership is in the hands of a small committed group of people. This might be a church-planting team that have been sent to the location to church plant, or a small group of Christians who have broken off from a 'mother church' to form the new church plant. They have had to work very hard to keep the whole thing going and usually have made great personal sacrifices in the process.

The next group of people who join the church are likely to be the converts of the original team of planters. When these people first join the church, they do so as new Christians who lack experience and are dependent on the spiritual mentors that brought them to faith in Christ. In time, however, this situation changes and those young and inexperienced Christians become mature Christians and begin to express themselves, wanting to shape the church, sometimes in a way that the original team might not like. Here is where tensions can arise which relate to this issue of 'ownership' of the church—tensions that can deeply affect the church planters and, if unresolved, can leave them hurt and disillusioned.

· ·

Perhaps the best way of illustrating the challenges of size and of ownership is to tell a fictional story. None of the characters in this story really exist, but the story is based on what has happened in real church plants in the United Kingdom. It will be told in the form of an occasional diary kept by John, the leader of a church-planting team that went into a large council estate to plant a church.

December 1998
The three couples who comprise our team have now been living and working in the area since January. It has been tough, but I am amazed at how much we have been able to achieve. The kids club and youth club we began in the local school now attract 40 kids between them. We have also begun an evangelistic bible study in our house which my wife and I run and three people are attending regularly.

March 1999
What an amazing day. Only 9 weeks ago, Charlie, a local gang leader got saved. He is basically a 20 year old thug and I still can't believe that he really became a Christian. However, he seems serious about it which is why we baptised him today. He has a huge amount of charisma and even though he is very rough and ready, he is a real asset to us because he tells everyone on the estate that he is now a Christian. This is a breakthrough with the adult world on the estate. We still meet as a team every Sunday morning for a short communion service in my house and now Charlie joins us along with Bob, a local pensioner who has been a Christian for many years and Rita, a backslider who recently returned to God

and attends our 'church' sporadically. The bible study in our house is still going on, though with a new group of people.

July 1999

We are running our first summer mission. Charlie is a good help, though sometimes he feels like a bit of a liability, not least because he has a big mouth. He is still a young Christian, with all the weaknesses that entails. However, at least he recognises this and is always sorry for any blunders he makes. Bob and Rita are also a help, though are never going to be leadership material. A couple of teenagers from the youth club got saved this term and are coming regularly to the 'Family Service' we have begun in the house, along with a family, the Irwins, who have just moved into the area. They are Roman Catholics, but not sure if they are true Christians. They are regular however and very nice. The living room is very full on a Sunday. With all these spiritual 'dependants', it feels like one big family. Can't believe things have taken off so quickly, we have only been in the area for a year and a half.

December 1999

The millennium is upon us. Can't wait to see the fireworks on the Sydney harbour bridge, makes great telly! We are going to use the local community centre for the very first time for our Christmas Carol Service. Charlie isn't too happy, he complains that it will make for a formal church service. However, we just won't have the room in our house for all the visitors we are expecting.

December 1999

The carol service went very well—even Charlie enjoyed it. We had about 20 visitors, half of them I didn't even get speaking to. It was a great morning. Best of all, a young girl became a Christian.

April 2000

The new millennium has been good to us. We have only been working on the estate since January of 1998 but already we have a regular Sunday attendance of 20 (not including the team). Not all of them are Christians and several came from other churches, but nevertheless we have had 11 adult conversions which I think is amazing. One of the couples on our church planting team intends to leave in the summer as their short-term commitment will be up by then. They will be missed. However, Charlie is getting so involved in things, he is almost like a part-time team member. He is still a bit rough and ready, but a natural leader and a very good evangelist. He has also begun a relationship with a girl who is a very committed Christian. She has brought a real stability into his life—I hope she makes an honest man of him. Church is great—still feels like a family, I still feel like a spiritual parent with all these new Christians relying on me.

August 2000

It has been a great summer. Our summer mission ended well, with a couple coming to faith at an outreach meal. Somehow, it felt different because it was Charlie who first made contact with them, then witnessed to them and led them to faith. Now he is doing a discipleship course with them. I don't really know them that well, however I guess that is progress.

December 2000

Charlie had a bit of a dip last month. Nearly broke off his engagement to Lisa. Thankfully they are still getting married in March. He seems to have bounced back and is firing on all cylinders again.

Church is still growing and we have just been joined by a couple, James and Julie, who have just moved into the area. They are mature Christians and both very gifted.

June 2001

Remarkable: a whole family (of 5) have come to faith this year. They have really brought a sense of excitement to the church. Things are buzzing and several people have joined us from other churches as we are closer to where they live. We now have up to 40 on a Sunday if you include the kids. I never thought church would grow so quickly, it's so overwhelming, it is sometimes hard to cope with. We have formalised our structures and now we have elders. Mark and myself (both on the church-planting team) and also Charlie. He is still a fairly young Christian, but really maturing and a natural leader. In fact he sometimes seems to be more in touch with some of our church members than I am. Hopefully be the end of the year James who is a great Bible teacher will become an elder. We need all the help we can get, given our sudden growth.

December 2001

In a couple of months time, I will have been here for 4 years. Hard to believe how much has been accomplished. Another conversion this month, a boy of 11.

May 2002

Easter went well with very good numbers at the special Easter activities. With 4 of us in eldership, I feel the burden is being shared. No one has become a

Christian this year; however I think we are in a period of consolidation which is good. People are beginning to mature spiritually. Partly because of the good quality bible teaching they are now getting, and partly because of the mature Christians who have joined us from other places over the past two years. With 40 regularly attending (including children), I feel that I can only maintain a close relationship with about half of them. I am so glad of help from Charlie and James.

December 2002

An interesting few months. The leadership is still intact, but one or two church members are becoming pretty vocal about things. Some of them are committed and helpful members and their comments are generally constructive. However, a couple of them seem to just want an argument.

May 2003

Growth continues, spiritually and numerically. Not just because we are doing some good evangelism, but also because of transfer growth. A church about 5 miles away imploded and we ended up with about a dozen imports, mostly good people. It still amazes me that we can get up to 70 on a Sunday (including kids), given that we only began the work at the start of 1998. The vocal people are still being vocal. We feel the need to appoint another elder next year, either one of the group who joined us recently, or one of our original church members, several of them have really matured spiritually. It is not that we as elders don't feel we can do the job, it's just that there are now several obvious candidates and it would go some way to quelling the restlessness.

December 2003

We have had good Christmas services, but my mind has been on next year and the big changes that will take place. We have just appointed an elder, earlier that we intended to. The new dynamic has resulted in us deciding on a complete restructure next year. With an ever growing congregation, there are needs we really can't meet. What is more there is still a lot of discontent. We cannot possible satisfy all the expectation of a church like ours by simply putting a few mature people into eldership. There are 5 of us now, but not enough, especially as we seem to be doing everything and consequently are not really giving focus to the job of being elders.

June 2004

The restructure has taken place and not before time. We now have two layers of leadership. The elders still maintain overall responsibility for the spiritual health and orthodoxy of the church, but now we have several leadership teams. There is a pastoral and prayer team responsible for caring for people in the church, an evangelism team that looks after outreach, and a programming team that co-ordinates all services and activities. In total, 14 people are involved in leading these teams, none of them being elders. We are also having communion in our house groups and making the family service a little longer.

December 2004

The new structure has been a very positive thing and I think that it will lead to further church growth. Personally, I feel a little wounded by the events of the past few months. I am very encouraged about all that has been achieved and feel that we are in a good place as a church. However, it has been disconcerting to have people question the leadership in general and me in particular. I also have some concerns about one or two of the people we have brought in to leadership. They have potential, but I would question their wisdom and I am not always happy with the way they do things. Still the church is growing and so I am grateful for that.

. . . .

I hope that the above story will help to illustrate the changes that take place as a church plant grows and also develops. It is important to remember that nothing is static, life is always changing. Every new person who joins a church will change the dynamic. The bigger a church plant gets, the more different the 'feel' will be. It is always dangerous to generalise, but the following is generally true of growing church plants.

Stage 1
Early days 10-20 members: it feels like a family. The church planter will be in a position to exert great influence over the members of the church, not least because they are young Christians who are still trying to get used to their new lifestyle.

Stage 2
A few years' later 20-40 members: it will become necessary to clearly define and articulate a leadership structure. The church planter or team of church planters will need to think about the issue of local leadership. If they do not then it will

look as if the church is being led entirely by visitors. What is more, the sign of a healthy church is that it can develop leaders from among converts.

Stage 3

Later again 40-60 members: by now, it becomes apparent that new structures are need to cope with the size of church. It can no longer simply be a family, now it is very much an extended family. Not everyone will know everyone else well; they will do well just to know everyone by their first name. Inevitably, groups will form within a church of this size. Some work will need to be done to keep a sense of unity and oneness. Leadership needs to be inspiring, so that everyone is willing to follow. Representation is also important, so that no individual or group within the church feels left out. The eldership will need to reflect the wide range of people within a church of this size.

Stage 4

When the church is firmly established 60+: by this stage, a church will have a number of strong and vocal characters who are not on the eldership. It is important to recognise these people because they have influence even though they may not actually be elders. They will want to be listened to and will have ideas to contribute, many of which will be good ideas. Unless the elders find some way of utilising these influential people, frustration will set in. Different levels of leadership and the extensive devolution of responsibility will be very important. If the energy and vision of these people can be captured and channelled, the church will have the potential for even more growth and development. The one sure thing is that you simply cannot run a church of this size and maturity in the same way as you would a church at stage 1.

CHAPTER 16

Handing over and moving on

John McQuoid

In 1974, my late wife, Valerie, and I began a new work in an unevangelised district of Addis Ababa, Ethiopia's capital city. Three years later, when the Communist government obliged us to leave, a little church with 35 members had been established. By 2011, these few believers had become a community of 17,000 in l50 churches (both urban and rural), and 200 evangelists have been commended and are supported by their local churches. What were the lessons learned in that initial church plant?

There is no joy like the joy of leading people to Christ, but the New Birth is, by definition, just the beginning of Christian life. Birth must be followed by growth, and growth in Christian lives occurs as we turn away from our sinful lifestyle and build new Christ-like graces into our day-to-day living (*2 Cor.* 5: 17 & *2 Pet.* l: 5-7). Growth, of course, takes time. The conversion of a soul is the miracle of a moment, but the growth of a saint is the occupation of a lifetime.

To leave or to stay?

How long should a church planter stay with his group of new converts? He has led them to faith in Christ, so is his work among them now finished? Might they struggle if he leaves them too quickly? What if they want him to remain with them long-term as a pastor and/or teacher? Could he then stay too long and be a hindrance? There is no simple answer to any of these questions, which will be considered later in the chapter. But one thing is certain: the care of a newborn church is important for the church's life and growth. What is the kind of care package that will help every member of the fellowship to grow in their knowledge of God, and become mature followers of Christ (*Eph.* 4: 11-13)?

Laying the foundation for growth—Phase 1

When people first trust in Christ, the church planter's immediate task is to establish the new believers in their faith, by teaching them some 'Christian Basics'. Clear, unhurried instruction is needed in such topics as the Good News (explaining sin, the death of Christ, repentance, and the implications of receiving Jesus as Saviour and Lord); what happened to me when I trusted in Christ? (I was forgiven, became God's child, received the Holy Spirit); prayer; baptism; the Lord's Supper; holiness; guidance; stewardship of money; and the daily quiet time (a time set aside each day for private bible reading and prayer). These basic studies will help the believers understand some of the blessings and responsibilities of their new life in Christ.

Inclusive leadership

In the early days of a church, the leader may find himself doing most of the work, while the other members simply observe. He sets the agenda, does the teaching, leads the prayers, and provides the pastoral care and counselling, because he is the only person equipped to do so. This one-man-does-everything situation is unavoidable, but the leader will aim as quickly as possible to phase it out, for the bible prescribes plurality of leadership in the church; and God gives spiritual gifts to every believer because He wants each and every one to be not just a spectator, but meaningfully involved in the life and work of the fellowship.

In fact, a church leader can do real harm by failing to involve others in work for God. When people are gifted and eager to serve or lead in the church, but are ignored or even deliberately excluded—perhaps by a leader who likes to be in control of everything—they will feel frustrated, become discouraged, and may respond either by suppressing their God-given aspirations or by leaving the church and seeking another spiritual home in which they can serve God as he wants them to do. If good people are allowed to drain away, a healthy church plant is unlikely to happen.

Leaders are meant to lead! However, a wise leader will be careful to include others in every aspect of the life and activities of the church. There are few churches that experience frictionless fellowship and seamless unity, but a church in which all the members are valued, and their gifts and godly desires encouraged, is a church to which people will want to belong, and where they are likely to be wholeheartedly committed, fulfilled and blessed.

Growth—phase 2

Having grounded new converts in Christian basics, the task now facing the leader is to build into the fellowship six essential features of the New Testament church. These are: teaching; worship; witnessing; every-member participation; training for service; and leadership structure.

1. Teaching

Programmed bible teaching, week after week, when the scriptures are read, clearly explained, and applied to everyday living, is the cornerstone of a church's health and growth. Feeding God's people with food that will make them strong in faith is, of course, a demanding task that requires serious, sacrificial commitment from those who teach and preach. James Black's book *The mystery of preaching*[1], is recommended reading for men aspiring to preach. Here are some snippets randomly chosen from the book:

> If you are called to preach, make your preaching the big business of your life. Preaching lifts men and women to God…Preach on issues, not on side-issues. It is the big truths that heal—and people need healing. Deal with the common experiences of men and women. Help and guide your people in the problems of their tangled lives, and show them the great way out…There is nothing more likely to tell in your ministry than your personal character. Cultivate above all things your own devotional and spiritual life…A ministry through which people are blessed is more often the fruit of hard work than the fruit of genius. Modest gifting plus diligent labour is a recipe for blessing…Don't waste your morning hours; use them to do your most important work.

2. Worship

William Temple's definition of worship is instructive, and worth pondering:

---

1   James Black, *The mystery of preaching*, Cambridge: Lutterworth Press 2003 (ed. Peter Cotterell) [first edition 1924].

> Worship is the submission of all our nature to God. It is the quickening of our conscience by His holiness; nourishment of mind by His truth; purifying of imagination by His beauty; the opening of the heart to His love; and submission of will to His purpose—and all this gathered up in adoration, is the greatest of human expressions of which we are capable.[2]

The more we know God, the better we will be able to worship Him; so it should be the chief ambition of every Christian to grow in our knowledge of God. Of course, we can never know God fully (*Rom.* 11: 33), but we can know him truly—not only by his attributes of holiness, truth, beauty, love, and so on, but also as a person (*Jer.* 9: 23,24), and as our Father (*Eph.* 1: 2).

In practical terms, there are three ways in which we can worship God. First, we can present our bodies to him (*Rom.* 12: 1), devoting our hands, feet, heart and mind to his service. Secondly, we can speak and sing his praises (*Heb.* 13: 15), as we are inspired by the awesomeness of his person (*1 Tim.* 6: 15,16), and by the marvel of his love (*Jn.* 3: 16). Thirdly, we worship him when we share our possessions with others (*Heb.* 13: 16), for generosity in his children is like perfume to our unstinting God (*Phil.* 4: 18).

The quality of our worship is not ultimately measured by the emotional 'buzz' we may experience from offering it, but by the pleasure God experiences from receiving it. And God has told us that what gives Him pleasure is worship that is 'in spirit and truth' (*Jn.* 4:23). Worship 'in spirit' is not outward ritual; it is a sincere reaching out to God from the deepest level of our being. And worship 'in truth' is worship that is doctrinally faithful, and is accompanied by integrity in the private, family and public life of the worshipper (*Ps.* 24: 5,6).

3. *Witnessing*

'Worship which does not beget witness is hypocrisy. We cannot acclaim the worth of God if we have no desire to proclaim it' (John Stott)[3].

God wants every Christian to be actively involved in the business of telling others about him (*Mt.* 28: 19,20 & *Acts* 1:8). Few believers are specially gifted as evangelists (*Eph.* 4:11), but all of us are required to be proactive in spreading the good news of what Christ has done in coming from heaven to die for men and women everywhere. A witness doesn't require extensive bible knowledge,

---

2   William Temple, *Readings in St. John's Gospel*, London: Macmillan & Co. 1939, p. 68.
3   John R W Stott, *Our Guilty Silence: The Church, the Gospel and the World*, Grand Rapids, Michigan: Eerdmans 1969, p. 35.

great intelligence or debating skill; witnessing is simply telling what one knows, however little that may be—and when this is done out of love for Christ, God will bless the effort made. In this connection, R.A. Torrey wrote: 'There is no joy like the joy of saving men and women, and it is possible for every child of God, no matter how humble or ungifted, to have this joy.'[4]

The members of the young church in Jerusalem believed this, and all of them—not just the leaders or the evangelists—made a habit of sharing the good news with non-Christians everywhere they went, even in days of persecution (*Acts* 8: 1-4). And God blessed their efforts and added to their number—not surprisingly, for in witnessing for Christ, they were each one doing exactly what he had commanded them to do, and God always rewards obedience with blessing. When a whole church, whether an existing church or a newly-planted one, gives its heart and lips to evangelism, blessing is inevitable!

How can we get people involved in witnessing for Christ? Church leaders must teach their people that it is part of Christian discipleship to witness. Christ has commanded it, as we have seen above, so if we don't speak to others about him, we are disobeying him. People can't believe in Christ if they don't know about him, and they can't know about him unless we tell them (*Rom.* 10: 17).

Leaders in the church must also lead by example, and actually teach their people how to witness. Below is one approach to personal evangelism which is easily learned. It is a gentle, non-confrontational method with which most Christians should feel comfortable.

i. Pray for God's guidance

> You can never speak to the wrong person about Christ, but you cannot speak to everyone, so pray that God will lead you to one specific person he wishes you to contact, and pray that he will bless that person when you have spoken to him/her. We will never see much fruit in witnessing unless we learn to pray from our heart.

ii. Use literature

> People sometimes don't remember, or understand, or even hear things that are said to them in conversation, but a clearly written message can be easily absorbed and retained. The literature must be written in language that unchurched people can understand.

---

[4] R A Torrey, *Anecdotes and illustrations*, Fleming H Revell Co. 1907, p. 23.

It should be concise, but should tell the reader everything he needs to know to help him find Christ, for you may not have another opportunity to tell him more. It should also show your church address for further inquiries. Attractive literature authored by an able writer is a good investment and an important tool in effective evangelism.

iii. Offer the literature with a simple comment

You may say, for example, 'I have found this little leaflet interesting; you might like to read it when you have time.' A lengthy conversation is not necessary, and often is not possible. Nor is there any need to explain the gospel, for the literature will do that. Furthermore, a simple, brief approach is often the most appropriate one, and is less stressful for the Christian who does not find one-to-one witnessing easy (which is true of most of us). You have now spoken to the person to whom God has led you. The word of life is in his or her hand. Now, thank God for helping you, and pray that he will bless what you have done. Finally relax, and leave the rest to God.

Courtesy is important as we approach people for Christ (*1 Pet.* 3: 15-16, NIV). Our business is not to criticize a person's lifestyle, nor to argue about his beliefs. We are simply witnesses, telling dying men and women about the Saviour who has changed our lives, and who loves and died for them too. Relax. Speak softly. Smile! God is standing by your side as you speak for him (*Mt.* 28: 20).

How often should I witness for Christ? There is no single answer to this question, but those who are new to personal evangelism might begin by praying for and then speaking to just one person each month. However, once the habit has been established, its frequency will likely increase. 'The joy of catching a soul is unspeakable. When we have got one soul we become possessed by the passion for souls. Get one and you will want a crowd' (J.H.Jowett)[5]

No work in the whole world is as important as winning people for Christ. The saving of souls was the Lord's singular reason for coming into our world, and we do well to make this our priority too.

---

5 J H Jowett, *Expositor and current anecdotes*, vol. 9, 1907, p. 155.

A church begins its evangelistic programme in its own neighborhood, but it must not finish there. The gospel is not just for domestic consumption; it is also for export. So it is important, early in its life, to acquaint the church with Christ's call to world evangelisation, and challenge each member to respond to that call. For some, the call may mean leaving home and taking the message to distant places. For others, it will be to stay where they are, praying intelligently for and giving sacrificially to support those who go. There is a price to be paid for winning men and women to Christ. The price to God was a cross on a hill! And whatever price I am called to pay, 'if Jesus Christ is God and died for me, then no sacrifice can be too great for me to make for him' (C. T. Studd).[6]

4. Every member participation

Just as each organ of the human body has a part to play in enabling the body to function, so each Christian has a task to perform in his/her local church (*l Cor.* 12). God gives to each believer the spiritual gift(s) needed to do the work that God assigns. Some gifts qualify people to teach the bible, and others equip them for practical service of different kinds (*Rom.* 12: 3-8). It is important for each person to discover what gift God has given him or her, to look for ways in which that gift can be employed for the benefit of the church, and then to use it for the help and blessing of all. As the believers try to find their niche in the church, the leader needs to be alongside them in his pastoral role, prayerfully advising and guiding, helping 'to prepare God's people for works of service' (*Eph.* 4: 11,12).

5. Training

Our Lord taught many people, but he singled out twelve men and trained them intensively for three years, for they were (almost all) to become key men in the future work of his church.

In the 1970s, in our new little church in Addis Ababa we tried, in a very humble way, to follow Christ's example by training key Ethiopian brothers and sisters for service in the church. As spiritual gifts were identified in these young believers, the gifted people were tutored for the particular work into which God was leading them.

For example, three of our young men were able communicators and had a keen interest in scripture, so they and the missionary met together every Wednesday to study the bible portion that was to be taught to the church the following Sunday. First, we worked at understanding the passage, then we

---

6 From a plaque that C T Studd kept on his desk.

discussed how its message could best be presented, and finally one of us was appointed to teach the whole church on Sunday what the four of us had learned together on Wednesday. This procedure proved to be valuable. It provided a forum in which the four men could grow together through serious, systematic bible study; it gave three new believers the opportunity to develop their gift; and it was an instrument for improvement, for each Wednesday session began by reviewing the preaching of the previous Sunday, both to commend what had been done well and to discuss any aspects of the presentation that might have been done better!

6. *Leadership*

A church is not complete without elders. The words 'elder', 'bishop' and 'overseer' are used interchangeably in scripture of the men who are in the top tier of leadership in the church. 'Bishop' means 'overseer', and indicates the supervisory nature of the work; 'elder' signifies the spiritual maturity required.

> *Qualifications for eldership* (*1 Tim.* 3: 1-7): Morally above reproach: self-controlled, mild-mannered, hospitable, not materialistic. Spiritually mature: able to teach, having a respectful, orderly family and a good testimony outside the church.

> *Elders' duties* (*Acts* 20: 28-31; *1 Thess.* 5: 12-14; *Heb.* 13: 17; *1 Pet.* 5: 1-4): To teach, guard, guide and warn the church of dangers. The Chief Shepherd will require elders to give account of their work.

It is the Holy Spirit who entrusts men with the sacred task of caring for the church (*Acts* 20: 28). The bible (for example, *1 Timothy* 3) tells us of the kind of men God appoints, so the church is able to identify God's chosen men by seeing in them the qualifications that scripture demands, and will thus acknowledge them as its leaders, formalising their appointment by whatever protocol seems appropriate.

Handing over and moving on

Having looked at the six key features of church life, we now return to the question with which we began, namely, how long should a church planter stay with the people and church he has come to establish? There is no single answer to this important questions, but there is a great deal at stake in relation to the issue.

If the planter decides to go but leaves too early, it is possible that the fledgling church could collapse or suffer from long-term problems. On the other hand, if the planter stays on long after a leadership structure has been established, his presence could prevent genuine growth and development in the church and instead create a culture of dependence.

So when should a church planter leave and move on? There are several inter related issues that need to be reflected on in order to answer this question.

First, it is important to ascertain whether or not there are natural successors in place within the church. It would be possible for all of the above conditions to be in place, including the establishment of a group of elders, and yet for the church to lack the confidence that it needs to go it alone without the church planter being present. If this is the case, the church planter needs to develop natural successors and wait until they are in place before moving on. If, however, they are in place, then the church planter should make plans to move on. There is a big difference between church members missing the person who began the church and their needing him to stay. Any good church planter will be missed if he leaves, but that is not enough reason to stay, especially if doing so could be counterproductive.

Secondly, is there a desire among church members to have the freedom to go in their own direction? If there is, then it is clear that the church has grown up and is ready to move ahead without the input of the church planter. There is no simple way of testing if this desire is present or not, but any church planter who genuinely understands the church that he has planted will know whether the church has reached that stage or not. Once awareness is recognized, then action needs to be taken.

Thirdly, is the church planter personally restless about being in the church? Some church planters are born for church planting. They love the challenge of a raw situation where they are reaching out to unchurched people, and they enjoy the comparative chaos of a 'new church' situation. Once the church becomes established, however, and they move into the routine of normal church life, restlessness sometimes emerges. They may find it hard to put their finger on exactly how they feel, but they are less motivated than they once were by the challenges of their ministry. This too may be evidence that it is time to move on.

It must be said that moving on can be an emotionally-disturbing experience for a church planter, as he leaves behind a work into which he has poured his whole heart and soul. I have known many parents who became depressed when their children grew up and left home. So too, church planters can find it very difficult to move on and leave behind a church for which they have sacrificed so much. This is part of cost of church planting! And his sadness may be increased if the church goes on to do things in a way that the church planter doesn't like. If this happens, what should he do? If the changes are matters that are clearly dishonoring to God, it cannot be wrong for him gently to express his concern; otherwise he should refrain from critical comment, and continue to pray for and encourage the church. It is important to remember that a church planter doesn't own the church he has planted; no human being ever owns a church, or has the ultimate responsibility for it. God is the sole owner of every church, and he can be safely trusted to exercise responsible ownership of his properties, and deal with any problems they present! This he does through his Son, who walks among all his churches, constantly monitoring and maintaining God's interests in each one (*Rev.* 2: 1).

This said, the handing over of the work needs to be a planned and continuous process, as the new believers' gifts have been identified, developed and put to use in the life of the fellowship; and elders are encouraged to lead the people forward.

Sometimes, a church doesn't want their founder to leave but to stay and help them long-term with the on-going work of the fellowship. This is usually the case when the church planter has significant gifts of teaching or pastoral care. If he accepts the invitation to stay, there should be caution and a process in place to avoid the dangers already mentioned. A mechanism should be worked out to prevent the planter from being overly dominant among the leadership of the church, or the church being overly dependant on him. There are two simple ways of doing this. Either he can remain on as a servant of the church, but not be in leadership, or he can step out of leadership for a period of time (e.g., 18 months), so that the other leaders can grow in confidence in his absence, and then resume leadership by invitation.

A church planter who is gifted as an evangelist, but not as a teacher, may feel that, having led people to faith in Christ he has done what God has called him to do, but is not competent to teach the important, substantial programme for growth that is outlined above. This is understandable, for no one can do everything; but in this case someone else must be found to teach and care for the young believers, so that they can be quickly and securely established in their faith. In such a situation, there are two options. One is for him to remain as part of the new fellowship and simply concentrate on evangelism, while leaving the leadership of the church to others. Alternatively, he may prefer move on to another location and plant a church again. Given the huge need for church planting, it would seem highly desirable that someone who has already proved his ability in church planting should keep going and plant another one while he still has the physical energy.

A final word for all Christian workers

'The Christian's chief occupational hazards are depression and discouragement'[7]. This solemn comment reminds us that serving God is a deeply challenging business. Satan, the god of this world, is driven by hatred of God, and is unrelenting in his efforts to oppose God's plans, spoil his work, and discourage us, his servants, in every possible way. We are in direct conflict with the Evil One (*Eph.* 6: 12), part of whose strategy is to blind the minds of unbelieving men and women—the very people whose blessing is the heart of our ministry—so that they cannot see how desperately they need the Saviour. What can we do in the face of such opposition? What can sustain us in our feeling of inadequacy when those for whom we pray remain unresponsive, and our witnessing falls so often on deaf ears? How can we rise above the depressions and discouragement that are the 'occupational hazards' of Christian ministry, and persevere in the work to which God has called us?

Here are some thoughts to encourage us:

1. In our moments of discouragement, we are in good company! Christian workers in every generation have experienced discouragement; indeed, they have expected it, for we are engaged in the Conflict of the Ages, the war of righteousness against sin. Christ himself, God's perfect Servant, wept because his saving grace was rejected by people he wanted to bless (*Lk.* 13: 34 & 19: 41), and those same people later crucified him! The apostle Paul suffered enormously, in body, mind and spirit, for the gospel's sake (*2 Cor.* 4: 8-11 & 11: 23-29), and every evangelist since that time, in every country of the world, has tasted apathy, rejection, or worse.
2. We will be helped as we grasp the fact that God's servants never walk alone. God is for us (*Rom.* 8: 31), Christ is with us (*Mt.* 28: 20), and the Holy Spirit is within us at all times (*l Cor.* 6:19). It is true that the strongest Christian by himself is no match for the evil forces against

---

7   John Stott in John Blanchard, *Gathered Gold*, Evangelical Press 1984.

which we struggle; but it is also true that every faithful servant of Christ will be helped by God to accomplish whatever task God assigns to him or her.

3. Human beings can plant and water seed, but only God can make it grow (1Cor.3:6). When God's servant has sown and watered, diligently, carefully and prayerfully, he has done all that the master requires. Any blessing that might result, or be withheld, is not the servant's responsibility; it is the business of God.

4. God will use us in his service if we keep our personal relationship with him in good repair, on a daily basis. We must be diligent in our private study of scripture, in prayer, in obedience, and in conquering temptations. God can use any vessel in his service, because he is sovereign; but he prefers to use a sanctified vessel, because he is holy.

5. Whatever difficulties or discouragements we experience in serving God, we are on the winning side! Christ is coming, and he will reward his faithful people (*Rev.* 22: 12). He will also destroy all God's enemies and deliver the kingdom to his Father, so that God's supreme authority over everything will be established for ever (*1 Cor.* 15: 24-28). So let us persevere, giving ourselves wholeheartedly to the work of the kingdom, gladly accepting all its challenges for his sake. Then, when we see him, with the scars of Calvary still visible upon his body, we shall fall at his feet in adoring worship, glad about any little sacrifice we ever made, or any hardship we endured in serving him. And our joy will be complete when, alongside those we have won for Christ, we join with the vast army of the redeemed of every nation, and sing the praises of God, who has made us one family in Christ. On that day, we shall discover, with glad surprise, that our labour for Christ was not in vain.

Chapter 17

Making decaying churches live

Graham Poland

Every year our garden morphs predictably from the colourful hues of autumn into the barren grey of winter and seems to lie lifeless, awaiting the magical kiss of spring to revive it again. New bulbs always need to be planted to replace the ones that die, yet other bulbs, dormant through the winter months, emerge with new life and vigour. So too with churches.

Church life cycles

Gary McIntosh, in his book *Taking Your Church to the Next Level*, points out that 'all organizations and organisms move through predictable stages of birth, growth, maturity, and decline.'[1] Drawing upon an earlier work by Robert Dale, he likens the life cycle of a church to the human life cycle, using the following bell curve figure:

Human Life Cycle

Young Adult

Emerging Adult — Middle Adult

Adolescence — Senior Adult

Childhood — Elderly Adult

Birth — Death

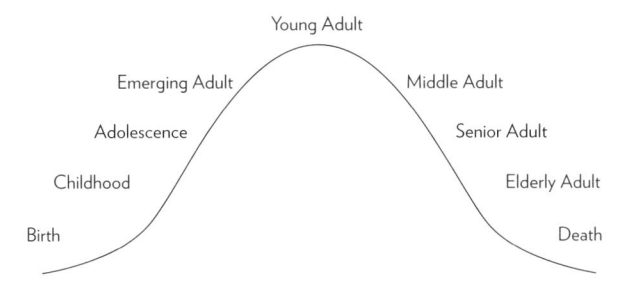

1 G. McIntosh, *Taking Your Church to the Next Level*, Grand Rapids: Baker Books, 2009, p. 13.

McIntosh's book then compares five stages in the life cycle of a church, calling them 'emerging, growing, consolidating, declining, and dying.'[2] He also refers to what has been called 'St. John's Syndrome'[3], an allusion to the pattern of decline seen in the seven churches in *Revelation*, and observes, from his research, that:

> A church is prone to rapid growth in the first fifteen to twenty years of its existence, followed by a levelling off of growth onto a plateau for another twenty to forty years. Then follows a slower decline over the next thirty to forty years until the church either closes its doors (dies) or eases into an unhealthy period of stagnation'.[4]

'Dry bones'

Ezekiel, under the inspiration of the Spirit, received a prophetic vision of the state of God's people, lying, seemingly dead, and scattered as dry bones across a valley (*Ezek.* 37: 1-14). Churches and denominations have identified themselves with that imagery many times through Church history and the image serves as a visual aid for this chapter. To Ezekiel, these bones appeared to be the only thing that remained from lives that had been lived and now, like dead plants, were discarded on the compost heap. Yet to God they were just dormant. He knew that with his breath of life they could be revived and rise to become a vast army. In the same way as new churches can be planted, old, seemingly dead, churches can be re-planted or revived.

My own call to Christian ministry came while visiting a bible study in a church that many would have considered 'dead'. The study was certainly 'dry', and the average age of the congregation made its appearance somewhat skeletal. But I heard the word of the Lord! On leaving bible college, I attached myself to another decaying church and witnessed the coming together of bones and the mobilisation of a willing army of workers that saw a period of revival. In more recent years, I have marched with yet another revived army that has risen from a valley where a remnant of about 30 people has become a church of over 300. So I know that bones can live.

---

2   G. McIntosh, *Taking Your Church to the Next Level*, p. 34.
3   G. McIntosh, *Taking Your Church to the Next Level*, p. 29.
4   G. McIntosh, *Taking Your Church to the Next Level*, p. 30.

How to identify a dying church

In reality, churches that still have people are alive. But there is a marked difference between a small, struggling church that is growing and a small or big one that is dying. The weakness of early childhood is not the same as the decaying weakness that sets in through disease. Like people, churches can die for a number of reasons. The following are warning signs:

An *unhealthy diet* can eventually lead to death. Whether it is the stodgy, high-cholesterol of 'fast food' imbibed by Christians who are too rushed to spend more than five minutes with their bibles, or an unbalanced diet served up to church members from the pulpit, a church body will die if it does not have a healthy diet. A diet of dispensationalism or legalism has squeezed the life out of many churches, while irrelevant preaching continues to leave many church members uninspired and unfed. When church leaders fail to ensure that they hold out the word of life through the activities of the church, then these activities will become acts that lead to death (see *Hebrews* 6: 1).

Another potential cause of death is *untreated wounds*. If allowed to fester, wounds that have been inflicted by insensitive and overbearing elders can become poisonous. Often bitter roots have been allowed to grow up 'to cause trouble and defile many' (*Heb.* 12: 15). Church members who fail to follow biblical principles for reconciliation cause deep and dangerous damage to a church and elders who turn a blind eye to such situations may appear to condone such behaviour. The presence of unforgiveness in a church is more common than we may be prepared to acknowledge and, like dirt in a car's petrol, may not only cause a loss of power but, if allowed to build up, can result in the engine dying.

Closely related to the last sign, but often harder to detect is *underlying illness*. The body may appear healthy and active, but all the activity may be masking a serious internal illness. Power struggles and family strongholds are often evidence of such illness. Human control can also fur the arteries, so that the Spirit cannot flow and eventually the body succumbs to the heart attack of division. Sometimes, this division is called multiplication and a new church is formed (which may be preferable to watching the body die).

A further warning sign that all is not healthy in a church body is the stunted growth caused by *undeveloped members*. In the early 1970's, Ray Stedman's classic book, *Body Life*, re-awakened some churches to the biblical imperative of every-member ministry (a value long espoused, in part, by the Christian Brethren). Churches that release their members to minister according to their spiritual gifts find that not only do their members grow spiritually, but the church grows numerically. Conversely, many churches that control 'from the top' and suppress the exercise of spiritual gifts because of fear or dogmatism stagnate and, ironically, many which have died have been from the Christian Brethren[5]. When limbs are not used they atrophy and when lungs are obstructed they cease to function. When a church does not use its members it may lose them and, when the breath of the Spirit is obstructed, life will ebb away. For some churches a lack of investment in children's and young people's work has been a short-sightedness resulting in death.

The mechanics of revival

Ezekiel recognised that revival has to be a *sovereign work of God* (*Ezek.* 37: 3, 5). If a valley of dry bones was going to be transformed into a vibrant army, then there was little that Ezekiel could do to engineer this miracle. From a realm of human probability, it was an impossible mission. As we observe the condition of some churches, it does indeed appear impossible that they will ever be revived. Not infrequently, zealous Christian workers have attached themselves to such churches in the hope of making a difference, only to find that eventually this spiritual graveyard has claimed them as another victim. The faith required to work in such circumstances is considerable, given that there is none of the vitality and excitement of a church plant. Energy for such work can only be found in prayer, crying out for God to move in sovereign power, knowing that only he can make a lasting difference.

Yet faith and prayer for God's sovereign intervention must be accompanied by a prophetic *sowing of seed*, as Ezekiel discovered (*Ezek.* 37: 4). The remnant that has remained faithful in a seemingly dying church needs to 'hear the word of the Lord!' and the people who are still dead in their transgressions and sins who might one day re-populate the church need to 'hear the word of the Lord!' I remember the late Ralph Shallis declare that the only kind of revival that God is interested in is one where evangelism takes place. Anyone called to work in trying to revive a dying church must believe in the power of the Word to bring life. Charles Finney, in his classic *Revivals of Religion*, states:

> In the Bible, the Word of God is compared to grain, and preaching

---

[5]   For general statistics see research by Dr Peter Brierley at http://www.partnershipuk.org/qwicsitePro/php/ docsview.php?docid=388

is compared to sowing the seed, and the results to the springing up and growth of the crop. A revival is as naturally a result of the use of the appropriate means as a crop is of the use of its appropriate means.[6]

It is not insignificant that Ezekiel is called to 'Prophesy to these bones' (*Ezek.* 37:4) and he prophesied as he was commanded (*Ezek.* 37:7). Clearly, as an Old Testament prophet, he preceded the full revelation of God's Word as we know it now, but that does not preclude speaking with prophetic authority and insight today when called to speak out the word of the Lord. The gift of prophecy is a critical part of the gift-mix in a person who is going to engage in ministry in a decaying church (or at least within any team of people involved in such ministry). I have witnessed its pivotal significance in a *forth-telling* aspect at crucial points in a church's life. If a church does not do what the word of the Lord is telling it to do at these crucial points, then the future can only lead to death.

A further development in Ezekiel's vision sees old *structures renewed*. The bones were still there; what they required were tendons, flesh, skin and breath (*Ezek.* 37:6). In many decaying churches, the existing structures may not in themselves be the problem; it is these structures that need to be revived and supplemented with their missing ingredients. For example, I recall working in a church where the structure of the gospel service had become no more than a pointless exercise. When the time and feel of the service was changed, and a new attitude of believing prayer prevailed, the missing ingredients of seekers and motivation turned the structure into a life-giving occurrence. Equally, boringly-predictable communion services, when renewed in structure or incorporated as part of a home group, can be infused with new life.

However, the most significant missing ingredient in the bones was breath. Revival is always a work of the *Spirit* (*Ezek.* 37: 14), the breath of God. When the Spirit breathes new life into a dying church, then the structures start to come together in a meaningful way and hope is renewed. The reality is that he breathes life into people, and these people will be inspired to revitalise the structures of the church. As people see the Spirit working in others, they too will be revived and start to recognise spiritual gifts awakening in them and use them.

---

6 C. G. Finney, *Revivals of Religion*, London: Morgan and Scott, 2nd edition 1913, p. 5.

The release of an army of Spirit-filled people can only result in a spurt of new growth for what has been a dying church.

A healthy, growing body

Much of this chapter has focused on the scene in *Ezekiel*. We turn now to the vision of a healthy body described by Paul in *Ephesians* 4: 11-16. This key passage should act as a reference point for every practitioner engaged in trying to bring life to a decaying church.

Gary Mcintosh engages with the question of long-term durability of a church, so that it does not succumb to terminal decline. He asks:

> So what makes a church durable over the long haul? Why do some churches seem to keep going while others fall into decline? In short, a church's durability comes, first, from the values that guide the creation of its program and ministry; second, from the development of processes designed to encourage the behavior that reflects those values; and, third, from leaders who function as architects of the entire process.[7]

A fundamental *value* reflected in *Ephesians* 4: 11-16 is that of every-member ministry. There are no 'spare parts' in this body. The *process* designed by Christ for the healthy functioning of his body reflects that value, as we shall see. Yet the role of *leaders* as architects of that process is crucial. Only God can create a healthy church body, but he has engineered it so that leaders are pivotal in the process.

It is difficult to paint the perfect profile of a leader who is most likely to facilitate growth in a decaying church. Church leadership in the New Testament appears to be plural, whether it is a group of elders who 'direct the affairs of the church' (*1 Tim.* 5: 17) or the combined gifts of *Ephesians* 4: 11. Yet, within that group, growing churches normally have at least one whose leadership gift is paramount. George Barna observes that:

> Highly effective churches...have placed a true leader in the position of leadership...Such leaders articulate vision, mobilize the people, motivate focused activity, consistently provide strategic direction and resources to get the job done efficiently and effectively...[8]

---

[7] G. McIntosh, *Taking Your Church to the Next Level*, pp. 33, 34.
[8] G. Barna, *The Habits of Highly Effective Churches,* Ventura,Ca: Regal, 1999. p. 32.

Maintaining the body analogy, leaders are like the *vital organs*, without which it is difficult to function. The 'five-fold ministry' reflected in v 11 is clearly not put in place by Christ in order to do all the ministry, but to give the members of the body the capacity to do theirs. It is debatable whether all five people-gifts function in the same way today as in Paul's day, or whether each has an equal importance for a church at a decaying stage. The list is front-loaded with apostles, prophets and evangelists, and it would seem from my experience that at least one of these people is going to be the catalyst used by God in instigating revival in a decaying church (as well as in planting a new church). Yet pastors and teachers are essential for the ongoing health of the body. They are likely to be the ones who will 'prepare (equip) God's people for works of service'. So, the presence of at least one from both front and back-end of the list would be a critical minimum in making decaying churches live.

Leaders must provide *a clear vision,* which is essential for the body to avoid stumbling down dangerous paths or dead-ends. Prophetic leaders act as eyes for the body. A church may have reached a stage of decay because the vision has grown dim and elderly leaders, like Eli (see *1 Samuel* 3: 1, 2), have ceased to see what they should be seeing. If a decaying church in these circumstances invites a worker to come in and help them, it is essential that the church allows the worker to catch and cast the vision of where God is leading the church. I have witnessed many willing and able workers perish on the rocks of an intransigent eldership, who would not embrace the worker's vision.

What is the vision that leads a decaying church into renewed growth? The vision reflected in *Ephesians* 4: 11-16 is of a group of leaders using their gifts, under the headship of Christ, to equip the body to reach full maturity. The 'works of service' done by the members of the body result in the body's being built up 'as each part does its work.' (*Eph.* 4: 16).

The vital organs of leadership require the *supporting ligaments* to hold the body together and enable it to function in a healthy manner. By equipping God's people for works of service, and releasing that equipped army, there will be growth in maturity and numbers. A healthy body will be a growing body.

In my present church, we call this process 'discipleship through relationship'; where each member is encouraged to act as a supporting ligament for other members, helping to bring them to maturity in Christ. Inevitably, being devoted disciples of Christ will result in the arms of the body reaching out to help and embrace the lost. A decaying church responds dramatically when it is injected with new life. The presence of new or non-Christians in a home group or a church service encourages the church. This may be the result of tireless effort by one of the church members who has built relationship with this work colleague, neighbour, family member or stranger. Seldom do evangelistic events produce growth in a church unless there is this background building of relationship as the arms of the body reach out.

Our church is currently recognising the shift taking place in evangelistic strategy across much of the UK, as churches mobilise their membership to move out and incarnate the gospel in creative ways. Gibbs and Coffey foresaw this in 2001 in *Church Next*, noting that:

> In contemporary society, which is increasingly permeated by postmodern thinking, maintenance-minded churches need to be transformed into Missional communities, which will entail decentralizing their operations. Church leaders will need to facilitate this transition by giving higher priority to working outside the institution, functioning as teams of believers located in a highly polarized and pluralistic world. From a strategy of invitation the churches must move to one of infiltration, to being the subversive and transforming presence of Jesus.[9]

Incarnational evangelism has the advantage of being kaleidoscopic in its variety: we have people who are passionate about the poor and needy, who will take a homeless person out for breakfast or mobilise a team to decorate a single-parent's house; others who will invite their neighbours in for a 'big breakfast' along with other Christians; or a lady who teaches English as a foreign language who will invite her students for a conversational class alongside other Christians who will converse about the gospel. All of the above initiatives are able to be done on a Sunday morning instead of, or alongside, a church service and can be seen as a stepping-stone to later inviting them to a home-based bible study or a church service. They also release church members to reach out in a style that suits their personality and is fired by their own passion, rather than in a way that is imposed by their leaders.

The paradigm-shift required to facilitate such a leap from conventional church evangelism is enormous, but if a church really is intent on reaching out and growing, a new mind-set is essential, otherwise churches that currently appear to be healthy will succumb to the inevitable decline that eventually leads to death.

---

9 E. Gibbs and I. Coffey, *Church Next*, Leicester: Inter-Varsity Press 2001, p. 212. For further reading on this matter, I recommend Stuart Murray's companion books *Post-Christendom* and *Church after Christendom*, Milton Keynes: Paternoster Press, 2004.

CHAPTER 18

Encouraging the church plant to maturity

David Clarkson

When first asked to write this chapter, I thought it would be helpful to do one or two preliminary surveys. So I spoke with several groups informally, asking them how they would define a 'mature congregation'. Several groups burst into hoots of laughter, saying, 'impossible—it's a contradiction in terms'.

Another friend said, 'Just do nothing and you'll end up with a mature congregation of elderly people resistant to change and holding fast to earlier times. That's the only kind of mature congregation you will get today'. This was not the response I had hoped for, nor is it the kind of congregation that is the focus of this chapter.

What we're writing about here is a church that will stand the test of time, maintain its spiritual vitality over the years, handle difficulties well and demonstrate a level of love and commitment within and beyond the fellowship, that will present a compelling witness to the community.

I am sure my friends were caricaturing the issue and perhaps not taking the matter too seriously. But there was, nevertheless, in their responses sufficient evidence to point to hurtful and sometimes damaging experiences inflicted by fellow Christians. Christian congregations can often be a theatre for conflict rather than a refuge for wounded people, but we need to strive for something better than this.

Maturity is difficult to achieve

The responses above, and the stories of church planting found in this book, illustrate how difficult the task is.

This is also borne out in scripture. The author of *Hebrews* expressed disappointment regarding the maturity of the believers to whom he writes (*Heb.* 5: 11-14). Paul describes the massive effort required in developing maturity (*Col.* 1: 28 – 2:2). *2 Corinthians* is a record of the difficulties he had experienced in planting and building the church in Corinth. It brought him to his knees, crying out 'who is sufficient for these things' (2: 16). Maybe he had been at the point of giving up, but he is driven to the conclusion that 'our sufficiency is from God' (3: 5) and this enables him to continue (4: 1, 16).

If the task is difficult, it is also ongoing. It will never actually be completed. By the very nature of a congregation, its members will be at different levels of maturity. Some will have been Christians for many years. Others will be new Christians, excited about their faith and with much to learn. Maturity in a congregation must be about something more than simply how long people have been Christians.

Maybe the picture of a family can help us here. The idea of maturity is seen in physical terms when a child is born into the family. The child develops physically, intellectually, morally and spiritually in that supportive relationship, and is able to become an independent adult. It requires the passage of time and exposure to a wide range of experiences. In the early years, the child is dependent on his (or her) parents, but as he grows he can begin to take responsibility for himself and, in due course, can contribute to the development of younger children in the family.

Similarly in a church planting context, the leaders will spend a great deal of time teaching new converts. But the new Christians will not remain 'babes in Christ' forever. The aim is for them to reach a level of maturity so that they will be able to teach others. A mature congregation therefore is one where people are at different stages, but everyone is contributing to the well-being of the whole.

Maturity is what God wants for us

When God blesses the preaching of the Gospel, his intention is not only to bring individuals out of darkness but to gather them into a community of saved people (*1 Cor.* 3: 6-9). These saved individuals are brought into a vital relationship with one another. They are 'baptised into one body' (*1 Cor.* 12: 13). God's intention is that this new community will manifest his glory in the world.

It is not God's intention to have communities of people behaving like children, fighting and squabbling with one another. God is looking for loving, serving, Christ-like fellowships. In *Colossians* 1:28, Paul describes the goal of his ministry as 'presenting everyone mature in Christ'. He expresses a similar thought in *Ephesians* 4, where he says that the risen Christ has given gifts to the church to equip the people of God, so that we might all come to the unity of the faith and 'become mature in Christ attaining to the whole measure of the fullness of Christ' (vv. 11-13). So, bringing congregations to maturity in Christ is one of Paul's primary goals.

God is not only looking for communities that will reflect his glory, but he has given us all the resources we require to make this possible. Christ loved the church and gave himself for it (*Eph.* 5: 25). The church is the supreme manifestation of the multi-faceted wisdom of God (*Eph.* 3: 10). Paul has a very high view of the church. He sees God's plan as to create colonies of heaven here on earth.

God's plan is to raise up communities all across the world which will reflect the life of heaven. In these communities, there will be peace and harmony. There will be no jarring conflicts or bitterness; instead, every member will show an unconditional commitment to every other member. These are the kinds of communities God is looking for with totally disparate people relating together in loving, trusting relationships.

What is maturity?

A mature person, unlike a child, is able to manage his or her behaviour and emotions, having regard not only to his or her own needs but to those of others. He or she will be able to handle problems or adversity in an appropriate and positive way. Maturity is generally something learned rather than being instinctive, and is not determined by one's age.

If maturity is something that is learned, then church leaders need to teach it. New Christians need to learn how to behave appropriately and relate constructively with fellow Christians. Too often we imagine that they will somehow get the message, so we can leave them to it. The analogy of the child and the family demonstrates how absurd this is. We would never dream of saying to a few-weeks-old child 'here is the cooker and the milk is in the cupboard. Just heat it up when you're hungry'. The child needs to be taught the basic skills which will enable him or her to become a mature adult. It is not so very different for those born into the family of God.

New Christians need to learn about the bible and what it teaches. They need to learn to pray, to share their faith and be involved in the life of the Church. All of these are so important for spiritual development. But they need also to be taught what it means to live as a Christian in the home, at work and in community. They need to see that the radical change which has taken place in their lives has practical implications for everyday living. The whole of life is affected by a decision to follow Jesus.

New Christians (and older) need to learn that the Christian life is not just continuing with the same values, lifestyle and presuppositions as before, with a few prayers and hymns thrown in, to give a kind of religious flavour. If this is true for the individual, it is also true for the church. On too many occasions, we try to conduct the business of the church on the basis of pragmatism or personal preference in exactly the same way as committees do in the secular world; and we imagine it is enough to 'baptise' our deliberations with an opening and closing prayer. But God has not been sought nor his word consulted.

We need to learn that we are not the same as before. There has been a radical change. There is a new standard of behaviour to adhere to, a new set of principles to guide us and new motivations to empower us. Because everything is different, there is so much that needs to be unlearned. Before we became Christians, we spent many years in the world, thinking, believing and taken decisions purely on the basis of our own desire or needs. We need to be taught how to think, act and behave in a new kind of way. This is why the discipling of new converts is so very important, for it is only as each individual Christian grows in maturity that the church will grow in maturity.

The discipling of individual Christians and training for community life, however, cannot be completely separated. No individual can reach maturity on his own. Christian growth can only be accomplished in association with other people. There are aspects of our character that can only be developed in relationship with others, e.g., learning to give and receive forgiveness or learning to submit to and serve one another.

So what does maturity in this collective sense look like? What are some of the features of mature, believing communities?

Mature congregations maintain a strong commitment to the core vision and values.

In defining the church that we are trying to build, we would certainly want to include statements about such matters as what we believe, the centrality of scripture, the place of teaching and preaching, baptism and the Lord's supper, leadership, and church order etc. For church planters, it is essential to have clarity with regard to these matters. Some kind of statement of faith and description of practice will probably be required.

But it is possible to have a congregation which has extensive biblical and theological knowledge and which is fully committed to a particular form of churchmanship, but which could not under any stretch of the imagination be described as mature. Knowledge and theology alone do not describe maturity. We need to look at such aspects as behaviour and attitude. This is where vision and values come in. A clear understanding of these will define where the church is going and how it intends to conduct its business.

But there is a further step. If we are to achieve maturity, it will be essential to keep the vision before the people. In the early days of a church plant, there is enthusiasm and energy. The members are united around and totally committed to the vision. But as the numbers increase, there often comes a subtle change in mindset. The leaders are no longer able to relate directly to each individual. New structures are introduced to provide pastoral care. A new building is perhaps being considered, all of which contributes to a change in the original atmosphere of the church.

At some point along the way, the focus gets lost. Instead of being driven by the vision, the members begin to look inward and become much more concerned about their own comfort or their own preference. The church has now become something that exists 'for us', to provide what we want, rather than 'for them', which was the original driving force. The emphasis now is on church structures and services, which often become the source of tension and conflict.

Leaders need to recognise that, if action is not taken at that point, the church will stagnate and eventually go into decline. The church must be brought back to a re-commitment to its original vision and values. It is the task of leadership to remind the people of their original calling. The vision must be an integral part of everyone's thinking, so that it impacts all the ministries and activities of the church and provides a strong motivating factor for Christian living.

Churches that stand the test of time remain true to their God-given vision.

Mature congregations give high priority to maintaining quality relationships among the members.

Whenever people live or work together in a close relationship, at some point there will be disagreement. It is common to all human relationships and it's perfectly natural. It can sometimes even be beneficial. What we don't need is to become alarmed or paranoid at the presence of conflict. What we do need is to be equipped with the necessary skills to handle and resolve disagreement constructively. As indicated in the section above, these skills need to be demonstrated and taught.

The tensions that arise in church do not normally have to do with theology. More often, the problem stems from a disagreement about some aspect of church practice or from a breakdown in relationships. Someone in the group wants a more prominent role. Others feel that they have not been given sufficient recognition or that their gifts have not been fully used. Whatever the reason, problems arise because of how people see themselves in relation to others.

Leaders will ensure new converts are aware that this is a normal part of the maturing process and will ensure that clear instruction is given as to the standards and principles by which members will relate to one another. They will also provide instruction on the procedures that will be followed in the event of a breakdown in relationships.

Clear instruction on this matter is given in the word of God. We are to love one another (*Rom.* 12: 10), build one another up (*Rom.* 14: 19), have the same care for one another (*1 Cor.* 12: 25), serve one another (*Gal.* 5: 13), bear one another's burdens (*Gal.* 6: 2) and a whole range of exhortation as to how we are to relate to one another (*Eph.* 4: 32 & 5: 21; *1 Thess.* 4: 18 & 5: 15; *Col.* 3: 9; & *Jam.* 4: 9, 11).

The sheer number of these references indicate that in the early church, loving, sacrificial, Christ-exalting relationships was the goal of essential Christianity. The mature congregation will major on ensuring that everyone is valued and welcomed, that everyone's gifts are used, that people in trouble are quickly supported, and that any underlying tensions are spotted and dealt with before they can develop into major incidents.

Lasting congregations give high priority to maintaining strong, healthy relationships and dealing with tensions or potential conflict early.

Mature congregations have developed skills necessary for handling change

One of the features of a mature congregation is openness to change. No church will stay the same forever. Some changes will be anticipated, others will not. Some changes may be planned or initiated by the leadership, others may be forced on the fellowship from outside. The attitude of the church is that the changed circumstances may present an opportunity to rise to something better. The culture is such that people are encouraged to try out things and even be allowed to fail. They quickly see the benefits of changing circumstances and are not afraid to take risks.

If maturity is seen in how the community responds to change or difficulty, then leaders need to explain how the church will deal with these when they arise. Leaders will take the opportunity to teach about how church problems were resolved in the New Testament, for example in *Acts* 15. This will provide a framework in principle, which will operate when actual decisions are required.

When changes are proposed, different reactions will be displayed. There is no church anywhere where everyone gets everything they would like. The changes will not suit everyone. Some will like what is proposed; others will not. Some will find the changes advantageous; others will be adversely affected. The outcome may be tension or, in some cases, conflict. It is at this point that the hard work involved in building strong relationships and maintaining a focus on the vision produces benefits. The climate has already been established where the issue is not about personal preference, but about seeking God-honoring solutions.

Different churches will have different strategies for handling change or problem circumstances, but the discussion above would indicate that the mature congregation will not duck difficult issues. They will acknowledge when change is necessary or a problem has arisen. The leadership will attempt to spell out, whenever possible, to the congregation the context and the implication of the issue, so that prayerful discussion can take place and consensus reached. This may not always be possible, particularly where sensitive personal information cannot be publicly disclosed, but the principle is to involve as many people as possible, especially the key influencers in the congregation.

This requires a different kind of leadership approach. It recognises that not all wisdom resides within the leadership group and that people within the membership are well capable of contributing positively to the discussion. Of course, this kind of strategy will only work if there is a high level of trust between the leaders and the members. But collective maturity is precisely about this. The days when leaders simply announce decisions without consulting the church have gone. In a post-modern society, people want to understand the reasons why particular actions are taken and want to be involved in the decision-making process.

The ability to do this well is a sign of maturity in the congregation.

How do we build this mature community?

Having attempted to define maturity in a church context, we must now address the issue of how we actually achieve it. I have deliberately devoted considerable space to describing what it is we are trying to produce. Stephen Covey in his book *The seven habits of highly effective people* states that we need to start with the end in view. That is, we need to know what it is we're trying to build. How else will we know when we have achieved our goal? But how do we build it?

Model it

Let us assume the leadership of the church has a clear understanding (and perhaps even a written statement) of the kind of community they are trying to build. How do they communicate the vision to the people? They can (and should) do some teaching about it or they could issue a policy document describing it. But, in all probability, this will have little impact on the actual life and behavior of the congregation.

Nothing will happen until the congregation sees the vision and values demonstrated in the life and behavior of the leadership. When the leaders deliver on their promises, observe confidentiality, make opportunities for others to develop their gifts, and are first to provide support in a crisis, then the congregation will see something of what maturity means.

Members of the church will only respond to the vision when they see it being worked out in their leaders. If the aim is to build a mature congregation, then the leadership team must behave in a mature way. Just as children copy their parents, so, in church, people copy their leaders.

Leaders must model commitment and care for others. They must be committed to the vision and live out the values. They must be able to demonstrate that they have developed the skills of handling conflict within their own group. There will be no power-seeking nor dictatorial attitudes. The leadership team will recognise the gifts of every member in it and, in different contexts, will allow different members to take the lead. This will be a team where there are no 'stars' or primadonnas. It will be a team committed to the glory of God and not the pursuit of some lesser agenda.

We can be sure that, if the leaders are not modeling maturity, then the congregation will never arrive at it. Conversely, we must equally be sure that, if the leadership is modeling something other than spiritual maturity, the congregation will follow the lesser example. This is very challenging for leaders, but this truth must be recognised if we are to be successful in building for maturity.

Teach it

Paul indicates in *Acts* 20 that he taught the church in Ephesus the whole counsel of God and he did it publicly and privately, night and day. We must follow Paul's example. The preaching programme of the church is very important and should include basic biblical and theological subjects. We do want our people to be sound in the faith and aware of the reasons why the church operates as it does. Living in a secular society requires Christians to be able to give a reason for the hope they possess. All of this needs to be taught.

In addition to the public teaching programme, building a mature congregation will require some kind of a mentoring structure where Christians can learn on a 'one on one' basis. It is in a secure trusting relationship like this that the deeper issues of life can be dealt with. Problems can be confronted, advice can be given, and correction can be offered.

Small groups too, where people trust and commit to each other, can be a major opportunity for learning how to receive support, handle different points of view, and openly share with other people.

The church needs to be intentional in its teaching provision if people are to reach maturity

Expect it

This is where the crunch comes. I suspect most of us will be able to sign up to most of what has been advocated in this chapter. But if that's all we do, we are merely living in the realm of dreams and ideas that will never see the light of day.

We must be intentional about making the dream happen. We need to hold our people to account. This will mean that we will talk often about the vision, asking how the people think we are progressing. We will regularly review the ministries and activities of the church to see how well they are contributing to the vision. Questions will be put to ministry leaders like 'is this the best way to do this activity?' and 'Are we using the gifts and experience of every team member to best advantage?'

We will also ask about the relationships within the church. 'Do you think there is a good atmosphere and team spirit around the church?' 'Are there any undercurrents of bitterness or jealousy?' 'Are you aware of any problems that need attention?' Similarly, in relation to change, we would want to review with key people, and maybe even the whole congregation, how a particular change process went. Was it conducted effectively? Were there any breakdowns in communication? How would we do it better next time?

At every stage and in every aspect, we need to challenge our people to do the very best they can for God (which means ourselves doing the very best that we can for God). We need to let it be known that we believe this congregation is capable of rising to maturity and doing great things for God.

This is a two-way thing, however. The membership will also be entitled to hold the leadership accountable. If it is felt the leaders are not behaving appropriately, or providing sufficient support, or showing the required level of commitment, the membership will wish to confront those questions. The membership will make it known to the leaders that nothing less than their very best leadership will do. They will point out that, if the church is to achieve its vision, then it will require the leaders to set the highest spiritual example for the church, and that the church is not prepared to settle for anything less.

Leaders need to call out the best in the membership and members need to call out the best in the leadership.

Leaders and members must hold each other to account. What a community that would be—leaders having credibility in the eyes of the membership and members having the confidence of the leadership.

It may be that all of this sounds like wishful idealism, perhaps even, as my friend said at the beginning, 'impossible'. But it is to this great task that God has called us. No doubt, there will be many disappointments along the way. But, as God begins to develop maturity in the people he brings to faith, we will be able to rejoice that we were part of God's plan to do something special in this group of people.

APPENDIX TO PART ONE

Church planting and emergent church

Stephen McQuoid

Over the past few years, a new movement within evangelicalism has come to prominence which is often referred to as 'emergent church'. The use of this title is in itself a little strange, because the movement does not like labels. However, it is a convenient hold-all term to describe those who form part of it. Key leaders in the movement would include well-known names such as Mark Driscoll, Brian McLaren and Rob Bell.

Emergent churches claim that they are trying to express their faith relevantly within a post-modern society and believe that their expression of Christianity is more satisfying for today's Christians than traditional strands of evangelicalism. It is actually quite difficult to categorize emergents, not just because they reject labels and categorization, but also because the movement is so diverse. Some emergent churches are best seen as a 'protest movement' which balks at the perceived sterility, calcification and formality of traditional evangelicalism. Others are creative communities who find new and relevant ways of being church. Still others are theologically radical groups that drive a strong theological agenda of their own and positively seek out new directions for Christianity. Understanding the movement requires a sophisticated approach and a fair assessment of the movement needs to steer away from comparing the best of mainstream evangelicalism with the worst excesses of emergent Christianity.

One way of understanding emergent church is to understand the spectrum(s) which this movement represents. There are two different axes that can be used to measure emergent churches.

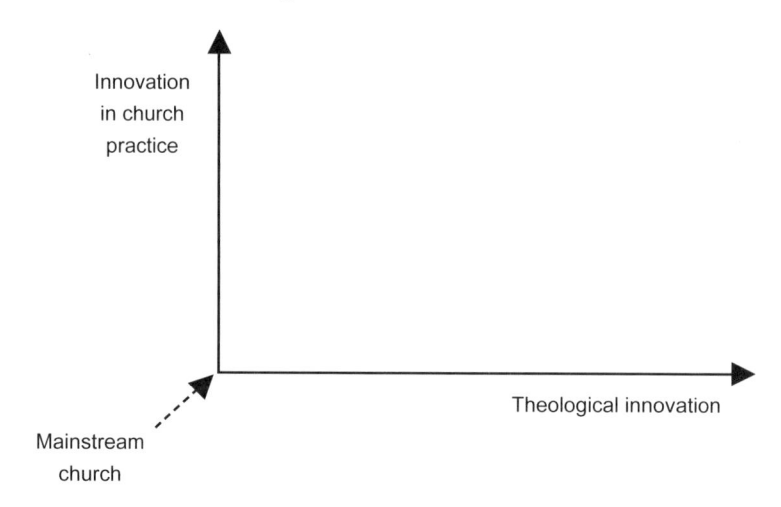

```
           Innovation
            in church
             practice
                ↑
                |
                |
                |
                |
                |
                |
                |————————————————————→ Theological innovation
               ↗
            ╱
   Mainstream
    church
```

The vertical axis relates to innovation in practice. That is, some emergent churches hold to theologically-orthodox beliefs, but in the way they conduct themselves, they look very different from standard evangelical churches. For example, they are creative and experimental in worship, relaxed in dress style and presentation, and preach in a less formal way or perhaps not at all. They might reject pews in favor of café-style seating. They will often prefer to incorporate question-and-answer sessions in their teaching programmes and emphasize the importance of the visual and the emotional in their church services. When they get together, they make a big issue out of community and authenticity, but are still orthodox in their theological stance.

The other axis by which they can be measured is that of theology. Some emergent churches are not only innovative in their practice of being church; they are also innovative in their theology. They tend to feel that traditional evangelicalism is too dogmatic and narrow in its focus and that, in a post-modern world, there needs to be greater flexibility and tolerance. Such emergents are cautious about reading, or rather interpreting, the bible too literally and feel that the church has often used scripture to oppress rather than help. Indeed, some emergent writers have claimed that the church has misread the bible for centuries and that they are trying to recapture the spirit of what the bible is trying to say. They resist dogmatic statements and express contentment and comfort with ambiguity. Their slightly-fuzzy approach to theology, which is of course deliberate, also spills over into ethics. For example, they might state that the bible is unclear on the issues such as homosexuality, so they are happy to take a flexible approach when dealing with it pastorally.

If these two axes or spectrums are held together, they can express something of what emergent Christianity means. Every emergent church will sit somewhere within the framework of these two spectrums, though that gives room for significant diversity. Consequently, we need to be careful not to narrow our definitions of emergent Christianity and certainly not make too many assumptions when we hear mention of the term emergent church.

One might well ask why there is an appendix on the emerging church in a book about church planting. The reason is that emergent church has done, and continues to do, a lot of church planting. It is true that in many cases emergent churches have not begun from scratch, but rather have simply recruited and absorbed Christians who have become disillusioned with traditional evangelical churches. However, that criticism could be levelled at lots of traditional evangelical churches too. Whatever critics say, the emergent church movement has certainly made its impact and will continue to do so for the foreseeable future.

As far as church planting is concerned, there are certainly lessons to be learned from the emergent church, both good and bad. Perhaps it is better to get the negatives out of the way first.

The biggest concern that many mainstream evangelicals have with emergent church is not actually with the movement as a whole, but with those parts of it that are very theologically innovative. There is a genuine concern that some segments of the emergent church play fast and loose with truth, and seem so unwilling to be categorical about even the simplest claims of scripture, that the gospel is not proclaimed clearly in all its fullness. Indeed, questions can be asked as to whether some emergent leaders really understand the true nature of the gospel. This sounds like harsh criticism indeed, but when emergent leaders seem unsure of what sin is, or question the atonement, or suggest that other religions have theological validity, doubts about their orthodoxy are bound to be raised.

A second concern is that some emergents are so quick to criticize church (though, of course, they thoroughly endorse their form of church) and so ready to use 'straw men' in their denunciation of evangelicalism, that they almost make 'church' a dirty word. Moreover, some of them are by nature anti-establishment and consequently suspicious of authority structures within church.

This position, if unchecked, could certainly make church planting, and the establishing of structures within a church plant, very complicated indeed.

Criticism aside, there are certainly positive lessons that church planters can learn from the emerging church movement. First, there is the willingness to try new and innovative forms of church which can be a huge benefit in church planting. It is the boldness of emergents to experiment that has resulted in much of their success, and this is an important lesson for anyone beginning a church plant. Secondly, there is the desire, which many emergents exemplify, to be truly relevant to culture and listen to the heartfelt cries of our age. This, too, is helpful. Evangelicals have often been accused of not listening to others and of being so dogmatic and forceful in preaching that they alienate rather than attract. Seeking cultural relevance is important, provided scripture and not culture forms is the guiding principle by which we operate. Emergent church helpfully emphasizes the importance of listening to culture. Lessons can be learned here. Thirdly, emergent churches tend to have a refreshing honesty about them, and a willingness to strip down church life to its bare bones. This approach helps church planters to see what is really important in church life.

History teaches us that radical movements die out, become heretical, or get absorbed into the mainstream. These, I think, are the options left open to emergent churches. In the meantime, those of us not involved in the movement, especially those of us involved in church planting, should observe carefully and ask what lessons are to be learned.

PART TWO

Ten living stories

CHAPTER 19

Starting fresh— Liberty Community Church, Bellshill

David Buchan

Viewpark Christian Fellowship, to be renamed Liberty Community Church when it moved out of the area in which it was born, officially came into being at a special dedication service in the local community centre on Sunday 5 March 1995.

This was, in fact, Year 7 of a church planting work that began in September 1988, when a resident GLO team of four people went to live and work in the area, following an invitation from Bothwell Evangelical Church. Although only two miles away, Bothwell was a very different community, had more of a village feel, and had significantly less of the social problems identified within Viewpark.

Through a 'Macedonian call' for help with a Sunday school that had been running for several years in a local school, the church in Bothwell soon realised the potential to do more. David and Jean Wood, and Jean's sister, Betty Weir, had taken on the task when they were younger, as part of the outreach from the Gospel Hall in Uddingston and as part of their desire to reach the community in which they lived.

The Gospel Hall being unable to do more and, the Woods feeling their age, they prayed about how to continue the work. Unknown to them, God had already placed in others in the area the idea of other Christians' coming to live in Viewpark: David and Eleanor Hall from the local Parish church; Jean-Marie Bell who attended a Church of the Nazarene in Glasgow, and Mary Theresa Travers, who attended the local Roman Catholic church. All later admitted independently, and without previously knowing each other, that they were praying for Viewpark and for Christians to come to live there.

Interestingly, Mary had been recently converted through an inter church prayer meeting when someone asked her if she had ever given her life to God! She said that she didn't understand their question, but on the road home told God that if that was what He wanted her to do, she was ready to cooperate! She became one of the GLO team's biggest fans and often prayed for us. She was also a natural evangelist, ready to encourage others to seek God's help in their lives, and with a smile and a spontaneous prayer would give out tracts and "Jesus Loves You" stickers!

More background preparations were taking place as God began to weave His designs. David and Sheena Buchan were completing a gap-year in Ipswich after completing the Training for Service Year with GLO in 1987. David had been a social worker and Sheena a teacher, but both felt called to leave their jobs to be part of a team that would take their Christian compassion into the community. The project was called 'Bridging the Gap' and would attempt to reach an urban community from within. All four team members moved into the heart of the housing estate, or "scheme" as it's known in Scotland.

At that time, reaching urban communities was seen as one of the biggest challenges facing the Christian church. Writers like Roy Joslin had launched the challenge through his book that claimed that, while almost 80% of the population lived in towns and cities, less than 1% of the British working-class ever attended church. 'When is the Church going to make an impact on the working class people of this country?' asked John Baigent at the launch of the resident GLO team. The answer, he believed, 'is when it adopts a radically different approach to the presentation of the gospel, in a practical, experiential way' demonstrating to people that God loves them.

Viewpark with a concentrated population of 8,500 had been designated by the Council as an "Area for Priority Treatment". Resources and facilities were to be directed to help the neediest parts of the community. With experience as a social worker, David Buchan had a conviction that Christians should be part of this work too; that Christians should be going to where the people are in an attempt to reach the 'whole person' with Christian care and compassion.

They were joined by Lorna Paterson, who sold her hairdressing business to respond to a growing burden in her heart to share her faith in practical ways. Her skills in hospitality, a listening ear, a praying heart, and ability to use her beautician skills with young girls, proved invaluable. She was really thrown into the deep end, dealing with one difficult lady who suffered from depression and who asked Lorna to help her as she had cut her wrists. 'Big Jane' responded to the compassion, prayer and practical help and later became a Christian and was baptised at the church in Bothwell. Her home needed some redecoration and the team soon volunteered to help her brighten it up. Someone arrived at Lorna's door one day with a large bag saying, 'it's curtains for Jane', which, after her suicide bid, appealed to our sense of humour and helped to ease the tension!

Colin MacPhie, a former manager in a Glasgow department store, initially came for one year and stayed for 21 years! He brought tremendous enthusiasm and skills in communicating to children and young people. He was ready in a reluctant way to get involved in delivering tracts or 'door-to-door' evangelism, but was pleasantly surprised that we in fact used more personal and innovative methods. He jokingly said he would love to play football and table-tennis, so that's what he did (some of the time!), showing the boys from the scheme that Christians can enjoy sport. The lads, curious about Christians, had asked one day what we did—'did we just pray all day?'!

When Colin married, his bride Margaret also married into the work and brought her creative talents as a great asset to the work. Once again, hospitality and their willingness to give practical help to people, opened people up to the message. Indeed, they really grasped the fact that people coming to church was often the last link in the chain of many links forged through friendships with people, engaging in activities of mutual interest and usually over a cuppa or a meal.

Debbie and Stephen McQuoid later moved onto the estate and brought much to the work. Debbie had become involved before she married and Stephen with his bible teaching abilities was appointed an elder on 11 February 1996. Together they saw the importance of engaging with people and persevering with them.

Many others gave their time and talents to augment the Christian presence and help in many ways. Some like Helen lived on the Estate, but many like Steve lived nearby and committed themselves faithfully to helping in one of the youth clubs or the Sunday Fellowship over many years. It was important early on to maintain the balance between locals and 'visitors', so that the young fellowship would maintain its own distinct identity.

Initially the team settled, tried to live and learn, identifying local needs and deciding on an appropriate Christian response. The authorities unofficially entrusted the team with much of the youth work in the scheme and were happy to allow it to supervise a disco run with the young people (who developed their DJ skills). Previously, discos had been banned, because of a lack of supervision and too many problems resulting from underage drinking and vandalism. In the early days, the team relied heavily, but not exclusively, on children and youth work, supplemented by two or three special mission weeks throughout the year. This helped towards our credibility and opened the door to families. However, we soon realised that, to reach adults, we had to spend time with adults too and not just rely on the children's work. Other Christians living or working in the area were encouraged; and often prayed, supported events or referred interested people. The local pharmacist, a speech therapist and two Christian GPs referred people for befriending and/or prayer.

One such person in her 30's had lost all confidence after a road accident. She slowly overcame her fears and rebuilt her confidence through the friendship offered. Moreover, she expressed an interest in spiritual matters and became a Christian, got engaged and married another Christian in the fellowship.

Simon, an elderly grumpy recluse was referred and, in true Victor Meldrew fashion, announced that he was interested in neither politics nor religion, but enjoyed social outings. He never became a Christian as far as we know, but some of his crustiness seemed to soften after consistent and practical help and friendship.

No one approach was *the* way to do things: family activities, small group bible studies, drop-in coffee-shop, and later Mums & Tots activities, all supplemented the work. In the summer, we took 'The J Team' to the grassy areas to play fun games (like parachute or rounders) and sing lively songs with the children, while some of the Team engaged with adults looking on from their doorsteps. We didn't want any confusion about who we were or what we were doing. 'Praise in the Park' combined a Bar-B-Q with praise in the beautiful 'Viewpark Gardens'—often a venue for wedding photos. This event took its name from the famous rock concerts called 'T in the Park', but it was felt prudent not to shorten the name of our event!

However, integration remained the key feature of the work in Viewpark and the above examples represent many cases guided by the fundamental quality of unconditional love. The team always tried to take a genuine interest in people whether or not they 'came to church'.

Liberty Community Church grew out of the seeds of Viewpark Christian Fellowship, where a mission-oriented approach always defined that church is about people, not properties. Indeed, 'the fellowship' was the term that new believers gave the gatherings, so although the church planted grew from a conscious evangelistic purpose, the expression of church came from the meaning given to it by those attracted by the shared life of the participants. Liberty continues to develop this within the community it now identifies with.

The change of name to Liberty Community Church came about as a result of a move to the Orbiston Estate, in a transition that was not straightforward. For a variety of reasons, the leadership of the Viewpark Christian Fellowship felt the time had come to move from the community centre where they met into a permanent building owned by the church. One of the elders was assigned the task of finding alternative premises and, in the course of investigation, came across an elder from the assembly in Bellshill which owned two properties, one of which was on the Orbiston estate, just two miles away from Viewpark. This building had been used for outreach over many years in Orbiston, but the Bellshill assembly were no longer able to maintain it.

Initially, the other Viewpark elders were completely opposed to even considering moving the church away from the Viewpark estate. However, through a day of fasting and praying, the Lord made his will clear and transformed entrenched views to bring the elders to a place of unity. This whole experience prepared the leaders for difficult conversations with members from the Viewpark area and in time we were able to take everyone along with the vision God had given us. As the name Viewpark Christian Fellowship was location specific and the church now met in a different place, a change was needed. The name Liberty Community Church was arrived at, partly because we liked what the name indicated and partly because the building was on Liberty Road

Looking back over the years, we can see the truth of the parable of the sowing of the seed, as so many made professions over the years, but a lot of them fell away. We praise God for the good seed and the work that continues to grow in Liberty Community Church.

Over the years and particularly in the early days, GLO teams played a significant part in the development of the fledgling church. They allowed us to impact the community on a much bigger scale in a concentrated period of time, and the blessings from those missions were often lasting, as people were followed up and relationships developed. The teams also had the effect of building up our members and proved to be significant times of growth in the lives of those who participated in the teams. The ethos of mission was in the DNA of the church and this has evidenced itself in the many outreach teams our own people have committed themselves to over the years—travelling all over Europe and beyond, spreading the Good News. We have also had the joy of commending some of our best people to serving God in mission and ministry elsewhere. For example, John Dick, who got saved as a boy in the early days of the work, studied at Tilsley College before doing an internship with a Church Planting Initiative-supported church in Cardiff. He then, again supported by CPI, helped with a GLO church plant in Johnstone on the west side of Glasgow, before becoming a community pastor at a church in Cumbernauld. The DNA of Liberty Community Church lives on.

CHAPTER 20

Mother and daughter— Kirkliston Community Church

Colin Haxton

Bellevue Chapel is a well-established church with a Brethren heritage in the city centre of Edinburgh. It had successfully grown its membership during the 1990s to almost 200 people. By 2005, services were full to capacity and there were often around 20 people who had to stand due to lack of seats! We were also blessed with many gifted people who were not being given sufficient opportunity to use their gifts as a result of others already being in position. Looking back, we realise that we were extremely fortunate, as we hear so often of churches that are struggling to keep going due to lack of numbers. During the latter half of 2005, as a leadership team, we shared with the church the God-given vision which we entitled "Stepping Out With God".

The vision for the following 6 years involved three primary elements:

- A new church plant
- An expansion of our focus on and support for world mission
- A further development of the core ministries in the community surrounding Bellevue Chapel in Edinburgh.

The church wholeheartedly supported this vision which was rolled out from January 2006.

God Answers Prayer

For over six years (since 2000), Christians of various denominations in the village of Kirkliston (on the western fringes of the city of Edinburgh) had been meeting together on a monthly basis to pray for a movement of God in the local area. Owen and Ruth Bramwell (members of Bellevue Chapel who had already established a weekly children's bible club in the village) were catalytic in this process and followed the Lord's leading by forming the '*Kirkliston Prayer Group*'. It became clear to many of the group that God wanted to do something big in the community and this coincided perfectly with the '*Stepping Out With God*' vision which had been given to the elders of Bellevue Chapel. At the Bellevue Church Weekend at Carberry Tower in June 2006, God spoke powerfully to a number of individuals within Bellevue Chapel and the seeds were sown for planting a new church in Kirkliston.

A *Church Plant Working Group* was established to act as the advance party to establish the infrastructure and content of what was going to take place. This team consisted of Owen and Ruth Bramwell, Iain Brodie, Sandra Lindsay as well as two of the elders—Daya Rasaratnam and myself. This team worked together from December 2006 to December 2007 to ensure that the roots of the new church were established.

Early Beginnings

Between January and April 2007, a group of Christians from Bellevue Chapel began to meet for times of fellowship and communion on the 4th Sunday morning of each month. We had successfully arranged to have the use of Kirkliston Community Centre for this purpose and we give thanks to God for the tremendous working relationship that we built up with all the staff at the Centre. In addition to these Sunday morning meetings, we also agreed to meet on the 2nd Tuesday evening of each month for fellowship and communion, with a special prayer emphasis. These meetings were held rotationally in different homes in the South Queensferry and Kirkliston areas.

The fellowship times proved to be very special, and many commented on their intimacy. We learned that when a small number of committed Christians meet together with a purpose and resolve, then the Holy Spirit has freedom to move. This was certainly our experience as we reflect on these early days.

There were 22 members of Bellevue Chapel who formed the original nucleus of *Bellevue West Community Church*—the name we came up with to identify the church plant! These 22 adults were well supported by 20 children' so we had a relatively strong base to start with.

Stepping Out A Little Further

The work amongst the children which Owen and Ruth had been leading was reinforced by additional support from Bellevue West and the new name of *Kidzone* became established on Thursday evenings at the community centre. We also set up a Sunday morning programme for children—a crèche and a kids' church group, which ran concurrently with the fellowship meetings. Additionally, midweek bible study groups for women and men were set up and these helped a number of people who were new in the Christian faith.

From May to July, we increased the number of fellowship meetings and started to meet on the 2nd and 4th Sunday morning, as well as the 2nd Tuesday evening. Through word of mouth and individual testimony, our numbers started to increase—primarily with other local Christians who had been attending other churches in the Edinburgh area. It seemed that the call to minister in the Kirkliston and Queensferry area had not only been on the hearts of those in Bellevue, but also on other 'commuting Christians'!

We saw God working very specifically in equipping many at Bellevue West with gifts which were used and developed each week. As well as those who moved from Bellevue Chapel, the newcomers were also blessed by the Lord and made incredibly valuable contributions to the life and work of the new church. There was tremendous harmony within the group as we started to reach out to meet the needs of the community as well as serve each other. Collectively, there was a strong new church identity, which few of us could have predicted would be so strong, so soon.

Church Launch Week

The highlight event of 2007 was definitely the Launch Week which took place from 4 August. During the lead-up to this week and throughout the week itself, the establishment of the identity of Bellevue West was a key factor. This was achieved, and a lot more besides! Every home in Kirkliston, South Queensferry and the surrounding area had been leafleted with details of the Launch Week activities. Additionally, we had two features in the local newspaper, dozens of posters around the village, as well as a radio interview to highlight what was going on.

The 'Tea In The Park' event was an outdoor family fun-day which was attended by over 300 people from the community. This took place on a sunny Saturday and was a fantastic way to start. The support of our friends from Bellevue Chapel was immense and gave us a very professional image within the community. At the event, many young people signed up for the 'Wastewatchers' Holiday Club and 'Teen Nights' Youth Club, which ran from Monday to Friday during Launch Week. Both these activities were extremely well attended and, as a result, Kidzone had its regular numbers boosted every Thursday evening. The success with the teenagers resulted in our establishing Teen Nights on a regular weekly basis and many of those who attended for the first time during the Launch Week come along each time the club is on.

We were also able to use the Launch Week to have several prayer walks and one-to-one conversations with folks in the community. This included several of the parents who dropped off their children at the holiday club. These contacts have been developed and we have seen several folks attend our weekly Sunday morning service or they have come to other special events such as the Christmas Carol Service.

Many of us participated in some community projects during Launch Week. This included the painting and refurbishing of the Scout Hall and its environs, as well as the building and landscaping of a community garden at the Community Centre.

The week culminated in our Launch Service on Sunday 12 August which was attended by around 90 people. This gave the kids an opportunity to show us what they had been doing during the week, and also allowed us to meet and greet many who had never been in a church setting before. Weekly services have continued since that day.

The overriding benefit from the Launch Week was that, as a group of Christians, we truly found our identity and we were fused together in Christ with a clear purpose and mission.

Post-Launch

The church established a regular set of activities. On Sundays, we have a prayer time prior to the main morning service at 11am. This service takes the form of a family service, and there is a crèche and kids' church which run simultaneously.

We have benefitted from a number of men within our church who are capable speakers, as well as using visiting speakers.

Our children's and youth work has flourished, resulting in many attending both Kidzone and Teen Nights on Thursday evenings. We have established groups for women and men which meet periodically. We meet midweek in various homes where home groups allow us to go deeper into God's word and to pray together. On the second Tuesday of the month, we meet together as a fellowship and pray. On the 1st Sunday of the month, our morning service includes Communion and we don't normally have a speaker on those occasions.

On Friday evenings, we have an hour of football with men from the community, which has been excellent. We have established contact with well over a dozen individuals who have no current church connection, and it is our hope that we can get to know them more as time goes on.

Church Pastor Search

It became evident to us all that to continue the work in the future, we would greatly benefit from the services of a full-time pastor. We needed additional resource in terms of pastoral and community work, preaching and teaching as well as providing additional leadership support to the elders group. A thorough recruitment process took place over the course of 2008, and into early 2009, and we were clearly directed in our search. We welcomed our new Pastor—Colin MacPhie—in May 2009 and he has done a great job to become integrated into the community and the church. He is fully funded by the church fellowship as a full-time employee, a major commitment by a relatively small number of people.

Our Own Church Building

In February 2008, we were made aware that the former Masonic Hall in Kirkliston was available for sale. The building is located in a prime location on the Main Street, between the main pub and post office. The building consisted of a large two-storey 'house' at the front, with a 'link area' in the middle, leading to a large multi-purpose hall at the rear (capable of seating 150 people). It had been neglected for years and was up for sale, as there was a diminishing number of men supporting the work of the Lodge. In April 2008, we were successful in purchasing the building.

The members and elders of Bellevue Chapel emptied all the monies in the church's reserve fund and gave a large donation towards the purchase of the building. This was added to by huge sacrificial giving of the members of Bellevue West to enable us to purchase the building outright (at a cost of £280,000) without the need of a loan.

We took ownership of 70 Main Street, Kirkliston on 2 May 2008 and quickly recognised that it would not be possible to use the facility for our activities until it had been completely renovated. The scale of the works was large, and we decided to begin the process by appointing a design team to work with us in order to optimise the facility for the needs of the church and also the community. We wanted to ensure that the finished building would be of a high standard and would be seen as a welcoming place at the heart of the community. The design team helped us establish the best layout and construction methods, as well as provide outline costs for the project.

By early 2009, we recognised that the initial construction and refurbishment costs were much more than we felt we could realistically commit to. We therefore obtained a number of alternative proposals, and eventually agreed to go with a contractor who was able to give us virtually all that we were looking for, but for a reduced amount of about £500,000. By early May 2009, we had raised just over £200,000 in our building fund. This was the target figure we had set to permit the contractor to start works. The project started on 18 May and was completed in early April 2010. God miraculously provided much of the monies needed to complete the refurbishment, although the church has borrowed a considerable sum for repayment over a ten-year period.

Open Week—and a new name!

Our times of meeting at the Community Centre came to an end on Easter Sunday 2010. We had been wonderfully supported by the team at the Community Centre, who were sad to see us go. The following Sunday, we held our first service in the newly-refurbished church building right in the heart of the community—an emotional occasion for us all. During the rest of that week, we opened the church building to the whole community to 'come and see' what God had done. Over 700 people visited us during 'open week' and all of them were in awe, as they saw the transformation which had taken place. The new building has enabled us to develop more ministries, including a café which has seen many unchurched people coming into the church building.

The new building also allowed us to formally rename the church as 'Kirkliston Community Church'. We felt that this gave a much stronger identity to the fellowship within the local community, although it was an emotional wrench for some of those who had been on the journey since the early days as a new church plant of Bellevue Chapel to see the "Bellevue" name dropped. We recognise that without the incredible support of our mother church, we could never have achieved what has been done in such a short timescale. Although we now have complete independence in every way, we remain closely associated with the folks at Bellevue Chapel and will always be grateful for their willingness to step out in faith and encourage us to 'live the dream'.

The Future

Kirkliston Community Church is a vibrant and growing church fellowship with around 100 to 110 people gathering together to worship God every Sunday. We have had the blessing of being able to send out some missionaries from our church to serve the Lord in other parts of the world, and to seek to support them financially as part of our response to the mission to which we have been called.

We have taken time to prayerfully establish a clear process for the development of the church fellowship which is called our Mission, Vision and Values. On these foundation stones, each ministry of the church is being established and developed, to ensure that we are utilising our resources in the most effective and relevant ways.

We have seen tremendous spiritual growth in our members and within our young people. We have been blessed with several people becoming Christians from the local area and would seek to disciple them as part of the expanding fellowship. The most noticeable thing about our church is its prayer life—both personal and corporate. This has been at the heart of what we do from the beginning and has increased in its expectancy as the church has grown. Without this, we could not have made any progress. May it always be at the heart of what we do!

We have often wondered at the awesome way in which God has worked during the last four years and need to pinch ourselves to recognise that it is real! It would have been so easy to have remained safely in Bellevue Chapel and just continue to 'do church', but we would have missed out on all the blessing and excitement we have experienced.

So let me encourage you to have the courage to leave your comfort zone and allow the Holy Spirit to lead you into the fullness of what God has in store for you.

CHAPTER 21

Mother and daughter—Bethany City Church, Sunderland

Dave Burke

There are plenty of 'churches' in Sunderland—almost-empty buildings waiting to be dumped onto the property market; it is heartbreaking. There can only be a couple of thousand believers in a conurbation of 280,000 people. Sunderland is crying out for mission-minded Christian communities.

Bethany Christian Centre is in Houghton le Spring; six miles to the south east. For many years we had been blessed—and been a blessing to others. When I became Senior Pastor in 1997, it was clear that we would plant a church sooner or later. During the first few years of the new century, three things brought the timetable forward.

First, our worship space was full every Sunday with a large number of people travelling from Sunderland to join us. If a significant number of these caught the vision to plant, we would have a core for a new congregation. Secondly, with the help of David Clarkson's *Learning to Lead* course, we had trained a new group of leaders who wanted to be fruitfully deployed in ministry. Thirdly, through prayer and reflection, the passion to plant grew, especially in my own heart: God was giving us our marching orders.

Most of Bethany's congregation were up for the challenge, but many had reservations; we were having such a good time, why spoil things? Nevertheless, the passion to plant would not go away.

Thinking outside the box

From the start we felt that the effort should involve the strongest leaders we could find—this would give confidence to potential volunteers and emphasise the importance of the project. Then someone challenged me personally, 'Would you be prepared to lead this yourself?' So the plan became quite radical; to commit the pastor, a squad of our strongest leaders, and a team of gifted people to begin a daughter congregation.

When we announced this plan at a church meeting, everyone was a bit stunned, but the majority was prepared to give it a go. We gave potential volunteers two weeks to pray and think about coming on board—seventy or so chose to join the pioneer team and we began meeting to pool ideas, form ministry teams and to pray.

Our plan was a bit too neat: start meeting on Sunday mornings, with a functioning Sunday school and youth work, so that our new community would be attractive to families. The Sunday mornings would provide 'entry level' worship and teaching for seekers and young Christians, but everyone in the church would belong to a cell group which would provide teaching and pastoral input to sustain the more mature believers. In all this, we felt that we had a church structure that would enable us efficiently to make disciples and bring them to maturity.

For a Sunday venue, we secured the use of a large conference room at the Stadium of Light; Sunderland's football 'cathedral'. The whole team met there for a dry run in September 2004 and the new church got cracking the following week.

The first two years

We had a lot of media attention from the start; our unusual choice of meeting place ensured this, as did our radical goal to be a 'church for people who didn't go to church'. Determined to keep the focus on outreach, we tried everything we could to engage un-churched people; that meant 'we-come-to-you' evangelism as well as the 'you-come-to-us' kind.

We ran the Alpha Course in pubs and cafés, as well as clubs for young people at a venue in the city centre. We grabbed every opportunity to get into the marketplace, with display stands at wedding fairs and Sunderland Air Show. We had a stand and ran seminars at a New Age health and healing exhibition, and gave away hundreds of Pot Noodles to students to advertise the church—there were no limits!

Sadly, Pot Noodles turned out to be an ineffective outreach tool, but when some of our team opened an international student café in a town-centre location, it just took off. Then came one wonderful Sunday morning when, just before we started, 20 Chinese arrived in one large group; we have relished being an international congregation ever since.

It was good to see people begin their Christian journey by receiving Christ through these efforts—God was gracious and the congregation grew. Yet, we were also growing through people coming to us from other churches. Most of these had valid reasons; churches closing down or those in need of recovery from legalism or extremism of one sort or another.

And so our congregation grew. We quickly became financially independent from the mother-ship and after the first year took on a second staff member— Pete Chilvers. At the end of our second year, Sunday gatherings averaged 180 to 200 people, but it was becoming clear that we had a great deal of consolidating to do. Young Christians needed nurturing; some older believers needed healing and restoration. Our own team needed this too; many were exhausted after two years of vigorous activity.

In 2008, the banking industry woke up to a crisis; after a couple of decades of 'thinking outside the box', it turned out that there was nothing left inside the box; catastrophe! By the summer of 2006, we had learned the same lesson; priorities would need to be re-adjusted.

Thinking *inside* the box

The strain was beginning to show. Some team members were frustrated with entry-level worship and messages tuned to reach the un-churched. New Christians were often slow to grow into anything like maturity—many had emotional issues that would take time to resolve. We had picked up a large number of people with significant personal problems and we were struggling to support them all.

Other aspects of our neat plan were not working as expected; not everyone wanted to join the cell groups; others loved the small group environment, but didn't like the Sunday mornings! One of the many things I have learned from church planting is that the people in Willow Creek and Saddleback all seem to do as they are told; this is not how it is in real life!

This was a difficult period for the leadership team; some of our friends became very critical and negative, and it was hard not to take this personally. A number of us were, though gifted, inexperienced, and there was a tendency to over-react and beat ourselves up. Leading the leaders was a struggle; personally, this was a very tough time indeed.

So after two years, we felt it right to shift the centre of gravity of our Sunday mornings to provide better nurture for believers. From now on, we would try to be seeker-friendly and, at the same time, provide an environment that would also challenge, encourage and nourish the spiritual life of established Christians. Trying to achieve this balance would occupy us for the next few years. Alongside this, we put more effort into 'capacity building'—the difficult task of trying to get new people into useful ministry. Everyone seems to think that this is easy; it is not!

Our mother church was struggling too. They had lost seventy people and their pastor; Sunday ministry became a lot less consistent, and they faced the challenge of sustaining their ministries with a smaller workforce. Their leadership had a difficult time and it was a year before a new pastor was appointed. His ministry helped to get things moving again, but Bethany was bruised.

Six years on the mother church has not quite recovered from the effort of birthing a new one; yet the church has grown, and gifted people have slowly emerged to fill the gaps. This is one of the great by-products of a mother-daughter plant; it creates an environment that encourages the emergence of gifts not spotted before.

Moving out again

After three years meeting in The Stadium of Light, we had find another venue—this reduced our visibility and our sense of being at the heart of the city. On top of this, after a couple of years of consolidation, our church was stronger, but less engaged with the lost. We needed to recover the creativity and drive of our first two years—but by putting our energy into sustainable ministries rather than exciting one-offs. 'You-come-to-us' evangelism had continued consistently, but we needed to find new avenues for 'we-go-to-you' outreach.

So in the last year we have helped set up *Street Pastors* in the city—working closely with the City Council, Northumberland Police and a dozen or so other churches. Some of us are part of a *Healing on the Streets* team—being available in the town centre on a Saturday afternoon to pray for people. We are investing time working with the management of our local shopping centre; there we have run an *Operation Christmas Child* stand, and on late shopping nights at Christmas, we do free present wrapping and carol singing, anything to bless people in the city centre. We getting a return in this investment: they let us do a lunchtime concert with the *African Children's Choir* recently, and are willing to let us do a proper evening event next year.

More recently, we have just begun *Sunday Night Live*—an evening of live music and gentle evangelism in Starbucks every month, right in the heart of the city. Recently, some Chinese contacted us, wanting to do outreach in Mandarin—they started this autumn and we now have a Mandarin group meeting every week. No-one would have imagined that six years ago!

So we have a better balance of nurture and activity than before: with more sustainable activity 'outside the walls' of the church. We are getting closer to the gospel-shop we want to be, learning to live and love like Jesus and getting the people of Sunderland into heaven.

Reflection – what have we learned?

What would we do differently the next time we plant a church?

We should pray more thoughtfully, more often and more strategically. We sleep-walked into problems that could have been avoided if we had remembered that the Devil really exists and that God answers prayer. One of our faults is a tendency to regard difficulties as opportunities for more management know-how, more ingenuity or (frequently) for beating ourselves up. This is changing, but slowly. Looking back, it is astonishing that God was prepared to use people like us; we have proved that He is gracious!

We tried very hard to maintain a close relationship with our mother church, but this was more difficult than we anticipated. Quality relationships are not sustained by joint meetings but by person-to-person friendships, and very busy people have limited time for this. Maintaining this relationship deserved more thought than any of us gave to it.

We were too influenced by Mega-church thinking and rhetoric. I love Willow Creek and Saddleback, but their programmes only work well because their catchment is so vast. In our smaller, European congregations, individuals are not hidden in a huge crowd. Irritating to management-minded leaders, real people will not jump through the hoops set up for them. It is a hard lesson; our culture treasures individuality, and we should too. This makes everything harder—and slower!

Finally, if anyone is ever desperate enough to ask my advice before planning a church, I would say two things. First, be utterly certain that God wants you do it; don't do it on a whim, or because you fancy a change, because you won't survive. Secondly, be aware that the Enemy will explore all your weaknesses in the process; he will try to break you. Church planting is serious warfare—count the cost.

CHAPTER 22

Mother and daughter— Abbey Church, Gloucester

Roger Chilvers

What do you do if the church grows and the buildings are expanded until adding further extensions is no longer a feasible option? For us the answer was, 'Plant a new church'.

We had been thinking about it for some time. After all, we ourselves were once a church plant, having been started by a group mainly from another Brethren Assembly in Gloucester a few decades before in the 1950's (Albion Hall—today called Southgate Evangelical Church). Now it was our turn, as we at Hillview Evangelical Church were going through an extended period of growth. One at a time, we bought several small plots of land from the Council which were adjoining our site and which once contained small garages for nearby houses. These had become surplus to the needs of the housing estate, so we bought them as they became derelict. At about the same time, the next door small detached former council house came up for sale. We managed to purchase it, to use it as much needed church rooms. This then allowed us to make a whole series of adjustments in the buildings on a fairly limited site, to add facilities and to extend the main worship area, until we more than doubled the size we were originally.

Of course, the church is not the building, and adding rooms and extending the main meeting hall was only undertaken to accommodate growing numbers of people. It was the people becoming Christians and joining the church that we were really excited about. We were not a large church, but gradually numbers increased to around 150 people, filling the expanded buildings.

Elements of growth?

People have often asked, 'What is the secret of growing the church so that such expansion takes place?' I have always found it difficult to answer. As far as we could see, the elements that came together to some extent just happened. They were in the Lord's hands and he was at work. However, looking back, there are several things that contributed:

1. Growth became part of the vision of the church

This was not a written vision statement that the church strived to live up to (though we did have one to help clarify our understanding), but it became the everyday outlook of the church. People began to look for new opportunities and new ways to invite people and to personally share the Gospel. There were regular baptismal services. In fact, in one period we had a baptismal service for several candidates every month for over a year. And all this was not because of special techniques, but because of a new passion for growth. The church grew because people wanted it to grow! It was easy to invite friends because many others were inviting theirs.

Of course, some people were better at contacting and inviting newcomers than others, but those who were not so gifted in this area supported, prayed for and encouraged those who were.

2. We worked hard at the basics

Simple things that often it is easy take for granted were planned with great care. Sunday evenings, for example, were planned very thoroughly. It was not a case of just selecting a few well-known songs, followed by a visiting speaker preaching the gospel. Items such as what was sung and how to make the prayer more effective and relevant were really thought and prayed about. So, too, was the music which was not extraordinary, but was done well and practised carefully. We asked ourselves, 'What content of preaching would really help newcomers as well as encourage and teach the faithful?'

3. Many small groups took place

For example, Discovery Groups, Discipleship Groups, and Nurture Groups etc. for newcomers; Marriage Classes, Baptismal Classes, Parenting Groups, etc. for those taking specific steps forward were all looked upon as part of the spiritual growth of the church. Training programmes for those involved in the wide variety of church programmes were also regularly undertaken. There were informal groups run in homes by anyone that had a few people that wanted to cover the foundational issues of what it means to be a Christian. They were typically very basic, lasting just a few weeks, usually six, round the kitchen table or in someone's sitting room, and the content was straightforward enough for anyone to lead.

4. Recognition that informality is not the same thing as being casual

We sought to be informal in the way we did ran things, so that visitors felt at home, but not casual. This meant that we looked carefully at all the programmes of the church, asking what they would mean to someone with no church background. We recognised that 'formal' often was mostly interpreted as 'stuffy' and 'boring'. But we did not do things in a casual way. Things were carefully planned and prayed about.

5. The leadership of the church (the elders) spent much time seeking the mind of the Lord

This was, in particular, about the way forward and how to lead the church. It is difficult to pinpoint exactly the areas that changed as a result, but it did mean that the overall atmosphere and sense of being united under God's hand grew and was significant. It was often costly in time and effort. Days away became important, sometimes in prayer and fasting during which, on our knees, we prayed for every person in the church individually.

The search

However, to read these few pointers—and there are many more—to things that helped the growth does not give the whole picture. There were many disappointments and failures, as in any church.

Internally, there were those that once ran well, but then fell by the wayside, and those that for years drifted in and out of the church activities. There were also some that became troublesome and needed correction, even reprimand and strong guidance. We occasionally heard of criticism from other fellowships, but we knew it was our duty to walk with our eyes on the Lord and not on other churches.

Externally too, there were pressures and disappointments. We knew well, both from experience and much national research that the time to look at church planting or other options that growth presents is not when the present building are full, but when the buildings are at 70-80% capacity. Growth slows once the buildings are approximately 80% full. The feel-good factor of crowded facilities may remain for some time, but the growth itself falls off. So once we started to grow significantly the question arose, where do we go from here? We looked at all the options, such as multiple services or moving to another site to grow a bigger church. We researched and sought to purchase larger sites and buildings nearby. At the same time, we considered a whole list of areas of significant population within about a 10-mile radius that needed to be reached with the gospel and that had no active church; areas in which church planting could be the answer.

Yet, as we looked at these, we talked with others and wrote to many official bodies, such as owners of buildings that we thought would be suitable and that had been vacant for many months or years; and approached trustees of church buildings in areas of need where the occupying church was too small and elderly to be effective. We also approached the local City Council, seeking various plots of land for building, but the negative responses seemed to increase. It was very discouraging to the church, especially when there were situations where a considerable amount of time and sometimes some money had been invested in research.

However, as this process took place over several years, we became more and more convinced that one area of new development was being impressed upon our hearts and minds, until we clearly knew it was the leading of God. The problem was, where do you find a building to hire or a plot of land to purchase for building when the new development is on a green-field site in which every square foot of land is allocated? Around 20-25,000 people were moving into the areas of Abbeydale and Abbeymead in Gloucester, with, at that time, no clear witness or work among them, other than a small group that had previously sought to start a church there. This group had eventually found the vision impossible to maintain until the remaining few had moved to Hillview and the work ceased. It was at this time that we felt sure that God was leading us in this direction, so the vision clarified and plans began to emerge.

The first and major step was the start of the new church. Who would do it and how many do you need for a viable church plant, knowing that there is no fixed plan for success? Over several months we prayed and planned. As leaders, we asked for clear guidance about how many existing members should be asked to make the break and start the new church. As church leaders, we felt that about 40 would be appropriate, but who? And what should the criteria be for selecting this critical group?

At this point, we regularly shared the whole approach and our thinking with the church, as we had done over many months. This was done in print, through papers explaining our thinking and process, in preaching and teaching, and in discussion. And greatest of all, the church shared in the most important planning step of all; prayer, with regular personal and group prayer, added to by days and half days of prayer and fasting.

We knew that some people felt very keenly that they wanted to be part of the start-up group. Others felt equally strongly that they did not consider it was for them. Our concerns were that we should not end up with either all the enthusiastic and gifted entrepreneurial types leaving to start the new work, which would be difficult for Hillview as they left; and that we should not have an unbalanced group of mainly the younger and inexperienced people offering their services. What we needed and prayed for was a balance of gifts, experience, ability and age.

A special church meeting was called and the situation was outlined. 'If there are too many offering to go, we might have to ask some to remain', we explained. 'If there are not enough in one area, we may have to seek further help.' And, 'It is unlikely that we shall be able to do all that we want to from day one'. Then forms were given out for people to complete and return over the following days, to ask how they felt God was leading them personally. It was to our amazement and with much thankfulness that when the responses were counted and analysed we had 42 people, with a cross section of skills that we had already assessed as necessary for the start of a new work. This, we felt, was God at work. We had no need to make any changes or ask for any to 'change sides'! So Abbey Church was born!

At first, we met separately on Sunday mornings and for many of the children's and youth activities each week, but in the Sunday evenings we combined with Hillview from where we had come, to receive more structured teaching and to keep a strong link with the parent church for spiritual and pastoral protection.

We had no building but as a temporary measure we began by using the primary school in the new area. It was not ideal as a church building, but was much better than many such schools, and we anticipated it would only be for a short while, so we were happy to use it. Little did we realise at that time that it would take much longer, running into several years before we could begin to see light at the end of the tunnel of getting our own building.

The very first Sunday morning was memorable. A young couple came who we did not know.

'Great to see you' we said as they arrived. 'Where are you from?'

'Oh, I've have just moved here from Malvern about 25 miles away,' she said.

'Did you have any church connection when you were there?

'Oh no, I've don't think I've ever been to church in my life'

'Well what made you come today?'

'Well my boyfriend said that, when we moved here, we should start going to church. So here we are!'

Not being used to church they sat in the front row. From the first note of the first song she burst into tears. After a couple of verses, I walked across and spoke to her quietly.

'Is there something with which we can help? 'Would you like to go to a quiet spot somewhere and talk about things?'

'Oh no', she said, 'It is all so wonderful, I don't want to miss any of it.'

Later, she explained that when she was packing up to move to Gloucester she came across the little New Testament she had been given at school. 'I was an atheist, but I read it to see what it said, but never thought of it as God's word. Yet when in church that Sunday morning, it was just as if God was looking at me and for the first time I began to understand.'

So Barney and Claire started their journey with us and became two of our best and most faithful workers.

Our aim had always been that, if at all possible, we would seek to build and manage a facility that would serve the community and at the same time be the home for the church we planned to start. We were unhappy to think about investing in a church building that would merely be used on Sundays and a few hours during the week. But in running a community-based project, under our control we could both realistically serve the needs of the community and meet as a local church with all that implies.

Our research showed that the City Council had an unused plot of land allocated for community use on a prime site in the centre of the development.

But rather than taking a few months to apply for use of the Council-owned site as we anticipated, it actually took several years of what turned out to be a long, uphill, sometimes seemingly endless struggle, though that phase has now been completed as the land has been granted to us for our use in serving the community. Through this period, the church found it hard, yet at the same time the work gradually began to grow. There has never been a sudden burst of growth, but a steady increase in numbers until at the time of writing we have around 90 people of all ages.

So where do we go from here?

Abbey Church is just about to embark on the first stages of a building project on a wonderful site in the centre of the community. We plan to put up a community-based facility that will be the home for the church, but will also enable the church to serve the community. It is planned that it will be open every day with a variety of rooms and meeting halls and café, in which there will be a wide variety of programmes, with dedicated staff seeking to help and support the local community. There are plans for crafts, sports, courses, per-school work, children's clubs, youth clubs and seniors programmes, as well as the wide range of activities that you would expect from any growing church wishing to share the greatest news of all. Once up and running, we want Abbey Centre in Gloucester to be like a light that is set on a hill that cannot be hidden.

And what will happen when these facilities are bursting at the seams? Well there are plenty of other population centres that need a new church. The time to begin praying for the vision and ability to plant churches there too is now, so we're excited.

CHAPTER 23

Outreach to church—
The Living Rooms, Inverbervie

Ken Dickson

Inverbervie is a small coastal town in south Aberdeenshire. My wife, Veronica (Vee) and I have lived there for over twenty five years, and for most of that time had worshipped and served in the small Gospel Hall church there.

As the new millennium began, there was a growing awareness that we were stuck in a deep spiritual rut. The struggling Brethren church we belonged to had closed and we wanted so much to leave Inverbervie. This was the point that the Spirit of the Lord began to move powerfully in our lives, revealing himself in a way that we had never known before!

I unexpectedly received a copy of *Fresh Wind, Fresh Fire*, the story of how God had blessed the faith of Jim Cymbala as he pastored the Brooklyn Tabernacle in Manhattan, New York. My faith level soared as I began to see that God does do amazing things today, if his people are prepared to believe him enough to make 'big asks' of their Heavenly Father.

Next, the Lord stunned us by telling us at a very important moment that he wanted us to stay in Inverbervie with the words, 'Where you are right now is God's place for you. Live and obey and love and believe right where you are' (*1 Cor.* 7: 17 (MSG)).

Once we had come to terms with such a clear message, we began a period of waiting on the Lord. Eventually, we realised that he was speaking to us his prophetic word from *Haggai*, a book which he had used twenty years before to bring us to Inverbervie in the first place! So he again said to us 'Build the House so that I might take pleasure in it, and be honoured' (1: 8). 'Be strong….be strong….be strong and work, for I am with you' (2: 4). 'The silver is mine, and the gold is mine' (2: 8). ' "The glory of this present house will be greater than the glory of the former house" says the Lord Almighty "and in this place I will grant peace", declares the Lord Almighty' (2: 9). 'From this day on I will bless you' (2: 19).

As a result of this, a charitable trust was established at the beginning of 2004 to oversee the work. The dilapidated old gospel hall building was donated to the trust. We then had plans drawn and applied for the planning permission and building warrants—a process which took two years! However, the time was put to good use as we set about 'Casting the Vision' to Christian friends, and renovating the part of the old building which was to be retained. Our original intention was to do as much as possible of the building work 'in house', to try and keep costs down, but we soon realised that the project was going to be much too big for that, and so tenders were sent out to local building contractors. As the quotes came back, it began to dawn on us that the cost of the project to build a house fit for the Lord was going to be much more than we originally anticipated—in fact by five times!

At this stage we decided that we would not become distracted by fundraising activity. We knew that the vision for this work had come from the Lord, and so we trusted that he would provide the means for it to happen. Ever since then, we have been amazed and humbled at the provision of the Lord again and again, and at the very sacrificial giving of the Lord's people. When the builder began the work, we didn't know where the money was coming from, yet at the end of the work all the bills were paid and all the equipment we needed was purchased. What surprised me most was that I never lost a night's sleep during the whole period!

At Easter 2006, Vee and I stood at the site as the builders began the demolition work. I said to my amazing, longsuffering wife that the old building had served its day and generation well. Vee immediately responded, 'And now there is going to be a new building that is fit for the Lord and to serve a new generation'.

By the end of 2006, the builders had completed the new building, and a team of excited volunteers set about decorating, laying floors and equipping what would become 'The Living Rooms Christian Centre'.

During this 'start-up' phase, we discovered an important lesson, that we were also engaging in spiritual warfare. Satan began to manifest himself in many guises, from smooth-talking serpent to roaring lion. Again and again, we have watched in awe as the Lord has answered prayer, and battles have been won. The Lord was teaching us that prayer must be at the heart of the ministry, and be the springboard for all that we do.

We were finally able to open The Living Rooms Christian Centre in May 2007. To mark the occasion, we organised a family event for the afternoon and hired in a variety of bouncy castles. The morning was very damp and misty, but the skies cleared at lunchtime and families began to flood into the centre—eager to find out what was happening in this new building! During the afternoon we released a pair of white doves—acknowledging our thankfulness to the Lord for his goodness and provision, and our dependence on the presence and power of his Spirit in the future.

Our main object is to reach out to the unchurched with the Good News about Jesus and the love of God, and then to nurture Christians to become fully devoted followers of Christ. To help us fulfill the first part of the vision, the Lord planted into Vee's heart that we must have a coffee shop. So in July 2007 The Living Rooms Coffee Shop opened to the public.

Before The Living Rooms was complete, we began to notice that tradesmen, building control officers, and others who had reason to visit the site would often comment 'there is something different about this place' or 'there is a peace here'. When we opened the Coffee Shop, we realised that customers continued to make similar comments. So we were able to tell them that 'God is here in this place'. Others wanted to know where the money had come from to build the Centre. We were able to tell them that we had trusted God to provide, and he had, for all the bills were paid. This led to lots of very interesting opportunities for discussion.

Our aim is to do everything for the glory of God, which includes the food and drink that we serve in the Coffee Shop. Each day starts with devotions, and all the stresses and anxieties and cares are left outside the door, to allow the Lord to have freedom to do his work. The Lord has blessed us with a small but amazingly passionate team of people who volunteered to clean toilets, floors, cook in the kitchen, bake, serve in the Coffee Shop and run the office. We also place an emphasis on being 'family friendly'.

The result was that the numbers of people coming began to grow to the extent that we very quickly opened a second 'overflow room'.

Weekly prayer nights, a youth group and Sunday evening worship services soon became a part of life at The Living Rooms, and it became apparent that

God was touching people's lives in exciting ways. As more Christians were discovering the importance of having an intimate relationship with the Lord, 24-hour prayer events began to be held every other month. Customers who were unchurched began to place prayer cards in our prayer box and the intercessory prayer ministry began to grow.

During 2008 we realised that several of the ladies who were our regular customers were expecting babies. One of the mums even did her pregnancy test at The Living Rooms and announced the good news to the staff! Vee saw this as an outreach opportunity, so we invited all those families with new babies to a service of thanksgiving and blessing—and they all came. From that initiative flowed our monthly family Café Church service. Families come into an environment which they are familiar and comfortable with, and we have complete freedom to present the gospel to them in a fun and contemporary way.

We held our first Alpha Course in 2010—a lunchtime course. Most of the people who came had been regular customers since we opened the Coffee Shop in 2007. Some had even gone on to become volunteers. After a few weeks, we asked them why they had decided to come to the Alpha Course. They told us that they had been very sceptical of Christianity before they started visiting Living Rooms, but after watching our lives for two years they knew that our faith was real and wanted to find out more! We were overjoyed and so thankful to the Lord for His protection and blessing.

We have built a good relationship with the local Social Work Department who regularly use our facilities. We have been able to help individuals and families during times of difficulty with regular free meals, as well as giving emotional and pastoral care. We have also helped some single parent families to enable them to go on holiday. We organise one-off events, e.g., free Christmas lunch for regulars, picnics, family outings during holidays, ladies nights, etc.

What have we learned so far? Too much to record right now, but let me give some examples.

- An authentic call and vision from the Lord will carry you through the difficult times
- A consistent, God-honouring, Christ-like life is so important, as we are the book which the unchurched read
- We need to be willing to be flexible, and change, as the Lord leads us out of our comfort zone, to do his 'new thing'
- It is essential to have a core team of leaders and volunteers who have

'caught the vision', and who will also be bold and sacrificial in serving the Lord and leading others to Christ.

And some of the challenges along the way?
- We have been seen as a cult, or a threat by other churches
- Having the ability to break through the set-backs, disappointments, and emotional and physical exhaustion of a long-term ministry
- Not having sufficient labourers, particularly in a rural ministry
- Keeping the vision fresh! Encouraging creativity and freedom to allow the ministry to grow and develop into a sustainable Church plant

CHAPTER 24

Purpose-driven style— Forest of Dean Community Church, Cinderford

Tim Cracknell

As I neared my late 30's, God began to cause havoc in my life! I thought that I would be a dairy farmer until I retired, using my spare time to serve the Lord whenever I could. Now God was calling me to turn that on its head and make my Christian service my primary commitment and allow the farmer in me to take a backseat. That was quite a change both for myself and my wife! Church is my passion—to see growing, healthy churches. God was calling me to step out into the unknown world of church planting in the Forest of Dean, an area often described as a 'graveyard for preachers and pastors'. True, there are many churches in the Forest of Dean, but sadly most are in serious, if not terminal, decline. How could new spiritual life be brought to this region?

Between us, my wife and I had a good range of skills and experience which would be helpful in starting a new church, but we didn't really know anyone personally who had successfully planted a thriving church. The first thing we did after being commissioned by our home church to this task was to spend several months seeking out and studying growing churches and plants of all denominations. Here, we learnt many vital lessons which were to stand us in good stead for the next phase of our journey. The number-one lesson was that God is still building his church in the UK; people are still interested in knowing God; but planting is a messy business and not for the faint-hearted! We also realised that we would need some way of keeping ourselves on track. Church planting is full of people who start well, but who soon get discouraged and drift away from their original calling. How were we to both start and then maintain the church on God's course of health and growth?

This for us is where a visit to Rick Warren's famous Saddleback Church in USA made such a difference. During my stay there, I was taught about the importance of balance and staying faithful to the *Acts* 2 fundamentals for the church, as I moved into church planting. In nature, all healthy things grow and are fruitful. As a farmer, I know full well the importance of this. In both church planting and church life in general, growth springs out of health. How do we know that we are healthy? *Acts* 2 lays down the measuring stick for us in this. To ask the question, 'How is our plant doing in regard to these five key areas: worship, fellowship, discipleship, service and evangelism?' Most churches do well in one or two of these, depending on the elders' particular gifts and interests. But it is hard to stay focused on giving equal attention to all five continually. What 'Purpose-Driven' has done for us as a church is to give us a simple tool through which we can evaluate our balance, which leads to health, and then, as God graciously gives, to growth. 'Purpose-driven' is no magic formula or special blueprint for success; it is just a way of clearly flagging up to the leadership each week what is really important. It forces us to ask the question, are we giving focused attention to ALL FIVE areas in a balanced way? Or are we neglecting one or more of these key areas? I find that it is so easy to drift, and become distracted by pressing pastoral issues or demands, that these five fundamentals can so easily be overlooked. And once that happens, we are on the slippery slope to becoming stagnant and unhealthy.

Back to our story. Initially we gathered together a small nucleus of about 15 people in Cinderford, Gloucestershire. They comprised the elderly ladies from the gospel hall that had closed and another family that had an interest in the church, together with ourselves. For nine months, we ran a low-key morning service aimed at drawing out like-minded people and building the core group. It also gave us a chance to make our biggest mistakes when there were not too many people around and they were very forgiving! When this group had grown to over 30 regulars, we launched the Forest of Dean Community Church with much publicity spending every penny we could muster on newspaper advertising, leaflets and local radio.

The focus for the launch was a programme called '40 Days of Purpose'. This proved very effective and on the launch Sunday over 90 turned up. Many came thinking they would be there for a one-off Sunday, but got hooked on the 40 Days material and are still with us four years later! When the dust had settled, we had a church of over 50 regular Sunday morning attenders. This was made up of three groups. The biggest percentage were Christians who had given up on church often years ago and decided to give it one last try. The second group were non-Christians who were actively seeking Christ. The third group were Christians who were new to the area. We actively discouraged transfer growth and thankfully saw very little of it.

The challenge for us, then, was to develop this unusual mix of people which included six different nationalities, and a number of special needs, into a Christ-centred church that would continue to be an effective light in the community around us. We were also in the process of refurbishing the old 'Gospel Hall' building which we had inherited and which desperately needed modernizing. So we were working on many fronts. What followed was an exciting and chaotic year of people coming back to God, with all their baggage, some coming to faith in Christ for the first time, quite a few joyful baptisms and the excitement of seeing the Lord provide over £100,000 to enable the building to be refurbished.

One piece of advice that we were very grateful to receive from another church planter was 'don't appoint elders before you have been going 2 years'. As we grew, the pressure was on to appoint an eldership team. With this advice in mind, we were able to take our time, to see people working under pressure, and also to take the time to help people discover what their spiritual gifts were, before diving in and appointing elders. We found God sent us just what we needed to take us forward at this fragile stage—men who were clearly gifted in servant leadership and well equipped in the Word of God.

People often ask what brings newcomers in? The answer is quite simple. People! When Christians are fired up and seeing God at work in their lives, they get excited and share the good news with their friends. We have seen God at work in many wonderful ways. A divorcé came along and his ex-wife saw the difference that God was making in his life, to the extent that five years on from their divorce, they re-married and are now key members of the church. A man who was far from God and dying from cancer trusted Christ twenty-three days before he died, and the change in his attitudes impacted all his relationships before his death in a powerful way. A Filipino who came along from the beginning, because he enjoyed the chance to play his trumpet in the church band, trusted Christ a couple years later as he got into God's word for himself. He has led many of his friends and family to faith since then. I get very disappointed when we have two Sundays in a row without any new people coming along. We expect to see new people each week to our main Sunday service and plan for it. After all, we are in the faith business.

Three years after our launch, our tiny little church building was 90% full most weeks. All the studies on church growth tell us that at that stage, if we don't make more space, we will plateau and eventually go into numerical decline. So the tough decision to move the main Sunday service to a local school was taken. It took almost a year of much prayerful work to readjust. We now have a situation where we have established a highly-visible presence at the school, which is part of the Sports Centre. Then, during the week we are able to use the old church building as a centre for our activities, attracting many more people and connecting us to the community in meaningful ways. This pleases us, as we are making good use of the building, while benefiting from not having to spend more money on building bigger premises.

As a 'Community Church', we had a challenge to live up to our name: to be a church that is active in the community. Following the success of the '40 days of Purpose' campaign, we followed it up with '40 Days of community'. Through the nine projects, we gained greater credibility in the town and a reputation for a church of action and not just the 'religious stuff!' We have now built these projects into our regular church life, engaging in painting at a day care centre and local schools, pointing up and relaying patio stones at school, practical building and gardening work in homes of needy families in town. We find the church love doing these things and we have gained the confidence of the community as a result. After all, as the saying goes, 'people don't care how much we know until they know how much we care.'

Before we launched the church, we did a survey of the town to find out why most people don't go to Church. The four main reasons were:

1. Church is boring.

2. Church is not relevant any more

3. Church is old-fashioned

4. Church is not worth making a priority for.

This gave us the challenge of setting up a new church that was not boring, old-fashioned or outdated, but stayed true to God's living and timeless word.

Interestingly, we discovered that music was a key reason why non-Church goers thought it was old fashioned and boring. Pipe organs were not a draw for most any more. In our area, most like music with a beat to it. After starting with 11- and 13-year olds accompanying me on my guitar, we have worked hard to develop a music team. Now the Lord has blessed us with a great team of gifted musicians. This has not happened by accident and many hours of patient pastoral work have been necessary to facilitate this. Thankfully, we are now reaping the fruit of this investment and the music is one of the big reasons new people join our church.

Rapid growth inevitably brings with it huge pastoral issues. Church is all about God and people. People have very many complex problems in life to deal with. It is therefore natural that, when we teach that Jesus is the answer, we find people calling on the church for help. This is an important part of what we do, but it is where being purpose-driven helps us not to get blown off track. Well, not for too long anyway. To this end 'Celebrate Recovery' is in our view an essential for all church plants. It is a Christ-centred recovery programme which has proven most helpful in enabling people with all sorts of hurts, habits and hang-ups to get going again in their lives without bogging us down as leaders.

Five years on from the initial start, much of my time is now spent in helping people to develop their spiritual gifts to use in service in the church and mentoring. I have never met a church that has too many leaders. We are determined to develop the people that God has sent us and hope that the next generation of leaders for all sections of the church will emerge, enabling us to impact the Forest of Dean community with the gospel more effectively in the years that lie ahead.

CHAPTER 25

A church-planting church plant— Lakeside, Brierley Hill

Andy Hodson

In 2003, I was appointed by Wall Heath Evangelical Free Church to assist them in planting a church. The Pastor at that time, Alan Burns, was burdened by the lack of new churches being started in the UK, compared to existing churches dying out. The location had already been decided by the church after prayer and consideration. This would be the Crestwood Estate, near Dudley.

One of the elders, Alan Dodd, was also heavily burdened and committed to partner with me in the work, along with Janet Shackleton, another member of Wall Heath. The church plant team was also assisted by others from time to time. Our combined experience was zero, and we had no plan at this stage as to how we would go about planting a church; we just believed that we were called. Prayer was a major part of the development stage and would continue to be throughout the project.

One of the ways that the Lord guided us in the development of Crestwood church plant was with a festival, during the summer of 2004. We made plans, contacted the council, liaised with the local community and booked the marquees, toilets and well-known Christian band. A week before the event, the open space that we had received permission to use, suddenly became a problem. Several local residents petitioned the council to stop the event, because they didn't want Christians taking over their park area. We called the church to pray;

two days before the start of the event, we were offered a new venue at the local school.

The council said we were within our rights to stay on the original location. However, we sensed the Lord's hand, and moved to the school. There we received free security and better facilities than the original site. Before this, the school had refused use of their land. God had used the local authority to change their mind. Further answers to prayer were the fact that on the eve of the mission, it rained so heavily that the original site became unusable. Only the Lord would have known that in advance. Also, the relationship we built up with the school that week led to a venue to start services.

From the festival, the church developed, slowly. We held our first service at Christmas 2004 when a small number of people joined us. A few families left other fellowships to help with the work and the church continued to grow.

In May 2005, a few new families joined us and made decisions for Christ, leading to others also being saved. By April 2006, Crestwood Church had grown to around 40 people, including children, and was commissioned as independent by Wall Heath.

In the early days of Crestwood, the church plant team had already sensed the Lord was guiding us, not just to plant a church, but churches, and a strategy was implemented as to how we could fulfill this. Several key factors had to be met: Crestwood needed to have its own full-time elder. It would need to have part of the finances to continue the planting, and would need the strength and maturity to stand without the existing church plant team, all of whom would be moving on to plant again.

By October 2008, the church had grown to around 80 regulars, the eldership had been strengthened, and discipling of new believers was under way. One of the greatest challenges was developing leaders from believers who had only been Christians for a few years; the corresponding blessing was to see the new believers absorbing the bible like sponges.

In spring 2008, after seeking the Lord in prayer, the Withymoor/Lakeside Estate was chosen for the next plant. This fitted the vision criteria of working on estates where there is no evangelical witness, and was within easy reach of the church plant team. The team, along with some of Crestwood Church, started to leaflet and visit on the estate. At the same time, Crestwood were looking to employ an elder, so that when the church plant team moved on they would have a replacement. At this time, the Rowe family had joined the church and Nigel Rowe would eventually become that new full-time worker at Crestwood.

Financially, it was a tough time. I joined the Church Planting Initiative (CPI) in September 2008 and was pledged a very generous gift, which certainly built our faith. However, after a few months, CPI suffered, like many ministries, a massive fall in their support and the pledge level was halved. This was a very testing time, as Crestwood had stepped out in faith to employ the new elder, while still supporting me in partnership with CPI.

When you take a step back, you can see the hand of God in it. If the finance from CPI had not been pledged at the original amount, would the church have had the faith to step out with such a massive shortfall forecast for the end of the year? Throughout the church planting process, we have always viewed finance from this perspective: God gives the vision; this becomes our aim; we ask whether we have the money to fulfil it; the answer is, "No"! We pray and wait for God to confirm the vision. On every occasion, the Lord has given us an encouragement, a lump sum, a new giving family, outside support, which has never covered the missing amount, but has significantly showed us that the Lord is with us. Each time we have stepped out, and believed for the rest, he has shown his grace and mercy to us and met our need.

As a church plant team, we want to operate in faith. We prepare a general budget of what we need for the work we believe we should do, and as we step out, the Lord provides. If this was a business, it would be foolishness. But we have a mighty God.

The first service at Lakeside was Christmas 2008. We held this in the local primary school. After Christmas, we met weekly on Sunday afternoons until July. This was a strange time; on one hand, it was great to see a small testimony developing on the estate, but it was also a massive drain on the team, as most of us were still heavily involved with Crestwood. For me personally, it was a difficult time as a family. We had three small children. The average Sunday started at 8:30 am to set up Crestwood, now in a community centre, leaving at 1 pm after taking down the equipment, and then at 3 pm starting all over again with Lakeside until 5:30 pm, and then back at Crestwood in the evening. By July, we felt as though we couldn't put the required effort into both Crestwood and Lakeside, and so we prayed about moving the Lakeside service to the morning. During the build-up to this, various roles were being filled, but there was still a massive amount to hand over. This was a difficult time for the leadership, as we were stretched to the limit and found that, even though it was the right time to move Lakeside to the morning, the handover could have been better prepared. Lessons have been learnt and noted for future church plants.

One of the lessons is the financial burden on such a young church. The aim in the future would be to gather support specifically for the next plant, so that it would not all fall on so few. Our aim is to see the church plant team funded separately from the church, so that the new church can develop and train leaders at a very early stage. One of the strains of planting this time was that, because none of the original church plant team stayed with the first church; training a leadership team from the start, or having someone within the team who would remain, would bring greater stability.

During 2009, our elders meetings were packed with church matters that related to Crestwood and Lakeside. There was a heavy burden on the eldership, especially as Lakeside began to grow, and more issues were revealed among people in need from the estate.

From July 2009-May 2010, the growth of Lakeside was slower than it had been with Crestwood. Doubt and frustration crept in and threatened to derail us. Sometimes we had little to show for our labours, even though a lot had been done. Throughout this process we persevered in faith, and when at times we felt like giving up, the Lord would bless us in practical ways and through his word.

It was difficult to motivate each other during this time, but the Lord gave us the grace to find a way, as we relied on him. When the church plant did turn around, it wasn't because of anything that we had done, but more a recognition that the Lord, not us, would build his church. We were to stop worrying and trust him. In April 2010, the church started to grow and we saw new faces attending every Sunday for 2 months; as a result the church doubled. Most of the new people were unchurched, or believers who had not been attending church regularly. It was during this time that Chris and Foluso Enwerem, missionaries with European Christian Mission (ECM), made plans to come and work with us.

As Lakeside grew and Crestwood adjusted to change, with the church plant team having less involvement, the still-young church was again stretched. However, in answer to prayer, believers who lived locally came to support Crestwood, bringing more maturity.

In July 2010, the need for separate leadership teams at Lakeside and Crestwood became apparent. The need for each to work with those people that the Lord had given us to serve became our priority. So in October 2010, Lakeside became an independent church from Crestwood. Independence signifies that both churches are seeking the Lord for their own finances, their own local ministry and their own pastoral care, but the aim is to continue to work together in declaring Christ to the communities around us and to plant new churches together in the future. We have learnt many lessons along the way, which can be carried forward to future plants. It is incredible what the Lord has done, with our little experience and small resources. All we had was a willing heart to serve and step out in faith, and the Lord graciously did the rest.

Church planting is a potential disaster for a young church; it has endless problems and opportunities for failure. Some things we planned never worked. If you are not prepared to see failure at times, don't start, but if you can accept that we might fail but the Lord will not, and he will bring about the increase in his way and time, then the joy and refreshment of serving the Lord far outweighs anything else that may get in the way. Personality will not build a church, only faith and dependence on the Lord. Our aim is to keep listening and waiting on the Lord for his timing, in order to continue his vision of church planting.

CHAPTER 26

Responding radically to decline— Strathaven Evangelical Church

Andrew Lacey

Strathaven is a market town of some 8,000 people, 25 miles to the south east of Glasgow. The original industry of weaving has died away, and most people in the town now work in the larger towns of the Central Belt of Scotland. Like many smaller Scottish towns, it has had a long history of active churches and there are many interesting sites and memorials around the area to the Covenanters of the seventeenth century.

These active churches included a Gospel Hall established in the 1870s. We still have in our possession the descriptions of the first converts and baptisms in the Avon Water. In those early days, rapid growth allowed a substantial and very attractive Gospel Hall to be erected very close to the centre of the town.

Despite being an active and innovative assembly over many years, a steady loss of numbers during the 1970s and 80s resulted in significant decline. Much to the credit of the elders and members of that time, a very proactive decision was taken. Rather than allowing the assembly to die, a number of other Christians were contacted. The elders were aware that these Christians travelled from their homes in Strathaven to various churches of different denominations in nearby towns. These folk were very directly asked if they would meet to discuss revitalising the work in Strathaven. This was a bold move, and was made in the full knowledge that these discussions would likely result in the putting aside of deeply-held traditions.

Several of those contacted agreed to meet, and it was decided first to spend time in prayer seeking the will of God. This was the birth of Strathaven Evangelical Fellowship in autumn 1989. An 'ad hoc' committee was formed of several elders from the Gospel Hall and others interested in moving forward. Following a series of monthly prayer meetings, it was agreed to arrange a series of mid-week evening teaching services on core aspects of the Christian faith in spring of 1990.

Given the wide denominational mix of those attending, it was felt that a very clear 'Statement of Faith' needed to be developed and a constitution put together that gave a clear sense of structure and direction to the new fellowship that was now being considered. Two smaller working parties were set up to explore these aspects, and the resultant proposals were discussed and approved in the months that followed. These documents reflected mainstream evangelical doctrines, and amalgamated a mixture of Baptist, Brethren and Federation of Independent Evangelical Churches practices. Again, it is a measure of the grace that was shown by the Strathaven assembly that they recognised early on in this process the need for the assembly to close down to allow this new and very different church to rise. A first Sunday morning service was planned for autumn of 1990. Although this was technically a 'trial' service, the momentum now was very much towards the creation of a completely new church.

That morning, an embryo church gathered, and we recall how exciting it was to see this meeting composed of all different ages, social classes and backgrounds. We were witnessing the calling out of Christians from the town, with a sense of God's leading to join together. At this initial service, a Baptist Pastor, Alex Hardie, spoke to us of the four friends who brought their paralysed friend to Jesus—going to the time, effort and trouble of taking the roof off the house! And this, he encouraged us, was a focus that should characterise us as a fellowship—friends, taking time, trouble and effort to bring needy friends to Jesus.

The sense of call was very strong, and further monthly Sunday meetings concluded the year. As we moved towards the formal start of the church, it was agreed that those who wished to join the church should consider the now-agreed Statement of Faith and Constitution, and sign a book if they wished to take on the responsibility of membership. The working title of 'Strathaven Evangelical Church' was adopted, and the assembly which was closing offered to transfer title for the 100-year old building to the new church—a very generous and practical endorsement.

Strathaven Evangelical Church had its first formal meeting in the first Sunday of January, 1991. There were 24 members, and these were exciting times, as the church grew rapidly. The ad-hoc committee was replaced by formally-elected elders and deacons, and further work was done to establish the role and responsibilities of a Pastor-Teacher. This provision was built into the constitutional bricks of the church from the beginning. In a fairly short number of years, numbers rose to 60 members, and a major building extension was required, this being completed in 1997. Much of this growth was by transference, as is often the case when new churches are established.

In the years following, the church saw further significant growth to just over 90 members. This resulted in consideration of church planting or seeking larger premises. However, two difficult times resulted in numbers dropping back significantly.

One issue related to a difference of emphasis over the exercise of 'charismatic' gifts within the public worship of the church. There were a number who sought liberty to express these gifts, and this resulted in some tension. The eldership at that time felt it important to set down their position, confirming the consistent practice of the fellowship over previous years. By mutual consent, a number left in 2001 to start an Assemblies of God church in the town. 'Outreach Community Church' has prospered, and there continues to be good relations between the two churches.

Secondly, an attempt to appoint a full-time pastor-teacher in 2005 failed by a narrow margin, and the resulting fall-out from this was very damaging, resulting in a significant fall in membership. By the grace of God, the fellowship worked through these difficult days, and has emerged perhaps more united in purpose and vision than previously. As I write, the church has just celebrated twenty years of witness, has a membership of 62, and has appointed their first full-time Pastor-Teacher, David Childs. We have always accepted that a major weakness of the fellowship was lack of pastoral care, given that the elders have generally been in full-time employment. We look to God for his blessing on this investment in his people and those who are seeking him.

. . . .

Strathaven was not a church plant in the true sense of the phrase. Rather, it was the re-birth of an existing work in a more contemporary 'wineskin'. But there are several significant lessons to note.

First, those involved in the original vision had a very clear sense of the 'call' to evangelical witness in the town, and this call has managed to transcend some of the traditional lines of denominational demarcation. To this day, Strathaven retains a slightly quirky independence in matters of services and practices that reflects aspects from many differing traditions. One major benefit has been the flexibility to respond quickly to opportunities when they arise. 'Tradition' does, of course, have a place in Strathaven—but it tends not to have the over-riding veto that can emerge in church life.

Secondly, we have maintained a formal 'independence', despite a number of discussions both at eldership and a wider church level of the benefits of formally affiliating to inter-church bodies. While such an independent approach has suited us, it is not right for every context. There have been times when we have had to 're-invent the wheel', and at times we have felt ourselves to be somewhat isolated. However, there have been significant benefits when trying to coalesce into one fellowship in a small town those from many differing backgrounds and viewpoints. Despite not being a member of a recognised network or denomination, we are grateful to those from other fellowships who, over the years, who have offered support, advice and prayer.

Thirdly, there has been a very clear vision of the 'main things' that were seen to characterise a church: the centrality of Christ; the teaching of the Word; reaching out to the community and close fellowship; and friendship and respect for others. This has worked itself out in close working relationships with other churches in the town. One of the very positive aspects of Christian work in our town has been the close co-operation of churches under the 'Hope' banner. This has resulted in events being carried through that would be beyond our resources to stage. But, in partnership with the other churches, it has been possible to embark on some exciting projects.

Finally, one clear characteristic of this church over the years has been a strong community engagement. From the annual participation in the 'Raft Race' for Gala Day (in our first year, the church suffered the indignity of being disqualified when our 'Noah's Ark' banner was adjudicated to be an illegal sail!) to the ASK Bus which served the late-night kids on the street, we have sought to share in the life of the community. As a result of Coffee & Chat, toddlers groups, and football training, we continue to make an impact at multiple levels in the town, and we look forward in the years ahead to seeing positive results as we continue with Christianity Explored and other outreach efforts to win these friends as converts for the King.

Strathaven is far from being a perfect church. But it currently represents some positive characteristics of 'New Testament' churches that bode well for the future, in the grace of God. We look forward with anticipation to the next chapters as Christ continues to build his Church in our small Scottish country town.

CHAPTER 27

The life and death of a church plant— The 145 Church, Hornsey, North London

Neil Summerton

Our natural pre-supposition tends to be that local churches have a beginning—they are planted—but they should never have an end. There is support for that idea in John's prophetic words to the seven churches in *Revelation*. The Lord of the churches' desire is that the lampstand of the particular fellowship should remain in place; it is in the hands of the fellowship itself whether it does so or not. ('If you do not repent, I will come to you and remove your lampstand from its place' (*Rev.* 2: 5).)

If we look across church history, the reality is that many local churches no longer exist. Often this is the responsibility of a particular generation, particularly leaders, in the local church; the warnings of the Lord of the church are either not heard or not heeded. Churches are also extirpated by persecution or genocide, as were the churches of North Africa in the post-Roman era and the young Brethren assemblies of the western Ukraine in the 1930s and 1940s, to take only two widely-differing examples. And some cultural and practical environments are more hostile for churches than others.

The experience of church planting is that sometimes particular efforts are not successful, despite the best exertions of those involved—no viable church is formed at all, or only one so fragile that, like some infants, it does not survive long. This can be demonstrated by many cases in the wave of church-planting that was initiated in Britain from 1985 onwards. It was very probably so in the early church: churches survived in Ephesus and Rome, but did every house-church, even among those mentioned in the New Testament? And mission history would show that this was the case as well. As Paul said, church planters and builders need to be expert and 'each one should be careful how he builds' (*1 Cor.* 3: 10 onwards), and the test may come well before that of final judgment to which the apostle refers.

The 145 Church in Crouch End in inner north London proved to be a shooting star, a flare. It illuminated the sky briefly and notably for a decade, but quickly fell to the ground. While it existed, it achieved some notable things. Its legacy lives on, in church planting elsewhere in London, in missions and development work in Lebanon, Rwanda and other countries, and in Christian life in the Wellington area of New Zealand, through people who were deeply influenced by it. Indeed, only when the final book is opened will it, as with all work for Christ, become clear just exactly what this church plant achieved.

Its story can be summarised briefly enough. It is the lessons that can be drawn which may be of greater interest.

The 145 Church had its origins in Cholmeley Evangelical Church (Cholmeley Hall of earlier years), whose building is located in Archway Road in Highgate, a mile or so to the west of Crouch End. Cholmeley Hall was itself a typical Brethren church plant of 1880s, formed under the influence of Clapton Hall in Stoke Newington, by Brethren who moved to the burgeoning suburbs of Highgate and Crouch End in the last two decades of the nineteenth century. In the early part of the twentieth century, it was a powerful and typical upper-crust English Brethren church, which itself engaged in church-planting, notably through the so-called 'Iron-Room' which became in due course Wilton Hall/Chapel in Muswell Hill.

By 1960, Cholmeley was beginning to be affected by the rapid social change being experienced by inner north London. The congregation was increasingly scattered, mainly under the influence of high property prices on younger couples. Turnover of membership was increasing, especially as younger couples chose not to remain in London and take the chance of state education there for their children. After a very sharp fall in membership in the 1970s associated with a change in the generation of leadership of the church, the 1980s saw a new resurgence, traceable in part to experiments with full-time leadership and more particularly thanks to the spiritual influence of Spring Harvest. By late in the 1980s, numbers were around the 160 mark, nearly a third of whom were between the ages of 15 and 20.

This growth was not the only sign of life in the church. Gerald West and I among the leaders were particularly concerned about the growing weakness of our kind of church in the inner London area. In particular, we believed that the Lord was encouraging us to reach out and encourage Wilton Chapel and Parkhill Chapel (the former Malden Hall) in South Hampstead. In conjunction with Gordon Holloway, then the Chief Executive of the Shaftesbury Society, who was also concerned to encourage church planting and growth in inner London, we had discussions with leaders of both these fellowships, and a full-time leader was identified to assist Parkhill Chapel. (That did not have the results hoped for and in the mid-1990s it was arranged that the Stable, a Charismatic church plant in a former Brethren building in High Barnet, should seek to plant at Fleet Road—a venture which failed after some ten years and the property has now been sold. Wilton Chapel also dwindled over time and arranged that St James's Anglican Church in Muswell Hill should attempt to re-plant in their building.) These attempts at church planting and resuscitation were part of the experience which led Gerald West to propose to Stewardship and others towards the end of the 1990s that the Church Planting Initiative should be established.

Secondly, it was clear that Cholmeley's building on Archway Road, which was approaching its centenary, would need either major refurbishment or reconstruction—it had been built so that it could be used alternatively as a drill hall, should that church planting venture of the 1890s fail! We looked for alternative sites but found none, and decided that, despite the inconveniences of location on Archway Road, the Lord was leading us to rebuild in situ and building work began in 1986. It was this decision which led more or less directly to The 145 Church. For it was essential to find alternative meeting space for Cholmeley while the new building was in construction. We approached the leaders of Park Road Hall in Crouch End, to ask if we could use their premises on Sunday afternoon for our main church meeting of the week. Their surprising response was that their fellowship would, in effect, take a holiday and the Cholmeley fellowship could use the space, full-time, provided that it would meet all outgoings on the building.

For a small, weak and elderly fellowship to cease to meet is a risky proposal, of course. Within a very few months, they decided that their hibernation would be permanent and the Park Road trustees agreed that, provided that Cholmeley was prepared to make in effect a payment to Echoes of Service of £30,000, they would transfer the hall and next door house to the Cholmeley trustees. Cholmeley was now rebuilding on Archway Road and had acquired these extra premises in Crouch End—projects entailing a capital expenditure of over £700,000 in the currency of the day.

The question was, what should the church do with Park Road, once the congregation moved back to the new premises in Archway Road, which were opened in spring 1989? Our first plan was to establish some community family work in Crouch End, using Park Road Hall as a base. Chrissie Hayman who had been associated with Cholmeley for a few years was just completing the year's course at the GLO mission centre, as it then was, in Motherwell. She had done community children's work with the Müller Foundation in Weston super Mare and had then moved on to similar secular work in north London. So it was easy for us to ask her if the church could support her to start some children's work based on Park Road Hall. We had not fully taken the measure of our woman! Though she was scarcely 22 when she began working with us, within a year or two there was a full-blown, full-time family centre operating in Park Road Hall, with parent and toddler sessions, baby groups, and pre-school sessions operating throughout the week. Such was its success that within a short time both Chrissie and we were asking ourselves what the next steps were, in particular should we not be adding a spiritual dimension to this work in some way? The answer was facilitated by the fact that we had agreed that the house adjacent to Park Road Hall should be occupied by a young couple who were members of Cholmeley, so as to help the completion of a Ph.D. thesis and to encourage the Cholmeley camps work[1] which had restarted in 1987.

By early in 1991, we had agreed that there would be a worship meeting each Sunday at Park Road Hall; it was to be aimed particularly at reaching the users of the family centre. Here, there was some uncertainty: the elders were inclined to think of it as an outreach from the parent church; those of us involved in the work saw ourselves from the beginning as aiming at church planting. Be that as it may, the work was funded in the first place by the parent church and remained so until the end of the 1990s. From the beginning, it had a leadership

---

1   Now, since 2004, the work of the Fleet Camps Trust.

team of four including myself as the link with the eldership of the parent church and Chrissie's line-manager. Three of the four were financially supported by the parent church.[2]

We began this spiritual work with a small group of about 10 people, including the leadership team (this was neither the 'normal' model across the world of planting by a couple and one or two other friends, nor the model of shearing off 50 or 100 people from an existing fellowship to form the basis of a new local church). There was an older lady, the one former member of the Park Road assembly who continued with us, a teacher who had spent endless hours in prayer and Sunday school teaching there, and who continued in the church plant until the last. There was my wife and I in our early fifties, and the rest were under 30. Frankly, we were feeling our way forward. (We began, foolishly, by sitting in a circle in our Sunday morning meeting, until we realised quite quickly that that made newcomers feel very embarrassed and self-conscious—they needed to be able to slip quietly into the back or side of the gathering.)

In fact, the group grew quite rapidly, to a peak in about 1997 of some 80 adults, for a number of reasons. First, early on, a Congolese political exile, who had been re-housed just along the road, came in with her seven children: she more or less doubled our numbers on the spot (and is still associated with Cholmeley). She was a Pentecostal and we were enriched by her worship and prayer in French. We had both effective worship leaders and instrumentalists to support them—I have claimed that what we did was to devise a form of renewed Brethren worship, led but cultivating throughout spontaneous contributions from the congregation (this reflected the Brethren roots of the leadership team). We remained committed to lively and serious bible teaching, but this style of worship was a key factor in growth. We also grew because the plant attracted a number—at one time, as many as 10—younger people who were in the UK from New Zealand on their Overseas Experience (none of these had a Brethren background, I believe). More problematically, a key factor was that the plant drained younger people out of the parent congregation to a significant extent, because they saw in the plant a greater willingness to be radical in adapting church practice to the needs of time and place. Some elders of the parent church had been anxious about this possible effect, and they were right. It troubled

---

2 At the time, I was significantly otherwise engaged at the Department of the Environment, first trying vainly to make the poll tax stick and then trying to make the privatised water system work smoothly.

me, but I knew that, whether or not the plant had existed, the parent church would be unlikely to hold the young people concerned: they would drift away elsewhere in any case, and it was better that they should find a spiritual home in an associated congregation. And, of course, being young, some quickly moved off into to higher education elsewhere in the country, in many cases and in the usual way never to return.

We saw only limited success in conversions among those from the neighbourhood whom we were in touch with in the family centre. There were a few, but it was hard work which required patient bridge-building over a long period. For some, the process of challenging their trendy north London philosophical assumptions took time (I can think of one person in particular who would stop coming whenever anything was said which did not fit with such assumptions—particularly on sin and judgment, but who would then drift back as if mesmerised by the candle). There was also a tendency to see converts move off elsewhere, almost as soon as they were converted, whether to the USA or Japan—these days any church in inner London is an international church. Almost our first convert (for whom we were a final link in the divine chain) promptly returned home to Japan. For the most part, however, the response of the centre's clients, despite inventiveness in outreach, was resistance to the gospel, much of it scarcely conscious: they were users of services which advantaged them and which they did not see any obligation to contribute to financially, let alone any obligation to stop to ask why all this effort, much of it voluntary and none of it at public expense[3], was being expended. There was sometimes admiration of what was seen as our public-spiritedness, even our generosity, but they carefully airbrushed out its Christian motivation. This is of course a very common phenomenon in community development activities undertaken by churches in Europe.

The centre did benefit greatly from the input from a series of Careforce and similar workers. It was our privilege to make a spiritual input into their lives at a critical stage and some even remained as members of the church.

It will readily be seen that the plant was largely a youth church. In the middle of the 1990s, almost all its members were under 30, many unmarried. This had its advantages: energy, of course; a willingness to do things differently; a willingness to be undaunted by risk and challenge; and a readiness to give

---

3   At no time did we accept public funds for the work of the family centre or the church, on the grounds that we wished to be free from the power of the purse in doing the work.

time to the church plant (the fact that the building was a full-time family centre meant that it could become their common room—if there was time on your hands, where better than to spend it than with like-minded Christian friends at Park Road?). The character of the church was well-suited to Crouch End, a young café society, where many of those we were seeking to reach were younger (in their case, often in unconventional relationships, which were in themselves a significant challenge to their becoming Christians). There were downsides as well of being such a young church: of course, necessary immaturity; but also the fact that, to anyone over 35, the church could seem like a spiritual Olympic training camp, a place where only dedicated high-grade performers had a place—there were quite a number of older people who liked what they saw, but who after a while concluded that they did not fit and sought fellowship elsewhere.

There were inevitably tensions with the parent church, some of them understandable given that they were so generously funding the operation. The idea of planting a separate church, rather than simply pursuing an outreach, was disturbing. The name that was selected was said to be naff—though to me the idea of using the number of the building, rather than the name of the street, seemed nicely traditional, as well as inventive. The parent was anxious to guide, even control, and sometimes prohibit. The plant thought that they were the people on the ground and therefore best placed to decide what was appropriate. There were also difficulties for the plant arising from serious leadership tensions within the parent church. It was eventually thought that these tensions could only be eased by establishing the plant as an entirely separate church as from 1 April 1998.

If the plant was strong enough for this to happen, why was it that, within five years, the decision was taken that the plant was no longer viable and that it should be brought to an end? Put simply, the answers lay in matters of leadership.

First, there was, even at the point of greatest success, a particular difficulty about which I still need to be suitably vague. But it had a serious impact, causing some key members of the church to think that they were not safe in the hands of the collective leadership of the church plant—when the fact was that the other leaders of the plant were completely unaware of a problem of which the critics themselves were aware.

More generally, the plant simply ran out of leadership and other burden-bearers. This was a reflection of the fact that for the most part they were young and still at the stage of life when the Lord was calling them on to other things. Thus New Zealanders returned home after their overseas experience. A key person was called to plant in east London (and from there to work in Lebanon). Chrissie after 14 years of remarkable work felt the call of God to community development work in Rwanda, where she is having a real impact. The key motivational leader from the early stages of the plant also moved to work in Lebanon. A couple of great talent went abroad in secular development work, which was always their intention. A number of other couples felt obliged to move out of London. Rather unexpectedly, we found ourselves as a couple in a significant relocation. All this reflected in considerable part calls into strategic full-time service of the Lord. But a background factor was that for church leaders the heat in the kitchen is sometimes well-nigh intolerable, and it is particularly difficult for young leaders who have not experienced it before. Be that as it may, these developments created holes in the fabric of The 145 Church which simply could not be filled quickly enough. It was a bold and reasonable decision in 2003 that the church should be closed down, though a concern is that certain of the converts of the church who remain in north London have barely found satisfactory alternative fellowship. The building is now being used by the Icthus Fellowship in a further effort at church planting, as well as a home for a small Tamil-speaking fellowship.

• •

What are the main lessons of this particular church-planting experience?

First, motivational leadership was very important to the successful launch of the project and its rapid growth in the early years. It was one individual who supplied this above all, and the church found life more difficult once he was no longer on the scene. It was not the only factor in rapid growth—the overall character of the group was perhaps at least as attractive—but it was important. Not everyone found the style of the particular individual to their taste and it was fortunate that there were other leaders around to moderate it and even to pick up the pieces on occasion.

Second, supporting leadership. Church plants need motivational leadership, but more than that is needed, and they need to find ways and means in which other leadership styles (pastoral, teaching, administrative, for example) can work together with, liberate and moderate motivational leadership. Goal-orientated leaders need others around them who can minister to people's emotional needs, including scars inflicted by the goal-orientated leaders themselves! Fortunately, for most of its life the 145 Church had a wide range of leadership gift at its disposal, as well as others who were prepared to bear the burdens of creating successful church life.

Third, for quite some time, the human resources were available to *focus on planting*. This amounted to four or five people, some full-time and some part-time. Planting needs time and focus. This was possible because the parent church was ready and able to provide the *money* to support those human resources to enable them to focus on the demanding task in hand.

Fourth, flexibility, fleetness of foot, willingness to take risks, grasp opportunities and take steps of faith. We live in an age which tends to emphasise rational planning, preparation, training and the minimisation of risk—nothing, we are inclined to think, should be undertaken without these. It is true that the particular church planting activity which has been described here began over 20 years ago, when the new push towards church planting associated with the DAWN movement was still in its infancy. There was an appreciation of the need for church planting, a desire to do something new, and recognition that there was an opportunity which ought to be grasped. The particular opportunity was grasped in an environment of outward-looking concern to support neighbouring, weaker churches and plant new ones if possible. But we did not know quite what we were doing at the beginning! The opportunity to plant in Crouch End was unexpected, the by-product of searching for a temporary home for the parent church. There was much ignorance on the part of those doing the work and of the parent church about what would be entailed. It is perhaps as well that there was, or we might not have begun in the first place.

Church planting is an entrepreneurial activity. It is like launching a small business. The risks are great and those doing it can lose their shirts! The initiators have to believe that they can succeed with God's help and invest all in doing so. Nothing ventured, nothing gained. It requires a sense of call, and trust that God will bless in what he has called people to. It must also recognise that failure is a possibility. A policy of safety first will not result in the planting of churches and potential parent churches need to remember that. At the same time, there should not be disappointment or recrimination in the event of failure. It happens in gospel work, as the apostle Paul seems to have experienced in Athens, for example. Like American investors, our attitude needs to be, 'So that project failed; what's your next one?'

Fourth, relationships with and impact on a parent church were important in this case, for good and ill. They will be likely to be so in every case where a church plants out another. Even if the parent is not obliged to shed a large number of people, very likely they will be shedding some of their best leadership to the plant. There is the possibility, even the certainty, that the act of planting will weaken the parent at least initially. This is a challenge to faith and prayer on the part of the parent. It also needs to be remembered that sacrifice is the default position of Christianity.

Relationships between the plant and parent call for tolerance, tact and realism. In the case of The 145 Church it was often my role, as a continuing elder of the united operation and a member of the leadership team of the plant, to manage the relationship as diplomatically as possible, and to act as something of a buffer between the two, frankly to protect the leadership of the church plant against unreasonable expectations. As in family life, the parent is often unrealistic about the extent to which their child want or will call for their advice! And sometimes the parent is right, though not always! A lot of attention needs to be given to maintaining good, constructive relationships, if frustrating, debilitating tension is to be avoided.

Fifth, church profile. There is no doubt that The 145 Church suffered, as well as gained, from being in effect a youth church. As explained, this was a key factor in its running out of leadership, even if it offered while it existed a remarkable leadership training ground for an astonishingly wide group of people who are now bearing responsibility in all sorts of settings across the world and in the UK. The age profiles of church plants are likely to be skewed towards the younger end of the spectrum. Bold risk-taking, initiative, and willingness to do things differently are more likely to be found among younger people than older people. Just like people, many Christian congregations start young, grow older and eventually die: the trick for any local church is to create a self-perpetuating turnover from generation to generation that ensures that the church group is more than simply a particular age-cohort growing old together. If church plants are simply youth churches, special measures need to be taken to ensure their future, depending on the particular social situation in which they are found. The problem may be more manageable in a small town than it is in the inner city.

CHAPTER 28

Growth delayed— Challenge Community Church, Hereford

Martin Erwin

Early Years – Sweet and Sour…

In September 1996 a group of 7 adult Christians, 3 children and 2 infants met in an upstairs room of the local community centre to break bread together. Just twenty minutes earlier, they had said the weekly goodbye to the 30 or so children who were the Sunday school known as 'Challenge', and which had for many years been part of the outreach of the Brethren church at Barton Road in Hereford. It was the first 'official' church meeting of Challenge Community Church.

As the evangelist who had met the Barton elders a year before to ask if such a plant could have their blessing, that first Sunday I was, to my shame, away preaching elsewhere. That tension between 'itinerant' and local did not help either me or the church to gain momentum in those early days, and it is a compromise that many of us have lived with and perhaps excused.

From 1996 to 2009 the numbers attending at Challenge on a Sunday morning (our main service) fluctuated from the handful at the beginning to 60 or so. The peak of regularly around 60 was hit only over a short period of time, when we ran the '40 Days of Purpose' programme in about 2003/4.

From 1999 to 2007 we were blessed to have Andy and Claire Gibson (GLO) work with us in fellowship with the Church Planting Initiative. A good core group in the church became established and worked incredibly hard to encourage evangelism and growth, and we continued to work towards a new building project, for which we had had a fund from the very beginning.

Those were very tough years. It always seemed to be a mix of some fruit and lots of discouragements. New believers who didn't 'stick,' others who moved to more 'exciting' churches, and a growing sense of lethargy among some to engage in the project, were just some of the disappointments. All the while, we were blessed by a core group of hard-working families and leaders.

We give glory to God that during that period, seeds were sown, adults were converted, and discipleship was taking place that was all to bear fruit later in our story. Looking back, I really believe that the Lord was taking us through those tough times, in order to prepare us for what he had in store. That is always how it is—isn't it? Billy Graham is quoted as saying, 'We all yearn for the mountain top experiences, but the fruit grows in the valleys.' Without a doubt, 'God's strength is made perfect in our weakness.'

Change is in the air…

Between 2005 to 2008, a number of events took place that would shake the church from its lethargy, and awaken us to follow God's voice in a new and exciting way.

First, in 2005 I got ill. It happens, people get sick, and I am not claiming to be a special case. However, I was diagnosed eventually, with Chronic Fatigue Syndrome (or M.E.), and had to completely empty my diary for 6 months. Looking back, I know now that I had been heading for a burn-out one way or another. Something had to give, and it was my health and, with it, my ministry. God now had my full attention!

Secondly, in 2006, sitting at an elders' meeting, we were reviewing where the church had got to. We knew that we were in the doldrums, but as we wrestled, we couldn't quite put our finger on why. I remember saying that if God gave us a chance to plant the church again that I would want us to do many things differently.

Thirdly, at the end of that year, Andy and Claire took a well-earned and long planned sabbatical. On their return, they informed us that they felt clear the Lord was calling them back to Newcastle. For many in the fellowship, it was a shock. In my heart, whilst very sorry to be losing them from Hereford, I knew God was at work. I had spent much of their sabbatical wondering how I should talk to Andy about how I felt God was calling me to take up the reins again at Challenge. I felt the Lord had been saying to me personally during those two years, 'I called you to plant a church, and you've done a rubbish job so far, but I'm giving you a fresh opportunity.'

Fourthly, at Easter 2007, the local council wrote to us, formally withdrawing the offer for us to build on land adjoining the local primary school. To that point, we had spent around £85,000 on the project.

Finally, that spring (2007) two other key couples also announced and made plans to relocate. One was our worship leader, the other an elder of wisdom and experience!

Please understand, the people that God was removing were pillars of the church. By the summer of 2007, the question being asked by many of those remaining (by now Sunday attendance was regularly below 30), was 'is it time to close?'

But God had spoken…

That spring, on an elder's retreat, we heard from God. The key words that He gave us were 'family' and 'Kingdom of God.' We were to be a church that was truly a family. Supporting people of all shapes and sizes, singles, families, broken, children, young people and not so young—we were to be a church that expressed God's Father heart, with 'family' as our watch-word.

That summer, we made three commitments:

- Rachel and I told the church that Challenge would be our major priority, not itinerant ministry (this had always been the case for Rachel, but it was a 'sea change' for me)
- As a fellowship, we recommitted ourselves to pray for an appropriate building to carry out God's purposes for Challenge
- We committed ourselves to appoint a family worker as a priority.

Renewal through the Word…

In the autumn of 2007, we began a preaching series in *Nehemiah*. Remarkably, God unmistakably rebuilt lives, renewed vision, restored passion and regenerated Challenge Community Church during that season.

About that time, it was brought to our attention that the local Royal British Legion Hall on Belmont Road, Hereford, was lying empty and was due to be sold at auction. We made an offer of £160,000, and a sale was agreed prior to auction, and was completed in August 2008. Around £480,000 has now been spent on the property, with loans and debts amounting to less than £50,000. The property is insured for just under £1 million.

In November 2008, we appointed Keith Baldwin to 3 days a week as the church Family Worker. Keith is a single dad, and was converted through the ministry of Challenge, and discipled by Andy Gibson. Keith's post is partly funded by two local schools.

In July 2009, we moved into a partially completed building. In our first week, we hosted the Counties 'Life' exhibition and welcomed over 400 children from local primary schools.

By November 2009, the back room was proving too small to accommodate the growing congregation, now numbering between 40 and 50. We prayed. By February 2010, not only had the £55,000 been found to complete the auditorium, but the work had been done and we opened that room with a Holiday Bible club.

Sunday mornings are now regularly attended by 70-80 people. However, the auditorium will comfortably seat 150, and we are praying towards the day when we will have to go to two services on Sunday morning.

In January 2010, we appointed Bella Rowe as a Christians against Poverty (CAP) worker. This is a joint initiative with other evangelicals in the city.

To God be the Glory…

We are not a big church, but God has a big heart. Our community, like yours, is made up of broken lives, broken homes, broken promises and broken dreams. It has been our joy to discover experientially, that God is in the renewal business.

A Teaching Assistant from our local primary school was sitting on the bus as it passed the old Royal British Legion Hall. She listened as some ladies, looking at the restored and renamed hall, remarked, 'Wow, haven't they done a great job on that building!'

The building in which we meet, is a parable to our community. I'd love to tell you of the broken lives that God is mending, the hearts that have been renewed and reborn, and the restoration that is taking place in people's homes. However, the story isn't finished yet. There is room for more. Dream dreams, have visions, and ask God to give you his heart for your local church—then pursue it with passion!

Further reading

Church planting

Graham Beynon, *Planting for the Gospel: A Hands-on Guide to Church Planting*, Tain: Christian Focus Publications 2010

David J Hesselgrave, *Planting Churches Cross-Culturally: North America and Beyond*, Grand Rapids: Baker Academic, 2nd edition 2000

Tom Jones (ed.), *Church planting from the ground up*, Joplin MO: College Press Publishing 2004

George Lings & Stuart Murray, *Church Planting: Past, Present and Future*, Cambridge: Grove Books 2003 (at present under revision)

Stuart B Murray, *Church planting: Laying foundations.* Carlisle, England: Paternoster Press 1998

Craig Ott and Gene Wilson, *Global Church Planting: Biblical principles and best practices for multiplication*, Ada MI: Baker 2011

Ed Stetzer, *Planting New Churches in a Postmodern Age*, Nashville: Broadman & Holman 2003

Ed Stetzer, *Planting Missional Churches: Planting a church that's biblically sound and reaching people in culture*, Nashville TN: Broadman & Holman 2006 (a revised version of *Planting New Churches in a Post-Modern Age*, Broadman & Holman 2003)

Church growth

David Beer, *Fifty Ways to Help Your Church Grow*, Eastbourne: Great Ideas 2000

Eddie Gibbs and Ian Coffey, *Church next: quantum changes in Christian ministry*, Leicester: Inter-Varsity Press 2001

Michael Green (ed.), *Church Without Walls: A global examination of cell church*, Carlisle: Paternoster 2002

Alan Howe, *Leading Ordinary Churches into Growth*, Cambridge: Grove Books 2005

Bob Jackson, *Hope for the Church: contemporary strategies for growth*, London: Church Publishing House 2002

Martin Robinson and Dan Yarnell, *Celebrating the Small Church: Harnessing the strengths of the small church*, Tunbridge Wells: Monarch 1993

Steve Sjogren and Rob Lewin, *Community of kindness*, Ventura, CA: Regal Books 2003

Rick Warren, *The purpose driven church: Growth without compromising your message and mission*, Grand Rapids, MI: Zondervan 1995

Rick Warren, *The purpose driven life: What on earth am I here for?* Grand Rapids, MI: Zondervan 2002

Emergent church

Steven Croft, *Transforming Communities: Re-imagining the Church for the 21st Century*, London: Darton, Longman and Todd 2002

[Graham Cray *et al.*], *Mission-shaped church: church planting and fresh expressions of church in a changing context*, London: Church House Publishing, 2nd edition, 2009

George G. Hunter, III, *Church for the unchurched*, Nashville, TN: Abingdon Press 1996

Evangelism

Stephen McQuoid, *Sharing the Good News in C21: Evangelism in A Local Church Context*, Carlisle: Paternoster for Partnership 2002.

Steve Sjogren, Dave Ping and Doug Pollock. *Irresistible evangelism: Natural ways to open others to Jesus.* Loveland, CO: Group Publishing 2004.

Leonard I. Sweet, *Postmodern pilgrims: First century passion for the 21st century world.* Nashville, TN: Broadman and Holman Publishers 2000.

Church leadership

Ajith Fernando, *Jesus-Driven Ministry*, Leicester: Inter-Varsity Press 2002

James Lawrence, *Growing leaders: reflections on leadership, life and Jesus*, Abingdon: The Bible Reading Fellowship 2004

Stephen McQuoid, *A guide to God's family: being part of your local church*, Carlisle: Paternoster for Partnership 2000

Stephen McQuoid, *Discipline with care: applying biblical correction in your church*, Leominster: Day One 2008

Harold Rowdon (ed.), *Church Leaders Handbook*, Carlisle: Paternoster for Partnership 2002

Harold Rowdon (ed.), *Serving God's People: Re-thinking Christian Ministry Today*, Carlisle: Paternoster for Partnership 2006

Alexander Strauch, *Biblical Eldership: An urgent call to restore biblical church leadership*, Littleton CO: Lewis and Roth, revised edition 2000

Alexander Strauch, *A Study Guide to Biblical Eldership: An urgent call to restore biblical church leadership*, Littleton CO: Lewis and Roth, revised edition, 1997

Alexander Strauch and Richard Swartley, *The Mentor's Guide to Biblical Eldership: Twelve Lessons for Mentoring Elders*, Littleton CO: Lewis and Roth 1997

Alexander Strauch, *Meetings that work: a guide to effective elders' meetings*, Littleton CO: Lewis and Roth 2001

Alexander Strauch, *A Christian Leader's Guide to Leading with Love*, Littleton CO: Lewis and Roth 2006

Neil Summerton, *A Noble Task: Eldership and ministry in the local church*, Carlisle: Paternoster for Partnership, 2nd edition, 1994

Background information to church planting and church growth

Jacinta Ashworth and Ian Farthing, *Churchgoing in the UK: A Research Report from Tearfund on church attendance in the UK.* Teddington, England: Tearfund 2007

Peter Brierley (ed.), *UK Church Statistics 2005 – 2015*, Tonbridge: ADBC 2011

Peter Brierley, *21 Concerns for 21st Century Christians*, Tonbridge ADBC 2011

Index

A
Abbey Church, Gloucester 233-239
Abbeydale, Gloucester 236
Abbeymead, Gloucester 236
Accountability 15-16, 40, 46, 47, 131, 205-206
Addis Ababa 67, 177
Albion Hall (Southgate Evangelical Church), Gloucester 233
Alpha course 15, 52, 132, 229, 242
Antioch 2, 73, 116
Apostles 26, 28
Apprentice, apprenticeship 24
Area for Priority Treatment 214
Ark of the covenant 35
Assyrians 32
Athens 52-55

B
Babylon 32
Baigent, John 214
Baptism 57, 115, 125, 127-128, 201
Barton Christian Fellowship, Hereford 114, 275
Bell, Rob 207
Bellshill 217
Belleview Chapel, Edinburgh 219, 220, 221, 224, 225
Belleview West Community Church 220, 221
Bethany Christian Centre, Houghton-le-Spring 227, 230
Bethany City Church, Sunderland 227-232
Bible reading notes 126
Bible studies 52, 56
Bible teaching 6, 11
Body of Christ 29, 33
Bothwell Evangelical Church 213
Breaking of Bread, Lord's supper, communion 33, 57-58, 71, 72, 82, 115, 125, 170, 201
Brethren, Brethren movement 29, 33, 112, 115, 161, 191, 233, 269
Brooklyn Tabernacle, Manhattan 241
Buckfast Abbey 91

C
Café Church 244
Catholicism 57
Cell networks 71-72, 84
Census information 109
Challenge Community Church, Hereford 111, 112, 275-278
Challis, Ralph 192
Change, adaptation to 45, 203-204
Children's (kids) club 11, 12, 15, 52
Cholmeley Evangelical Church, Highgate 266
Christendom 1
Christianity Explored 132, 263
Christians against Poverty 87, 118, 278
Churches
  activities 1
  apathy 9-10
  attitudes to church planting 153-154, 155
  attendance 4
  criteria defining 57, 72
  decline and death in the UK 4, 5, 69
  dying, identifying 191-192
  evangelistic effectiveness 4
  growth 2, 7
  incarnational 84
  large/larger churches 6, 7
  life cycles 189-190
  missional 5, 84
  New Testament requirements 9
  numbers in the UK 3, 81
  programme 14
  relationship with local community 11
  renewed structures 193
  reviving dying 192-193
  size 169-176
  sizes in the UK 78-79, 82
  social action 1
  tradition, history 2-3, 4, 8, 9, 12, 207
  vision 5
Church building(s) 9, 12, 13-14, 68, 80, 85, 135-152, 236
  architects and other professional advice 137-138, 140, 141-142
  car parking 136, 137
  condition 148-149
  energy performance 149

equipment 136
funding 138
health, safety and disability considerations 146-148
impression 138-139
insurance 141, 148, 151
leasing 150-152
legal questions and requirements 143-148
location 139
maintenance 136, 149
mortgage 142-143
need for? 135-136
ownership, purchase, renting etc 139-143, 143-144, 150-152
planning and change of use matters 145-146
sports and amenity areas 136
trust and covenant restrictions 144-145
value and valuation 145
vision and buildings 135-138
Church catholic (universal Church) 31, 32, 37
Church, definition(s) of 27
Church discipline 57
Church leadership 10
Church membership 127, 128
Church planter(s) 3, 55, 58, 184-187
Church planting
  adjusting to growth 170-176
  approaches 64-75
    adoption 68-69
    cell network 71-72
    collaborative 70-71
    dispersion 67-68
    mission team 74-75
    mother/daughter 64-66
    parent by accident 66
    pioneer planters 74
    planting at a distance 69-70
    spontaneous generation 73
  difficulty 2-3
  doctrine and practice 114-115
  effect on sending church 5
  effectiveness of 7-8
  emergent church(es) 209
  encouraging maturity 197-206
  ethnic 9, 67-68
  failure 8
  flexibility in 21-22
  financial pressures 20
  involvement of churches in 2
  means to growth 179-184, 234-235
  models 51-61, 63, 77-88
    house church/organic church 77
    ministry-driven 78, 86-87
    program-driven 78, 79-81
    purpose-driven 78, 83
    relationship-driven 78, 84-85
    seeker-driven 78, 81-82
  mother/daughter model 15, 64-66, 219, 227, 233
  numerical growth 124-125
  priority 7-10
  reasons against 2-7
  reasons for 7-10, 154
  relationships with other local churches 58
  stages 51-61
    pioneer 51-53
    parent 56-57
    participant 60
    partner 58-59
  stages of growth 175-176
  strategy 18, 65, 70, 72
  structures 8, 59, 65, 116
  team 3, 12, 18
  vision 18, 65, 114, 120, 160, 201, 235, 242, 255
Church Planting Initiative (CPI) 218, 255, 276
Clapton Hall, Stoke Newington 266
Coffee morning 52
Collaboration 70-71
Communication 40, 44-45
Community engagement 92-93, 262
Co-ordination 40
Courage 39
College 24
Complacency 43
Conversion 123-124, 177
Corinth 198
Creativity 63
Crestwood Church, Dudley 254
Crestwood Estate, Dudley 253
Cross-cultural
  differences 100-104
  mission 99-100
  understanding 108-109
Cult(s) 12
Culture, cultural relevance 100, 210

D

Dependency 131, 132
Determination 19, 39
Disciple, discipling, discipleship 11, 23, 56. 72, 83, 86, 115, 120, 123-134, 177-178, 195, 200, 202
Discouragement 14, 19, 42-43, 187-188
Driscoll, Mark 117, 207

E

Easterhouse housing Scheme 90
Ecclesiastes 27
Eden Partnerships 107
Ekklesia, 27-29, 31, 33
Elder(s) 10, 16, 37, 45, 118, 159, 161, 184, 194, 235
Emerging church(es) 27, 84, 207-210
Emotional baggage 130-131
Encouraging gift(s) 23
Establishing relationships 52
Ethiopia 67
Ethnic diversity 67-68, 108
European Christian Mission 256
Evangelical Alliance 115
Evangelical Christians
  authority 1
  commitment to church planting 2
  proactivity 1
Evangelism 11, 72, 83, 84, 120
Evangelistic services 52
Evangelistic dinner 52
Evangelistic methodologies 79
Every-member ministry 183, 191, 194
Exile 23

F

Fall 55
Family, family-life 6, 20
Family service 83
Favouritism 45
Fellowship 83, 117-118, 120
Friendship 19
Forest of Dean Community Church, Cinderford 247-251
Forgiveness 90, 124
Forty Days of Purpose 249, 275

G

Gifts, gifting 6-7, 10, 17, 23, 39, 65, 88, 115. 194-195, 261
GLO 73, 91, 93, 96, 116, 213, 214, 218, 276

Gloucester City Council 236, 238
Goals 41
Gospel meeting 82
Greco-Roman culture 8

H

Habit(s) 12
Harmony 43
Healing on the Streets 86, 231
Hillsongs London 82
Hillview Evangelical Church, Gloucester 233, 236, 237
Holy of holies 35
Holy Spirit (Spirit) 3, 28, 32, 33, 36, 37, 115, 124, 184, 193, 226
Home group 132-133
Hospitality 20
Hotel 13
Housing development(s), estate(s), scheme(s) 9, 14, 67, 90, 95, 104
Hybels, Bill 81, 121

I

Identification 107
Imagination 63
Incarnation, incarnational evangelism 55, 93-94, 106-108, 196
Inner cities 4
Innovation 208
Intensity 96-97
International student café 229
Inverbervie Gospel Hall 241, 242
Investigative learning 94-95
Involvement 95-96
Israel 30, 32

J

Jerusalem 116
Joslin, Roy 214
Judaeo- Christian worldview 55, 129

K

Kirkliston Community Church 219-226

L

Lakeside Church, Brierley Hill 253-257
Leader(s), local leadership, leadership team 6, 10, 16, 37, 43, 46-47, 58, 59, 60, 116, 153-167, 184, 201, 235
Leadership development and selection 153-167

appointing leaders 160-167, 249
attitudes to church planting 153-154, 155
consulting the church 165-166
developmental leadership 156-157
encouraging plural leadership and ministry 178-179
entrepreneurial leadership 155
initiating leadership 154-156
modelling maturity 204-205
pastoral leadership 157-160
supporting leaders 167
teaching on leadership 164-165
visionary leadership 155-156, 195
Leisure/community centre 13, 21, 52
Letham Road Gospel Hall, Strathaven 259-260
Liberty Community Church 96, 213-218
Local community 12, 21, 87
Loneliness 55

M

Maiden, Peter 134
Mandarin Chinese 231
Manpower 15
Masonic Hall, Kirkliston 223
Materialism 21
McIntosh, Gary 189-190, 194
McLaren, Brian 207
Message, Manchester 107
Minster church 85
Mission organisation 16, 20
Moral baggage 129-130
'mother church' 5, 64-66
  implications of planting for 66
Music 6, 23

N

New birth 177
New covenant 36
New towns 4
Northern Ireland 73

O

Obedience 124
Office of National Statistics 109
Old covenant 36
Orbiston Estate 217
Outreach Community Church, Strathaven 261

P

Park Road Hall, Crouch End 267
Parkhill Chapel, South Hampstead 267
Parking 68
Participation 183
Pastor(s) 6
Pastoral care 18, 22
Pastoral gift 22
Paul (the apostle) 27, 28, 31, 40, 52-55, 94, 118, 159, 162, 198, 199, 266, 273
Pentecost 27, 36
Persecution 67
Peter 27, 31, 159
Piety 25
Pillar of cloud 35
Piper, John 117
Population shift 4, 9
Post-modern society, postmodernism 8, 55, 84-85, 121, 128-129, 204, 207-208
Prayer breakfast 9
Prayer chain 52, 56
Prayer meeting 14
Presence of God 35
Proclamation 19
Professionalism 6-7
Prophet(s), prophecy 28, 193
Protestantism 33, 73
Pub 13, 52

R

Reformation 57
Relationship building 195-196, 202
Repentance 124
Research 105, 109-110
Resource church 85
Retirement 18
Roles 41-42

S

Saddleback 230, 231, 248
School, 13, 52
Secular society/secularism 8
Self-motivation 19
Servant evangelism 78, 86, 196, 250
Service 120
Shaftesbury Society 267
Sin 55, 129
Sinai 31
Social gospel 94
Socio-economic deprivation 59, 67, 72, 104, 105

South Queensferry 220, 221
Southgate Evangelical Church, Gloucester 233
Spring Harvest 267
St James, Muswell Hill 267
Stadium of Light, Sunderland 228, 230
Station Road Gospel Hall, Cinderford 248, 249
Stamina 19
Starbucks 231
Statement of doctrines and practices 115, 201
Stephen 28
Strathaven Evangelical Church 259-263
Strathaven Evangelical Fellowship 260
Street Pastors 87, 231
Suburbs 4
Succession planning 24
Sunday School 9, 11
Sunday service(s) 52, 56
Support 65
Synagogue(s) 32, 37

T

Teaching 71, 72, 83, 179, 205
Teams, teamwork 39-45, 56
Team dynamics 47-49
Tearfund 78-79
Temple 32, 33, 34, 35, 36
Temple of Solomon 35
The 145 Church, Hornsey 265-274
The Living Rooms, Inverbervie 241-245
Tilsley College 24, 91, 116, 218, 268
Toddler group 14
Training 24, 59, 69, 183-184
Transformation 91, 200

U

Uddingston Gospel Hall 213
Unchurched 19, 55
Urban Aid 95

V

Viewpark Christian Fellowship 91-92, 213-218
Vineyard Church, Cincinatti 86
Vineyard Church, Causeway Coast, Northern Ireland 86
Vucovar 73

W

Wall Heath Evangelical Free Church 253
Warren, Rick 83, 105-106, 119-120, 248
Willow Creek 81-82, 230, 231
Wilton Chapel, Muswell Hill 266
Withymoor/Lakeside Estate, Dudley 254
Witnessing 180-183
Women's meeting 9
Worship 22, 83, 84, 120, 169-170, 179-180

Y

Yahweh 29, 30
Youth club 14, 15, 52, 95, 222
Youth fellowship 9, 14

Z

Zagreb 73

The Church Planting Initiative (CPI)

CPI has been encouraging and supporting church planters throughout the United Kingdom since 1999. It is a joint venture of four organizations: Gospel Literature Outreach, Counties, the Church Growth Trust and Partnership.

The aim is to see planted a growing number of self-governing, self-supporting churches which are led by teams of gifted leaders and use the gifts of all their members in worship and service—churches which are bible-based and open-hearted towards all committed Christians.

CPI is concentrating on building a network of church planters across the country, with three essential components

- informal networking and relationship between planters which involves fellowship, attendance at events and exchanges of information for prayer, help and advice.
- more formal membership of the network for those who are church planting, have been church planting, intend to church plant or who are very supportive of church planting and are practically encouraging church planters in various ways. Such membership is for those who embrace the values and ethos of CPI (and the statement of beliefs), who are not an integral part of another denominational network or stream, and who are will to accept mutual commitment and accountability between themselves and CPI.
- financial support, either regular or occasional, for formal members of CPI if funds are available and CPI judges such support to be appropriate in the individual circumstances.

As the network of relationships grows, CPI is gradually developing regional networks or hubs across the country.

To learn more about being involved in church planting and being part of the CPI network, please contact:

Julian Marsh, Director of CPI
3 Cedar Way
St Mary's Park
Portishead
Bristol
BS20 6TT

E-mail jpm@jmarsh.freeserve.co.uk or jpmebm@gmail.com
Tel: 01275 848770
Mobile: 07802 312000 or 07727 106219